CW01662653

The MALABARI Who LOVED His FERRARI

The MALABARI Who LOVED His FERRARI

MEMOIRS

DILEEP HEILBRONN

Memoirs

Title: The Malabari Who Loved His Ferrari
Author: Dileep Heilbronn

Printing Permit: MC-01-01-6064517

ISBN 978-9948-727-46-0

Copyright © 2024 Dileep Heilbronn
© All rights reserved

To maintain privacy, some names have been changed.

This book is sold subject to the condition that it shall not, by way of trade or otherwise, be lent, hired out, or otherwise circulated without the publisher's prior consent in any form of binding or cover other than that in which it is published and without a similar condition including this condition being imposed on the subsequent purchaser.

Printed at Thomson Press India Ltd.

To my close ones and
to everyone who walked beside me,
inspired my resilience and
made this story possible.

Contents

An Opening Word

At the core of these pages lies not just my journey, but the intertwined stories of countless souls who've walked alongside me. To those who've lent me their strength, guidance and love, I dedicate this humble tribute.

My gratitude extends to my pillars of support—my parents, family, children, spouse and cherished friends. To the mentors who shaped my path, the colleagues who shared my vision, the clients who entrusted me with their dreams and the tireless staff of my company, Heilbronn, I owe a debt of deep gratitude. Even to the encounters with adversity, the challenges that tested my resolve and the lessons learned from both triumph and setback, I extend my appreciation.

And to Dubai, UAE, a city that embraced me as its own and offered unlimited opportunities, I owe a debt beyond measure.

My heartfelt gratitude to His Highness Sheikh Mohamed Bin Zayed Al Nahyan, the esteemed ruler of the UAE, for his exemplary leadership of this remarkable nation. Under his guidance, the UAE has ensured peace, prosperity and security for over 10,000,000 residents and citizens.

My gratitude pours forth to His Highness Sheikh Mohammed Bin Rashid Al Maktoum, whose visionary leadership ignited the dreams of millions, including mine. Through his resolute commitment to progress, he has sculpted a landscape where aspirations take flight.

This book reflects the transformative power of resilience and perseverance. From the uncertainty of a young man armed with only a diploma and a handful of dollars to the heights of achievement, it chronicles the 33-year odyssey of a dreamer. Within these pages, you'll find the echoes of my dreams, the echoes of my struggles and the echoes of my triumphs.

This life story is presented through brief snapshots. Together, these snapshots evoke a macrocosmic portrait of a journey—a mosaic of moments, small yet deep, creating a panorama of a life lived fully.

Every tear shed—be it in defeat or in joy— shows the human spirit's capacity for metamorphosis. And within these stories lie the wonders of miracles.

My love to all those who played a part in these extraordinary moments. For it is through their collective support that I've been able to turn the pages of my life's story from nothingness to abundance.

In solidarity with those in need, I commit the proceeds of this book to uplifting the lives of the less fortunate around me.

Prologue

In the cramped living quarters near Santa Cruz station in Mumbai, shared with five others, I reached a breaking point. There was scarcely enough room to move, let alone stretch out for sleep without bumping into someone. The stench from the communal toilet, used by many, was unbearable, forcing us to pinch our noses before entering. I realised I could not take it anymore.

Over the next seven months, I changed accommodations a few times, but none were satisfactory. Sitting outside luxurious hotels, watching pricey cars zoom by, I couldn't help but wonder: "Will I ever step foot inside or drive one myself?"

From childhood, my dream was to live and work in Dubai; the desire had embedded itself deep in my subconscious.

Each day, navigating the crowded Mumbai trains, enveloped in the scent of cheap perfume and sweat, I clung to my dreams. While diligently working as a draftsman at Niranjan Pandya and Harshad Dholakia Architects, I continued to pursue opportunities in Dubai, scanning newspapers and visiting agencies.

Then, fortune smiled upon me. Representatives from UTCC Wade Adams, a prominent engineering contractor in Dubai, offered me a job with a monthly salary of AED 900. I was elated. I resigned from my job in Mumbai and bid farewell to roommates and friends.

Returning to my hometown of Edappal, Kerala, to be with my family and friends before departing for Dubai, anticipation filled the air.

Everyone was happy. Achan was. Amma was. My siblings and friends were.

However, my excitement was short-lived. The outbreak of the Kuwait-Iraq war halted all recruitment efforts by UTCC Wade Adams, leaving me in despair.

The truth hit me hard. I left my job in Mumbai and the one in Dubai had vanished into thin air.

Feeling lost and hopeless, I decided to return to Mumbai and start anew. I thought: would my former bosses take me back? Or would I have to go through the whole process of finding a new job? I was reminded of the cramped quarters and the stench from the toilet.

At Kuttipuram railway station, as friends gathered to bid me farewell, the weight of my struggles overwhelmed me. Tears streamed down my face as I waited for the train, uncertain of what the future held. Everyone was silent.

"Nothing seems to be working for me," I told my friends.

I could not control my emotions and broke down, plunging into despair.

I could hear the siren of the Mumbai-bound train pulling into the station.

The MALABARI Who LOVED His FERRARI

THE EARLY YEARS

1

Made in Madras

My story begins in Madras, a city that now throbs under the name Chennai. Its cacophony has always been a melody to my ears—an endless hum of honking rickshaws and the spicy sizzle of street food. This extraordinary place holds a piece of my heart, forever marked by my dramatic arrival. Here, in the bustling corridors of Stanley Government Hospital, on a crisp January 29 in 1969, I announced myself with a squall. Amma, no doubt, wrestled with labour pains, while nurses likely held their breath in anticipation. And there I was, a tiny human blinking at the harsh lights of a new world.

My name, Dileep, a homage to the legendary Dilip Kumar, was a choice inspired by Achan, a Bollywood fan. Achan and Amma, A. V. Narayanan and Sarojini, were kindness itself. Achan hailed from a simple farming family in Edappal, Kerala. He owned a small plot of land, the kind that could have easily seen him tilling the soil under the harsh sun. But Achan craved more. In 1967, with ambition as his guide, he packed his bags and ventured to Madras, determined to change our family's fortunes. The city offered him a chance—a sturdy steering wheel as a bus driver for the Pallavan Transport Corporation Ltd, part of the Tamil Nadu State Transport service.

Achan was all about that self-made life. Chop your own wood and it'll warm you twice. This was his mantra. And he made sure I soaked up every bit of that wisdom. It's like he wanted me to have that same fire in my belly, that same drive to carve out my own path.

I'm this mix of Malayali and Tamilian. I practically grew up with Tamil as my second language. Even with all the Tamil classes and being in Tamil Nadu, we never lost touch with our roots. Malayalam was still flowing strong in our household, thanks to Amma's dedication.

I love Tamil. It is an ancient treasure trove of culture and history. I've been a fan since I was knee-high to a grasshopper. It's like every word, every syllable, tells a story that's been passed down through the ages. From the moment I began learning, I was hooked.

Let me take you to Tondiarpet in the northern neighbourhood of Chennai, formerly Madras, where I spent my childhood. Its very name, Tondiarpet, holds within it the echoes of a saint's legacy—Kannangudi Mastan Sahib, a figure from the 17th century whose birthplace near Tondi in the Ramanathapuram district still whispers secrets of times long past. The word, 'Tondi' or 'Tondai' bears the weight of ages, tracing its lineage back to the ancient province of Thondaimangalam. Here, amidst the fertile lands cradled between the Pennar rivers of Nellore and Cuddalore, Tondaimandalam flourished under the rule of Tondaiman Ilam Tiraiyan—a steward of the illustrious Chola family, whose influence stretched far and wide from the grand city of Kanchipuram.

Close your eyes and envision with me the lively Butchammal street, where the air hangs heavy with the scent of spices and washermen's calls. The simplicity of days gone by remains in the air.

As a child, my world revolved around the open grounds where kites danced upon the wind, their colourful tails painting streaks across the azure sky. There, in the background of shouts of joy, I learned the art of letting my dreams take flight, tethered only by the string in my grasp.

But it was not only the skies that captured my imagination; the earth beneath my feet held its own treasures. Marble games, with their intricate rules and strategies, became a picture of skill and precision. The distance between Goli and the player, measured not just in metres but in moments of anticipation and concentration, taught me the value of patience and dexterity.

During these childhood pastimes, my love affair with colours and designs began. Each swirl of a marble, each flick of a kite's tail, betrayed a world of beauty and possibility.

Cycle rickshaw and luxury cars

Fresh in my memory is Model School, a place where my sisters Pushpa and Sajana and I began our journey of learning. Like me, my sisters too were born in Chennai. Clad in our crisp white and red uniforms, we entered the convent school's gates each day. In contrast, the uniform for students in government schools were in green and white.

But behind the facade of education lay a reality tinged with humility and resolution. With my father's modest income unable to meet the demands of our education, it was my uncle, Cheriyachan, who generously shouldered the burden of our educational expenses.

As we made our way to school each day, the contrast between privilege and simplicity was stark. While affluent children arrived in sleek Mercedes and Jaguars, we trudged along in a weather-beaten cycle rickshaw, the name of its silent driver lost to time's tenuous march.

My young mind churned with questions. Why did my father struggle? Why do some people prosper? Why did some ride in luxury while we journeyed in simplicity? Though these questions went unanswered, they ignited a fire within me—a resolve to ensure that no child should ever feel the weight of inequality.

I thought: if I become a father, I want my son to have a more privileged life. I don't want him to face the uncertainties and hardships that I did. I aspire to provide him with the best, ensuring he never feels sad or embarrassed about his financial situation. It wasn't my fault that I was born less privileged, but it is my responsibility to change my circumstances. As many great men have said, the guilt of remaining less privileged must be overcome.

Right from those days at the Model School, I developed a lifelong craze for cars. After all, you crave what you don't have. And so, as I watched the gleaming cars glide past, my imagination took flight.

In the quiet of night, I found comfort in the kaleidoscope of colours that danced in my dreams.

From Madras to Edappal

My father's unexpected declaration shattered the tranquil atmosphere at home.

"Let's pack our bags and head home. I've landed a job in Bahrain," he announced.

The news sent shockwaves through our little household, disrupting the routine we had grown accustomed to. In Madras, I had enjoyed the simple joys of childhood—games with friends, kite flying and roaming the quaint alleyways.

But as we bid farewell to the familiar sights and sounds of the city, I couldn't shake the feeling of apprehension that gnawed at my heart. Leaving behind my friends and the immeasurable energy of Madras was a daunting prospect, yet I knew deep down that adventure awaited us in our ancestral home in Edappal. Tucked away in the scenic beauty of the Malappuram district of Kerala, Edappal graces the vicinity near the busy town of Ponnani.

The journey back to Kerala was filled with a mix of emotions – nostalgia for the memories we were leaving behind and anticipation for the new chapter that awaited us. As the lush greenery of Kerala came into view, I felt a sense of peace, a feeling of coming home.

Life in Edappal was a stark contrast to the hubbub of Madras, yet it held its own allure. Surrounded by the warmth of our joint family, our ancestral home, *tharavad*, became a sanctuary of love. Even as I missed the excitement of city life, I couldn't help but be drawn to the simplicity and serenity of Kerala.

But just as we were settling into our new life, fate intervened once more. Two years after we arrived in Edappal, my father returned from Bahrain, bringing with him a newfound appreciation for the bonds of family and the comfort of home.

"I'm back for good," he declared.

Blissful Childhood

In the middle of swaying arecanut trees and the gentle murmur of the Manoor Kayal waterway, stood our *tharavad*, where laughter echoed alongside the clucking of chickens, the lowing of cows and the playful gambols of goats. As raindrops danced upon our roof, we children revelled in their arrival, collecting them in cupped hands.

The thatched roof of our house was made of dry coconut leaves and grass. We lived there as a joint family. The joint family system where several members lived under one roof was common in our country at that time. But today such a practice has passed into history. We didn't even have electricity in our house at that time. All nightly needs were fulfilled by the light of a kerosene lamp.

We were six children at home—my Valiachan's (father's elder brother) three children and me and my two siblings. Our father and mother were staying with us.

We kept chickens, two cows and goats. The scent of cow dung permeated the air. A childhood with animals living close to human beings opened up new vistas of love for me.

With the sun's emergence, its golden rays painted ethereal pictures within our home. We pressed our palms against the sun's radiant glow, marvelling as the light revealed the intricate patterns of veins coursing beneath our skin. I found bliss in the serenity of dawn's light. I would walk into the vast ground around the house, thick with vegetation. We had a variety of trees and plants, including coconut, arecanut, papaya, ginger, tamarind, banana, tomato, chilies and jackfruit. The ground was a tad elevated. I would walk under a bunch of arecanut trees, craning their necks as if to touch the sky.

My simple ablutions beneath the open sky became a communion with Nature itself. From the toilet, with its side walls made of coconut leaves and small branches, I looked upwards and saw the beauty of the sky. Sunlight would filter in through the coconut leaves. Birds, in a variety of shapes and colours, chirped endlessly. The birdsong would take me to another world.

As I sat there, as if in a trance, my mother's voice would pierce the tranquility, calling me to the duties of the day.

"Honey, how long have you been gone? Are you ready to go to school?"

Her gentle inquiry would fade into the morning breeze.

Ignoring her pleas, I would stick around in moments of bliss until her patience wore thin. "Go to school soon," she would urge, wielding a rod.

The bath itself, in a big bathroom under the trees, was an invigorating sensory experience, as I shivered under the cold water from the well. The coldness would rise surreptitiously from beneath the feet to the crown. The brightest light of my childhood was certainly the experience of growing up in a joint family in a quaint little house built on a vast ground in the lap of Nature.

Parutty Chechi

Among my fondest recollections of Edappal, none are as prized as those of Parutty (Parukutty) Chechi, our neighbour whose love knew no bounds. Her son, Devan, along with his sisters Raji and Sajana, were close companions throughout my childhood. Set within a verdant yard adorned with fruit-laden trees, Parutty Chechi's home became my second home.

Behind their house, there was a large pond where we children spent our days fishing and swimming. We paddled paper boats and gathered flowers from the homestead for Onam. We also enjoyed fruits from the orchard, making our childhood both adventurous and joyful.

In addition to our playful adventures, the pond and orchard became our classroom for learning about Nature and life. We discovered the different types of fish inhabiting the pond, learned to identify various fruit trees and observed the changing seasons reflected in the landscape around us. Our exploration often led to impromptu lessons on the importance of preserving and respecting the environment. These experiences not only filled our days with excitement but also instilled in us a deep appreciation for the natural world and the simple joys it offered.

"You are like a son to me," Parutty Chechi would often declare, her words carrying the warmth of a mother's love.

Even after my family relocated to a new house built by Cheriyachan a little distance away, I continued to traverse the path to Parutty Chechi's doorstep for several years. In her, I found the familiar embrace of my own beloved mother.

Parutty Chechi's words resounded in my heart long after I left her doorstep. Her affectionate declaration resonated deeply within me. Despite the physical distance between us, her love remained a guiding light, a constant source of comfort and reassurance. Every step I took towards her house was a step towards home, towards familial love that transcended blood ties.

A whiff of the Gulf

Among the constellation of my childhood memories, one figure shines brightly: Cheriyachan (A. V. Balakrishnan), my father's younger brother. He was my childhood hero. He pursued a demanding career as a civil engineer in Bahrain, but always found time for his extended family.

Working for the Bahrain Petroleum Company (BAPCO), Cheriyachan had impeccable appearance, refined manners and eloquent speech. His tales from afar painted a picture of adventure, sophistication and inspiration. Cheriyachan's room, a picture of orderliness and cleanliness, mirrored the purity of his character and his commitment to excellence in every aspect of his life. His annual return home from Bahrain on leave brought immense joy to our family. His genuine interest in our well-being endeared him to us even more, as he treated me and my sisters with the same affection as his own children. We never got similar affection from anyone else.

He always brought gifts, each one carrying the distinct scent of the Gulf. Even the aroma of the bag filled with gifts captivated me, sparking dreams of the Gulf. With wide-eyed wonder, I would open his bag and marvel at the clothes, pencils and chocolates neatly packed inside, all waiting to be given to us. I accepted the gifts from Cheriyachan with great pride, cherishing each one.

None of my friends had the good fortune of receiving gifts from the Gulf. For this, I was deeply indebted to Cheriyachan. I owe most of my sweetest childhood memories to him.

The story of a pencil

Among the treasures Cheriyachan brought from the Gulf, a simple pencil held a special place in my heart. Its yellow and black hues, coupled with the comforting scent of its soft wood, sparked my imagination and curiosity. An eraser was attached to the top. It was the first time I had seen a pencil with an eraser, and my wonder knew no bounds. When I took a razor to sharpen the pencil, I discovered the soft, high-quality wood used in its manufacture.

It carried the name, Staedtler.

"Do you know where it is made?" I asked Cheriyachan one day, holding the pencil aloft.

"This is made in Germany," he revealed, opening my eyes to a world of quality and innovation that extended far beyond our shores.

I instantly liked the pencil, Staedtler and Germany. If the Germans instil such perfection in the making of such a tiny pencil, I wondered, what would be the precision and innovation they invest in their other products?

Starting from my hometown, Edappal, India, my imagination took flight, soaring across continents and cultures. The world became my playground, ignited by the limitless power of imagination.

I wondered how many countries existed outside of India and what unique products each one manufactured. The variety and craftsmanship of these products fascinated me, as each represented a blend of human intelligence, creativity, talent and labour.

The pencil has a fascinating history, tracing back to ancient Rome where scribes used a stylus—a thin metal rod—to leave light marks on papyrus. Early styluses were made of lead, which is why we still call pencil cores 'lead', even though they are actually made of graphite.

The true pencil revolution began in 1564 with the discovery of a rich graphite deposit in Borrowdale, England. I remember that it was the pencil gifted to me by Cheriyachan that first ignited my passion for travelling beyond India. It also kindled an interest in chasing quality and excellence. How do these countries achieve quality? How do they raise the bar? What are the main products of each country? I wanted to find the answers.

The humble pencil opened new doors of understanding.

Books and magazines from Cheriyachan's travels too opened windows to the world. One particular book, with its captivating image of dense forests, ignited a desire within me to explore distant lands. The forests were so think that sunlight would refuse to peep in.

"Where is this place?" I asked him.

"In Korea," he told me, his voice filled with the magic of discovery.

"What a wonderful place!" I exclaimed.

My curiosity did not end there. I decided I should go to Korea one day. And to different parts of the world. I wanted to see the beautiful sights there. I longed for the exquisite dishes there. I desired to savour those unique cultures.

Cheriyachan's wisdom extended beyond material gifts, teaching me the life-changing power of travel.

Every person should travel. Journeying offers a fresh lens through which to view life and one's own identity. It introduces you to diverse people, cultures and experiences, guiding you through a spectrum of adventures that may reshape your understanding of existence.

Much later in life did I realise the extent of Cheriyachan's influence on me—something he himself was not aware of.

That pencil and the book on Korea took my life into a totally new direction.

The 'Kannimanga' lessons

In our lush yard and sprawling fields, a bounty of trees and plants flourished, bearing succulent fruits and berries. My constant childhood companion was my cousin Kuttan, Valiachan's son. Each morning, our ritual began with the task of gathering Kannimanga, small green mangoes, and indulging in their tangy goodness dipped in salt. If we picked more, we would give it to the household for making pickles. The competition between us was fierce; the first to rise claimed the richest pick, turning mango-picking into a spirited contest.

Driven by my competitive spirit, I would rise early, eager to secure victory. But Kuttan, less inclined to rivalry, often yielded the prize to me. Yet, one day, witnessing his disappointment, I learned the joy of sharing, offering him a portion of my harvest and experiencing the warmth it brought to both our hearts. He picked the mangoes I picked and ate them, much to my joy. It opened my mind to a new realm of benevolence.

In a reciprocal display of friendship, when I got feverish and rose late one morning, Kuttan, recognising my absence, set aside a stack of for me, ensuring I wouldn't miss out.

As I walked out of the house, I saw a stack he had kept for me in a corner — the same way I did for him earlier.

"That's your share, you have it," he said.

His gesture brought tears to my eyes, teaching me the ever important lesson of empathy and generosity. It was my first lesson that one's achievements and success should be shared with others.

When I shared my winnings with him, he also learnt a lesson in magnanimity. The learning was mutual.

This childhood game of mango-picking also instilled in me the virtue of early rising, a discipline I uphold to this day. If we rise early, we feel that we have a lot of time in our hands. We may start our preparations early. We may gear up for facing the challenges of the day. We may plan the day with a clear mind and achieve results. For in the quietness of dawn, drowned in the chorus of waking birds and the gentle caress of the morning breeze, lies the promise of a new beginning—a chance to seize the day with vigour and purpose. Whether through a brisk run, moments of meditation or simply basking in the fresh air, the early hours offer a time for mental clarity and creative rejuvenation.

By adhering to a regular sleep schedule and awakening with the dawn, I take in the unique inspiration that each morning brings.

I consider this a good habit I learnt in childhood.

Usually, I hit the bed between 10 p.m. and 11 p.m. unless there is something urgent, a sports contest I take part in, an irresistible game to watch or a journey. And as I start each morning's journey, I am reminded that true winners are those who greet the dawn with open hearts and minds.

The most important lesson the 'Kannimanga' game taught me was that our success mantra, sources of inspiration, survival strategies and tales of triumph should be shared with others. The bottomline: we shouldn't be selfish. Indeed, the wisdom and life lessons from many people have made me what I am.

To a public school

From our ancestral *tharavad*, we made an unforgettable move to a new house, courtesy of Cheriyachan, near Govinda Talkies in Edappal. The land, a sprawling three acres, was acquired from the owner of Udayannur Mana, setting the stage for a concrete bungalow that would comfortably accommodate all of us. In a nod to our heritage, the house was christened 'Lakshmi', in honour of my paternal grandmother.

This transition marked an important moment in my life, ushering in a gradual shift in my outlook and overall quality of life. As we settled into our new surroundings, I found myself on a journey of adaptation.

My educational journey reflected this evolution. Up until the fifth grade, I attended Vijayamatha Convent in Ponnani, in the comforts of an English-medium education. Among my friends at school were Ajay, Preeti, Beeda, Princy, Stella, Vinesh and Sheeja. There were only 10 students in our class in 1978. However, the sixth grade saw me crossing over to Verur Government Upper Primary School, where the language of instruction shifted to Malayalam. It was a new experience, one that required adjustment.

I remember my classmates Bala, Shanmugham, Sheeja, Bhasi, Saeed, Aramugan, Janikutty and Dileepan.

It was at Verur school that I encountered Pramod, a dear friend whose simplicity and warmth endeared him to me instantly. Coming from a family of blacksmiths, Pramod's humble background only served to deepen our bond. "Come Dileep, let's go to my house," he would often invite me, leading the way to the Laksham Veedu Colony. It was one in a long row of houses built under a housing project for the landless initiated by M. N. Govindan Nair during the C. Achutha Menon Ministry (1970-77).

Our friendship flourished in the simplicity of those moments spent together, devoid of any material expectations. Whether engaged in conversation or lost in play, the joy we found in each other's company was enough to sustain us. Together, we explored the world of cinema, frequenting the Govinda Theatre near my house to indulge in the magic of movies.

As time passed, and circumstances shifted, our friendship endured. Pramod remained my constant companion until the day my father's new house beckoned, leading us down separate paths, yet forever bound by the memories we shared.

Imagination soars through clay-modelling

Ah, those childhood days spent immersed in the dirt, sculpting and crafting with clay, building miniature towns and energetic communities from soil, leaves and whatever odds and ends we could find lying around. I foraged for fallen leaves, weathered twigs, and reclaimed lumber. Even broken pipes and discarded cables found new life in my creations, transformed from cast-offs into something beautiful. Idleness was a foreign concept to me back then—I was always buzzing with creative energy, eager to bring my imaginative visions to life.

Whether constructing playhouses, roads or bridges, there was never a dull moment. My hands were perpetually in motion, shaping and moulding the world around me. And when I wasn't knee-deep in clay, I found joy in pencil drawing, channeling my restless spirit into yet another avenue of expression.

I remember the excitement of discovering new materials to incorporate into my creations—twigs that became trees, pebbles that turned into boulders and pieces of discarded fabric that transformed into flags and banners. Each day was an adventure, a new opportunity to explore and experiment. The thrill of watching my ideas take form, no matter how simple or grand, filled me with a sense of accomplishment and wonder.

But there's something special about doing what you love, isn't there? It's not about the income or the recognition; it's the sheer joy and satisfaction that comes from engaging in work that resonates with your soul. That's the real secret to happiness, I think—finding fulfillment in the things you do, regardless of what others might say or expect.

Life deals us a series of blows, no doubt about it. But when it comes to our careers and passions, we have the power to chart our own course. We shouldn't settle for anything less than what makes us truly happy, because at the end of the day, that's what allows us to enjoy each moment and live life to the fullest.

Journey to the fields

Transitioning to Kuttipuram Junior Technical School marked a new chapter in my high school education journey. Around the same time, changes were afoot within our extended family as we collectively decided to pursue separate living arrangements. Cheriyachan facilitated this transition by dividing his property between my father and his other brother, with my father securing his own share in the process.

My father acquired land near Edappal, a quaint locality known as Annakkampad. Here, he constructed a new home for our family.

The call of the soil beckoned my father back to his roots, and he eagerly answered, turning his gaze towards the vast fields of paddy, the sturdy coconut palms, the precious arecanut trees and the thriving plantains.

Heir to Achachan's farming legacy, my father cultivated more than just crops. God's own country revealed its wonders. Our home transformed into a heaven as our garden flourished with an abundance of fruits and vegetables. My father's agricultural endeavours took a significant turn with not one, but two plantain farms. One piece of land, a treasured inheritance steeped in family history, became a canvas for his agricultural dreams. The other, acquired on lease, represented a new chapter, showing his renewed vigour. In this agrarian odyssey, my father's life story emerged.

Many years later, as I faced the ardent sun, I reminisced about those evenings with my father in the agricultural fields, where the soil held stories. My father and I had a routine that added a unique rhythm to our days. Regularly, he would lead me to the agricultural fields after school, where I became his companion in watering the banana trees. Holidays were especially fond, as they stretched out into entire days spent alongside him in the fields. This harmonised perfectly with my natural inclination to stay active. Every moment engaged in the work was a source of genuine enjoyment.

As I returned home from school, my father would greet me with a familiar call, "Son, let's head to the banana plantation."

Despite the weariness of the day, I always found comfort in these moments spent alongside my father, tending to our land. Contributing my bit to the family income filled me with pride.

Yet, a small pang of longing remained in my heart, especially when it meant missing out on football games with my friends. The trek from one plantation to another, about two kilometres away, was bittersweet, as I watched my friends play.

Achan would carry the kerosene engine on his head, while I carried the pipes on my shoulder.

"Hey, aren't you joining us?" my friends would inquire.

"Not today, I've got some work to do," I'd reply, masking my disappointment as I trudged towards the farm, laughter and shouts fading behind me.

Despite the occasional yearning for play, I understood the importance of prioritising family and responsibilities. Reminding myself of this, I pushed aside any residual regrets and plunged into the tasks at hand.

Sports, however, remained an integral part of my life, offering not just physical strength but also a sense of camaraderie. It was through sports that I forged lasting friendships and learned valuable lessons in sportsmanship.

Perhaps it's because I value integrity and strive to achieve success through honest means that I have such a deep love for games. My passion for sports led me to introduce cricket to my native place, making me one of the pioneers in bringing this beloved game to our community. Cricket took root there in 1987, starting modestly amid many limitations. Despite the challenges, we nurtured the sport with enthusiasm. Those early days, filled with the excitement of playing and the camaraderie of the team, remain some of the most precious moments of my life. The memories of organising matches, practising in makeshift fields and the sheer joy of hitting a well-timed shot or taking a crucial wicket crowd my mind. These experiences not only deepened my love for cricket but also taught me lessons about teamwork, perseverance and the spirit of fair play.

Reliving the magic of movies

The thrill of watching movies at Murali and Govinda theatres in Edappal was the highlight of my teenage years. Little did I know then that those cinematic experiences would shape my perspective on life. Movies have also inspired my passion for journeys and cars. I used to visit the cinemas with my bosom friend Pramod.

Movies have the power to transport us to different worlds and broaden our horizons. They've certainly had a deep impact on me. After watching films set in foreign lands, I couldn't help but yearn to visit places such as Singapore, the U.S., and the U.K., eager to witness the sights and sounds firsthand.

And it wasn't just the exotic locations that captivated me—it was also the lives of the heroes and heroines on screen. Their glamourous lifestyles and grand adventures vivified my teenage fantasies of living in big houses, driving nice cars and having close-knit friendships.

There were also films like 'Arante Mulla Kochu Mulla', a Malayalam mainstream movie, that left a lasting impression on me. Directed by Balachandra Menon, it taught me that even an ordinary person can make it big—a lesson that has stayed with me ever since.

In this movie, Balachandra Menon plays an ordinary man who turns wealthy and goes about driving a silver-coloured Honda Civic. That scene is still vivid in my mind. It was a moment of revelation for me, showing that with strength of will and effort, anything can be achieved, even the most expensive cars.

Dreaming brings immense satisfaction to our minds, filling us with hope and aspiration. I still love watching movies, though my tastes have evolved. Now, I am particularly drawn to films that address contemporary issues, reflecting the complexities of our current world.

While I may not be an avid reader of books, I do enjoy flipping through magazines. I find great pleasure in talking and engaging in long conversations on a variety of topics. I especially love reading inspirational features in magazines and newspapers. Stories of successful people and their journeys captivate me, as they offer valuable lessons and insights. Learning about the role models who influenced their lives can deeply impact our own paths. These narratives of perseverance and achievement serve as powerful motivators, reminding us that we too can overcome challenges and reach our goals.

2

Dream it, you can achieve it

Those were the days at Kuttipuram Technical High School, where friendships blossomed and memories were made. Viswanathan, an ace singer, Ramachandran, Sasikumar, Suresh, Ashraf, Sajeeve, Mani, Nandan, Babu, Sreeni, Jayaprakash, Pradeep, Anand, Aravindan, Ashraf Ali, Latha, Leela, Manikantan, Surendran, Haris and Sayed—names etched in the annals of my heart.

Though I may not have been the brightest student, the support of my friends saw me through, culminating in good marks in my final exams. Back then, our school was just a modest building. After my school days, the institution got relocated to a building with better facilities.

Our beloved teachers—Santhakumari, Balabhaskaran, Sukumaran, Sudhakaran, and the ever-inspiring Ramachandran—were the guiding lights. Their dedication and wisdom not only imparted knowledge but also instilled in us the values and principles that would shape our future.

But it was the bond of friendship that truly enriched my life. Without my friends, I often wonder how different my journey would have been. Their firm support and encouragement bolstered my confidence at every turn.

In Edappal, my closest companions—Prakash, Hari, Rajesh, Babu, Pradeep, Giri, Akbar, Abu, Sudheer, Rafeek, Devan, Saifu, Bhasi, Jayan and Salam—were my pillars of strength. Together, we dreamed of a future filled with success and prosperity.

"I'm going to make it big in Dubai one day," I would declare to my friends.

And they would reply, "Dream big, my friend. Your desires have the power to manifest your destiny. If you can dream it, you can achieve it."

Listening to my plans for the future and the confidence I exuded, my friends must have been sure that I would get somewhere. However, I often wondered if my constant talk about my ambitions annoyed them. Eventually, I decided to stop bringing up such topics in our conversations. I realised that what truly mattered wasn't sharing our dreams with others, but working hard to achieve them. I am not someone who forgets friendships. I still make an effort to keep in touch with old friends. I find time to call them and maintain close ties with them.

Around the chessboard

The memories of Bindu Kalasamiti in Edappal bring a smile to my face. It was more than just a club—it was a hub of togetherness where friends gathered to bond over indoor games like carrom and chess.

I still recall the days when the membership fee was a mere INR 1, a sum we couldn't even afford back then. But thanks to the tireless efforts of people like Sasi, who served as the club's secretary, and the support of the Local Committee of the Communist Party of India (Marxist), we were able to enjoy the camaraderie and competition the club offered.

Mohan, whom we called Mohan Chettan, our resident chess prodigy, ruled the chessboard with unmatched skill. However, I'll never forget the day I managed to defeat him in a game of chess after just two weeks of learning. The victory was sweet and I could feel the confidence surging within me.

With a steely determination in his eyes, he offered me a challenge. "How about playing one more game?" he proposed, his voice laced with confidence.

I accepted the challenge without hesitation. "Okay, let's see," I replied, masking my nerves with a facade of assurance.

As the game started, our friends gathered around, their eyes darting between us in anticipation. With each move, the tension mounted, until finally, against all odds, I emerged victorious for the second time.

The silence that followed was deafening, broken only by the thunderous applause of my friends. Mohan Chettan, his pride wounded by defeat, could barely conceal his disbelief. "Well played," he conceded, a hint of admiration shining through his defeat.

I never got the opportunity to play against Mohan Chettan again.

But for me, the victory went beyond the chessboard. It was a reminder that with courage, anything is possible.

Life, like any game, is filled with challenges and obstacles. But it's the thrill of overcoming these hurdles that drives us forward. Failures are not the end—they're simply checkpoints on the journey towards success.

And just like in a game, where every loss steels yourself to win the next, every setback in life teaches us valuable lessons and strengthens our resolve. Every time I lost a game, I prepared myself to win the next one. The point is: never repeat your mistakes. Learn from the mistakes. If you despair over defeat, you risk losing everything. New paths to success are discovered through the lessons learned from failure. I remained confident that I would win the next game.

That's why Sparrow, the cricket club we formed, became more than just a team—it was a symbol of firmness of purpose, where players like Mohan Chettan, Satyettan (Satyan), Bawaka, Sainuddinka (Sainuddin), Liyakath Bhai, A.P., Vallettan, Jabirka (Jabir), Sadanandettan (Sadanandan), Pradeep, Rajesh, Prakash and many others came together to play the game they loved.

Whether on the chessboard or the cricket field, I've learned that every victory and every defeat shapes us into the person we're meant to be.

The bonds we formed extended beyond the games we played. We often discussed our dreams, shared our worries and celebrated our small victories together. It was within the walls of Bindu Kalasamiti that I realised the impact of community and friendship on personal growth. The support and encouragement we received from each other were instrumental in shaping our perspectives and ambitions.

Beyond the games, the club hosted various events and gatherings that brought the entire community together. Festivals, cultural programmes and impromptu talent shows were regular occurrences. These events created a sense of belonging and unity, making Bindu Kalasamiti a cornerstone of our social lives. The club was a melting pot of ideas and talents, where everyone, regardless of their background, could find a place and a voice. It was in this nurturing environment that many of us discovered our passions and honed our skills, laying the foundation for our future endeavours.

Nuggets of wisdom: timeless proverbs

I've always found it easy to connect with people of all ages, especially the elders. There's something truly enriching about engaging in conversations with them. Their life experiences offer such valuable insights and wisdom. I'm particularly close to the fathers of many of my friends. Many of these elders are above the age of 50.

The inspiration I got from them has been invaluable. We can never walk the paths they did because time never travels backwards. Each pearl of wisdom they share, gleaned from the richness of their experiences and the starkness of the realities they faced, enhance our lives.

One of the elders who left a lasting impression on me is Babyettan, the father of my friend Prakash. His wisdom and warmth always left a mark on me.

I also have a deep fascination with proverbs. They're little nuggets of wisdom for the benefit of humanity. They are timeless truths that have been passed down from generation to generation. They are thousands of years old, with layers of meaning embedded in them. Proverbs do not just spring up one fine morning. On the contrary, they are a repository of history and culture. They serve as commentaries on life and reflect an ancient tradition of knowledge transfer. They have rightly guided me more than anything else in my life journey.

Like proverbs, I've also been drawn to the verses from

the 'Thirukkural', or 'Kural' as it's commonly known. This classic Tamil text is packed with 1,330 couplets that explore the virtues of everyday life.

The beauty and meaning of those lines, which have become an inspiration and life lesson for generations, hold eternal value. Thirukkural, where big ideas are concealed in little verses, deeply impressed me during my days in Madras. Such wisdom and observations become truly meaningful only when practised in real life. If not, what relevance do they hold?

Polytechnic days

My journey from high school to pursuing civil engineering at Seethi Saheb Memorial Polytechnic College in Tirur is deeply rooted in my passion for architecture and design. As a child, I crafted playhouses and figures from clay and hardboard, igniting a fervent desire to see my creations materialise. This childhood passion enlivened my dreams of constructing grand buildings and villas, driving me towards a career in civil engineering.

At Polytechnic, I found companionship among friends, reminiscent of the bonds formed in high school. Together, we shared laughter, occasional escapades to the cinema and precious memories that still warm our hearts today. Our reunions reflect the enduring friendships forged during those formative years.

The lectures and practical sessions not only equipped me with technical knowledge but also instilled in me an appreciation for the intricate workings of civil engineering. Each day brought new challenges and opportunities, pushing me to expand my understanding and hone my skills. Yet, it was not just the academic rigour that defined my experience at Polytechnic. It was the sense of belonging and camaraderie that permeated the campus, promoting a supportive environment where friendships flourished and memories were made. Whether it was collaborating on group projects or cheering each other on during sports events, the bonds forged at Polytechnic became an integral part of my journey.

While my academic performance may have been average, my mind teemed with lofty aspirations and calculated plans for the future. I meticulously plotted my life's trajectory. From Tirur to Dubai, my visions expanded. While I dreamt in 1986 that I should work in Dubai one day, my mind perhaps imagined the metropolis we see today.

Dubai, once a mere speck on the world map, beckoned to me with promises of opportunity and prosperity.

Despite the skepticism of others, I harboured an unfluctuating confidence in Dubai's potential for growth and development. Though still undeveloped, Dubai had a strong brand value. My decision to pursue my dreams in Dubai showed my willingness to defy convention and woo the unknown.

Cheriyachan's influence, coupled with my penchant for unconventional thinking, guided me towards new horizons beyond the borders of India. With each step, I dared to challenge the status quo, refusing to settle for mediocrity.

My soundtrack of love

Back in college, English pop songs were like a lifeline for me. There was something about the beats and lyrics that just resonated with me deeply. But getting my hands on those pop cassettes in Kerala was like trying to find a needle in a haystack. I did what any music enthusiast would do—I hopped on a 12-hour train ride to Madras, all in pursuit of Michael Jackson's music.

Now, picture this: me, eagerly popping that cassette into my recorder back home, ready to groove to some classic MJ tunes. Instead of the King of Pop's signature voice, I'm greeted with the sound of a female vocalist. Talk about a plot twist! For a moment, I questioned everything – had I been duped? But then it hit me, the sheer genius of Michael Jackson. His ability to morph his voice into any form was nothing short of mind-blowing.

Moreover, Jackson's impact extended beyond his musical prowess. He was a cultural icon who used his platform to address important social issues, advocating for unity, equality and humanitarian causes. His philanthropic efforts and commitment to making the world a better place inspired millions around the globe, including myself. Jackson's music became more than just entertainment; it was a catalyst for change and a beacon of hope in times of adversity.

Of course, alongside my love for Western hits, Malayalam movie melodies also had a special place in my heart. It was like having my own musical universe. Whenever life got a bit overwhelming, I'd retreat into the world of music.

Now, let's talk romance— about those fleeting encounters that peppered my college days. Some were like shooting stars, bright and intense, while others fizzled out before they could really take off. With many distractions around, I made a conscious decision to prioritise my studies and ambitions. After all, love is great, but I wasn't about to let it derail my dreams.

Looking back, I don't dwell on the what-ifs or the could-have-beens. Instead, I see each relationship as a chapter in my life story, shaping me into who I am today.

A government job amid Nature's serenity

Having earned my Diploma in Civil Engineering from the Polytechnic College, I knew I needed hands-on experience in the construction sector. I dived into the world of local construction firms, where my monthly salary was a modest INR 300. Places like Meena Constructions in Kuttipuram, Muralidharan Contractors in Guruvayur and Universal Constructions in Edappal became my training grounds.

But it was at the age of 21 that my journey took a pivotal turn. Landing a job at Peppara Dam, in the heart of Thiruvananthapuram's lush wilderness, was like stepping into a paradise. Surrounded by dense forests, away from the city, the dam stood as an oasis of tranquility. The reservoir, always brimming with water after the rain, served as a lifeline for an entire city.

Every day was a marvel of Nature's beauty. Wild animals could be spotted every now and then. The verdant greenery, towering mountains and the majestic Agasthyakoodam hills painted a picture-perfect backdrop. And, in this haven, my bosses Pereira, Mohanan and Sasidharan were a source of inspiration.

But it wasn't just my colleagues who left a lasting impression. Gunman Sudhakaran, Electrician Sudhakaran, Chechi at the Post Office, the Postman, Office Boy Muralidharan, Boat Driver

Divakaran, Driver Dhanarajan, Overseer Kuttappan Nair, the Canteen Owner and the Maid, all embraced me with open arms.

As night fell, I often found myself lying under the star-studded sky, pondering the intricacies of Nature's design. Each twinkling star felt like a silent whisper, reminding me of the precision with which the universe operates.

I was amazed at how precisely Nature has arranged everything. If the sun were to move a little closer to Earth, human beings would be unable to survive due to the heat. If it were to move a bit farther away, we would face extreme cold. The Sun and each planet travel through precise orbits, arranged perfectly by Nature without a single mistake.

If the wind strength were greater than it is now, flames would engulf many places. This same Nature provides air, water, food and clothing to human beings. Human beings revere unseen deities, yet ironically, they destroy Nature, the real God. From my youth, I have been keenly observing and learning from everything around me. I respect Nature and have constantly learnt from it.

Whenever a question arises in my mind, I do not rest until I find an answer. I persistently think about it, driven by the same compulsion to achieve my desires and dreams. Call me naughty, stubborn or crazy if you will, but I strive to be different from everyone else.

And as I gazed at the wonders up above the world so high, I couldn't help but reflect on the wisdom imparted by my grandmother's bedtime stories.

"Let me tell you a story," she would say, her voice a soothing melody in the quiet of the night.

"Once upon a time..."

Granny had an endless collection of stories — like Scheherazade, the vizier's daughter. The tales did not end any night. And they looked like they would never end. They continued even after Bulukiya explored the seas and the Garden of Eden in his quest for the herb of immortality, after Abdullah the Fishermen discovered an underwater submarine society, and a bevy of characters flew across in the form of jinns, mermaids, talking serpents and talking trees. The stories never stopped.

Those stories were my gateway to a world of knowledge, guiding me through the trials and triumphs of life. They made me a better human being and took my imagination on a magic carpet.

Resigning from job

Four years had passed since graduation and, still, my dreams of working in Dubai seemed like distant stars in the night sky. Despair began to weigh heavy on my shoulders.

In my darkest moments, I confided in my friend Ashraf, pouring out my frustrations like a torrential rain. "Nothing is going right," I lamented, my voice heavy with defeat.

But Ashraf, ever the optimist, spoke with unwavering confidence. "Everything will be all right, Dileep. Time will come. Never despair," he reassured me.

A visit to the tribal families of Kanikkar section near Peppara brought a glimmer of light to my troubled soul. Witnessing their simple yet irrepressible way of life reignited a spark within me. In the face of adversity, they thrived, living in harmony with Nature and drawing strength from their deep-rooted connection to the land. Their confidence and courage to overcome obstacles amazed me.

And so, without much fanfare or deliberation, I made the bold decision to resign from my job at Peppara. The air was heavy with tension as I returned home to Edappal, my parents' disapproval hanging palpably in the air.

"Why did you leave your job?" my father's voice boomed with disappointment. "People are struggling to find any job and here you are, giving it up."

I remained silent, knowing that my actions went against the grain of societal expectations. In their eyes, securing a government job after graduation was a pinnacle of success, a modicum of stability in an uncertain world.

But I was not one to conform to the status quo. I had dreams that burned brighter than any societal norm. And so, with resolve in my heart, I made a daring declaration to my father: “I am selling my bike. I’m going to Bombay with the money to find work there.”

Shock and disbelief painted my father’s face as he struggled to comprehend my audacious plan. “Why are you selling the bike?” he exclaimed, his voice tinged with confusion and concern.

Before he could object, I vanished from before my father’s eyes, determined to go to Bombay and then get a visa to reach Dubai.

One summer day, while chatting on the road with my friend Hari, we bumped into Ummer, a friend from Kuttipuram Technical High School. Ummer, a year junior to me, had not only been my schoolmate, but also a fellow student at the Polytechnic College, where he studied Civil Engineering.

The sight of Ummer was a stark contrast to the memories we had. He trudged under the scorching sun, carrying rolled-up carpets precariously balanced on his head. Sweat and exhaustion streaked his face. His clothes, an unkempt shirt and ragged pants, spoke of hardship.

Deeply moved by his condition, I urged him to put down the carpets. I then took him home, where I requested Amma to offer him tea and snacks. As we sipped our tea, Hari and I caught up with Ummer.

My concern prompted me to ask, “Why are you carrying these carpets, Ummer? With your civil engineering diploma, shouldn’t you be able to land a good construction job?”

Ummer offered a tired smile. “Finding a decent job hasn’t been easy, but my family needs me to provide for them.”

His words hit me hard. Reaching into my pocket, I found only INR 50. I offered it to Ummer, wishing him well in his job search and sharing some tips I thought might be helpful. Back then, INR

50 was a significant amount for me and Hari. We often struggled to afford even a masala dosa, which cost around two and a half rupees. Sometimes, we even had to borrow a rupee or two from the grocery store owner Unniyettan just to make ends meet.

Seeing Ummer that day turned into a valuable life lesson for me. His situation underscored the importance of hard work and taking on any available opportunity to support one's family until the ideal job comes along. I'm grateful to Ummer for reminding me of these crucial truths.

Thankfully, things turned around for Ummer. He eventually landed a decent job in the construction field. There's no doubt that our experiences that day inspired each other.

The call of Bombay

Rajettan (Rajan), a friend of my father, had borrowed some money from him. But due to financial constraints, he couldn't repay it. However, he came to us with a different offer of help. One day, he said to my father, "A close friend of mine, Maniyettan (Mani), is in Bombay. He has connections and influence there. If Dileep goes to Bombay, I'll ask him to lend a hand.

Intrigued, my father asked, "Can Maniyettan help him find a job and accommodation when he gets to Bombay?"

Rajettan assured him, "Of course, everything can be arranged. I'll make the call."

With Rajettan's words, a sense of relief enveloped my household. My parents, reassured that I wouldn't be alone in Bombay, agreed to send me off. In 1990, at the age of 21, I started my journey to the metropolis of Bombay, a place I had only heard of but never seen.

On the day of my departure, my friends Prakash, Babu, Pradeep and Rajesh gathered at Kuttipuram railway station to bid me farewell. Babu kindly offered me a ride on his scooter, while the others arrived at the station by bus.

With a suitcase packed with essentials, I held onto the seat in front of me as Babu maneuvered through the busy streets. As I boarded the train, the weight of my dreams hung heavily on my shoulders.

I couldn't shake the sense of nostalgia that enveloped me. The streets I had traversed countless times, the faces of friends chiselled in my memory, and the comforting embrace of family—all seemed to blur into a bittersweet tableau of the past. Yet, amidst the tinge of sadness, a spark of excitement ignited within me, fired my resolve to forge ahead. With every passing moment, I felt the weight of responsibility and the exhilaration of possibility intertwine, propelling me forward into the vast expanse of the unknown. Though uncertainty loomed on the horizon, I clung to the faith that guided my steps.

No pain, no gain, I reminded myself, wiping away the tears. My mind was set on my ultimate goal: Dubai. Bombay was just a pit stop on my journey to the land of opportunity.

BOMBAY BECKONS

3

'It's a promise'

As the train chugged along towards Bombay, now Mumbai, the journey felt like an eternity. Surrounded by the clatter of wheels and the rhythmic swaying of the carriage, I found comfort in the company of my fellow travellers. Among them, one stood out – Rev. Fr Joseph. Our conversation flowed effortlessly, as if we were old friends catching up after years apart.

Fr Joseph, with his gentle demeanour and wise words, seemed to understand the turmoil within me as I set off on this journey away from home. As we talked, he listened intently, his eyes reflecting kindness.

When I shared my aspirations of finding work in Bombay and eventually making my way to Dubai, his encouragement was like a balm to my soul. His words rang with assurance.

"You've made a brave decision, my brother," he said. "With hard work and perseverance, your dreams will surely come to fruition."

His words touched me. In that moment, I felt a sense of relief, knowing that someone believed in my journey as much as I did.

Throughout the journey, I also crossed paths with a group of engineers, each with their own dreams and aspirations. Unlike me, they harboured no desire to venture beyond the borders of India. Their reasons were their own and I respected that diversity of dreams.

The experience within the train was equally rich. Vendors hopped on and off at each station, selling everything from steaming cups of chai to savory samosas, their voices adding to the sounds of the journey. The bonding among the passengers was heartwarming; stories were exchanged, meals were shared and there was a sense of collective anticipation. The rhythmic clatter of the wheels and the gentle swaying of the carriage created a soothing lullaby that, despite the length of the journey, offered a strange comfort. In this lively atmosphere, Fr Joseph's presence was a constant source of reassurance.

After three long days of travel, we arrived at Bombay's busy Dadar railway station. The train was late by a day. Fr Joseph remained by my side.

As my co-passengers bid their farewells and disappeared into the crowd, I realised that Maniyettan was not at the station to receive me. He did not know the time of my delayed arrival. With no cellphone or similar facilities in those days, communication was difficult. I felt a pang of anxiety grip my heart. Rajettan had given me Maniyettan's address.

It was then that Fr Joseph stepped forward, offering to accompany me to my destination. Grateful for his kindness, I accepted his offer, and together we made our way through the crowded streets of Bombay.

Stepping onto the streets of Mumbai for the first time, I felt as though I had entered a dynamic mosaic of human activity. Every corner teemed with life, a whirlwind of sights, sounds and smells enveloping me in a spirited sensory experience. The sounds of honking horns, vendors' calls and the chatter of passersby filled the air, creating a rich urban soundtrack that seemed to pulse with the city's energy.

I found myself swept along by the flow of humanity. From the labourer carrying a heavy burden to the office worker rushing to catch the next train, the streets painted a bright picture of the city's diverse life. Every alleyway and thoroughfare revealed a new chapter in Mumbai's story. It was an overwhelming sensory experience, yet amidst the chaos, there was a palpable sense of life and vitality that left me both exhilarated and awe-inspired.

Arriving at the address provided by Rajettan, we were met with surprised expressions from Maniyettan's wife Sudha Chechi (Sudha) because she saw me with a priest.

Before parting ways, Fr Joseph offered me one last piece of advice.

"When you've made it big in Dubai, don't forget to spare a thought for the less fortunate," he said with a smile. "Remember the orphanage I run and perhaps a small donation from your first paycheck wouldn't go amiss."

I nodded solemnly, touched by his selflessness. "Of course, Father," I replied. "It's a promise."

Thriving in a small space

Exhaustion weighed heavy upon me and the absence of Maniyettan only added to my weariness. I fell asleep.

Three hours later, I awoke to the sound of Maniyettan return from work, his presence a welcome sight in the unfamiliar surroundings. I apprised him of all that Rajettan told me and my family.

With his daughter Nisha's arrival, the house gained a sense of warmth and she reminded me of my own sisters. She quickly became my first friend in Bombay.

"Let's go," Maniyettan announced after a while. With a firm grip on my suitcase, he led the way as we went through the chaotic maze of Mumbai's local trains. The crowded compartments reverberated with the chatter of strangers, the aroma of Vada-Paav filling the air as vendors navigated through the throng. All of them talked in Hindi. It was a totally new experience.

The cityscape of Mumbai presented itself as a dynamic tableau, where towering structures cast long shadows over age-old temples and markets bright with merchandise. The skyline was a blend of sleek modernity and historical grandeur, each building telling a story of ambition and legacy. The streets were alive with a mosaic of human activity, from the precise rhythm of office-goers to the spontaneous choreography of street vendors. The air carried the mingling scents of freshly ground spices, ocean saltiness and the unmistakable hint of industry. Every corner revealed a new facet of the city's character, from serene coastal promenades to the intricate warren of narrow lanes brimming with life and colour.

Finally, we reached our destination – Santacruz station. The station pulsed with the constant ebb and flow of commuters. Its platforms, adorned with weathered advertisements and worn tiles, served as transient stages where the city's strange rhythm played out with each passing train.

Maniyettan had arranged a residence for me. Ganesh Darshan, a modest building two kilometres from the station, would be my new home.

As Maniyettan bid farewell, I was left to face the reality of my new living quarters. The room, miniscule at three metres by three metres, offered a glimmer of refuge. Its tight dimensions pressed in on all sides, but it was undeniably shelter. Yet, the prospect of sharing this cramped space with strangers cast a shadow, dampening the spark of hope that the room had ignited. In addition to the bedroom, there was a small kitchen and a washroom.

"I'm Seeb," my roommate greeted me.

"And there will be four more joining us after work," he added, a statement that filled me with trepidation. A weak smile played on my lips, barely masking the disappointment.

The arrival of the others marked the beginning of my first day in Bombay. Memories of solitary nights in my hometown haunted me as I lay on the floor, the absence of a bed a stark reminder of my new reality.

All of us lay on straw mats. We even shared the pillows. I still remember my first day in that drab living quarter. Tired, I fell asleep immediately. With no better options in sight, I resolved to make the most of my situation.

Simple. If you are left with no option or opportunity, you adjust to the new situation immediately. For me, there was no option other than the one arranged by Maniyettan. There was no one else I knew in Mumbai.

Before long, I felt in sync with that living quarter and the people there.

Bathroom queue blues

As I stumbled through the darkness of our cramped quarters, the urgency of Nature's call propelled me to seek out the bathroom. But what I found there left me stunned and bewildered.

My roommate led me to the end of the second floor, where a solitary shower stood in place of the facilities I had expected. The realisation dawned upon me with a jolt – this room was ill-equipped to fulfill even the most basic of needs.

Surveying the scene before me, I saw only three toilets for the entire floor, a pitiful number considering the multitude of residents sharing this space. The ratio was disturbing—three toilets for 30 people!

The queue of weary souls waiting their turn stretched on endlessly, a grim reminder of the harsh realities of communal living.

Reaching the toilets, I found myself facing a formidable queue of four. In that moment, I couldn't help but long for the comforts of home, where a bathroom was a sanctuary reserved for personal use. But as my mind wrestled with disappointment, a voice within urged me to press on, reminding me of the dreams that lay ahead.

"Yes, these may be thorns in your path," it whispered, "but they are but temporary obstacles on your journey to greatness. Keep your eyes on the prize and let nothing deter you from your goal."

No one is born with Aladdin's Magic Lamp. No pain, no gain. The road to success is long, but with grit and determination, we can climb every mountain.

With resolve renewed, I braved the foul stench, redolent of cigarette smoke, that permeated the air. Memories of that noxious blend of mould and neglect still irk my nostrils. The toilet, though far from inviting, served as a reminder of the sacrifices I was willing to endure in pursuit of my dreams.

The rumble of aeroplanes

In those days, communication with loved ones was a painstaking process, devoid of the instant gratification we've grown accustomed to. With no mobile phones or landlines in my house in Edappal, the only option was to put pen to paper and send letters, hoping they would reach their destination.

I remember the sense of anticipation as I penned down my safe arrival in Bombay, pouring out my heart onto the page before sealing it with hope and sending it off into the unknown. Days would pass like eternity as I waited for a reply, longing for the familiar voices of home to reach me through the written word.

My roommates – Seeb, Ansari, Raghu, Pratap and Hari — welcomed me with open arms, eager to share their own experiences of the city with a newcomer like myself.

As they imparted their wisdom on navigating the labyrinthine circuit of local trains and the names of neighbourhoods, I listened with rapt attention.

A warning hung in the air like a dark cloud – "Bombay is full of thieves and pickpockets. Be careful" — they would caution me whenever I ventured out.

Undeterred, I threw myself into the rhythm of daily life, quickly picking up the nuances of the Hindi language and learning to handle the intricacies of cooking alongside my newfound friends. Together, we would chop vegetables and wash dishes.

Outside our window, the constant roar of planes taking off from Bombay airport permeated the air. While my friends cursed the noise, I found music in the distant rumble, dreaming of the day when one of those planes would carry me towards my dreams in Dubai. This contrast underscored the power of perspective. After all, different people interpret the same experience differently.

New beginnings

As the days passed, I realised that Maniyettan's busy schedule left little room for him to assist me in my job hunt. I took matters into my own hands, diligently scouring the pages of *The Times of India* for any vacancies that matched my skills as a draftsman.

One fateful day, armed with will power and a map scrawled with directions from helpful strangers, I arrived at the office of Niranjan Pandya and Harshad Dholakia Architects. In the absence of GPS or Google Maps, the kindness of strangers guided me to my destination just in time for the interview.

Confidence buoyed by my convent school English, I faced the interview with aplomb, impressing the bosses Mr. Pandya and Mr. Harshad enough to secure a promising job offer on the spot.

Excitedly sharing the news with my friends, their incredulous reactions filled the room. "A job on the first interview? You're lucky!" they exclaimed in unison, their disbelief tinged with admiration.

The next day marked the beginning of my new career, with the rampant chaos of Bombay's local trains becoming my daily commute. I would get down at Victoria Terminus, later renamed Chhatrapati Shivaji Terminus (CST). My new workplace was in Dalal Street, just a short, refreshing 15-minute walk away from the station.

Stepping off the train, I soaked in the sheer energy of Bombay. Every sight, sound and smell was a delightful novelty. My gaze was particularly drawn to the street vendors, their stalls overflowing with treasures. Clothes in every imaginable hue fluttered in the breeze, while the enticing aromas of exotic perfumes mingled with the cacophony of street life. Shoes gleamed under the evening sun, each pair a silent promise of adventure in this new city. The sheer variety and affordability of the wares were a constant source of fascination.

The wares at luxury shops teased me with tantalising glimpses of a lifestyle beyond my reach. Yet, with each passing day, I vowed to turn those dreams into reality, setting my sights on the day when my hard-earned salary would grant me access to those coveted treasures.

Proud to have become a part of Bombay in such a short time, I gazed at the opulence of luxury cars that lined the streets, each one a symbol of wealth and status. Standing in awe outside banks and institutions, I couldn't help but wonder – if they could achieve success, why not me? "Be patient," I told myself. "Your day will come. Then, I'll buy cars like these."

Chapati and curry à la Kuttettan

As months passed by at work, the itch for new horizons grew stronger within me. With a renewed sense of purpose, I set my sights once again on the path to my dreams, this time honing in on opportunities in Dubai.

Scouring the newspapers for any inkling of job vacancies in the big city, I seized every opportunity to attend interviews during my lunch breaks. But alas, my lack of experience beyond India proved to be a stumbling block.

Yearning for a reprieve from the cramped confines of my current accommodation, I turned to my old high school friend Surendran, who worked in the maintenance department of Indian Airlines as an engineer.

"Surendran, the room I'm staying in now is far from comfortable. Do you know of any other options?" I pleaded.

Without hesitation, Surendran offered a solution. "Stay with me until you find a new place. I'll talk to my roommate and sort it out," he assured me.

Surendran's generosity lifted my spirits, and soon, I found myself settling into a new abode in Bhandup Housing Colony. The debt of gratitude I owed him was immeasurable, a debt I vowed to carry with me always.

Later, I moved to a new room at Bhandup (W). In my new living arrangement, I found companionship in Gopalettan (Gopalan) and Kuttettan (Kuttan). Kuttettan, a humble and hardworking soul, took me under his wing, treating me like family.

Despite his modest stature of five feet, Kuttetan was a giant in kindness, his simple meals, mostly chapatis and curries he rustled up every morning, filling my heart as much as they filled my stomach. His vegetable curry, made with love and a dash of milk, became a special part of my daily routine, packed into my lunch box and enjoyed at the office,

Essentially, Kuttettan and I were different. He had very few desires, unlike me. But we shared something deeper – a belief in the inherent goodness of humanity.

I could not afford the rent there and I moved to another room soon, leading me to new roommates—Sreeni, Anil and Gopi. Though lacking in material wealth, they were rich in generosity.

Anil was a skilled welder. His biggest dream was of owning his own welding machine.

An opportunity overseas

As months passed by at work, the itch for new horizons grew stronger within me. I set my sights once again on the path to my dreams, this time honing in on opportunities in Dubai.

During my seven-month stay in Bombay, thoughts of going abroad were never far from my mind. Interview after interview, I sought the opportunity to spread my wings beyond India's borders. But it wasn't until I received an offer for a job in Oman that the possibility of working abroad became a reality. However, Oman wasn't where my heart longed to be. Similarly, a job offer in Qatar and a few in other countries failed to capture my interest. My sights were set firmly on Dubai.

Then, like a whisper in the wind, news of a job offer at UTCC Wade Adams, a prominent building and civil engineering contractor in Dubai, reached my ears. The company representatives, Mr. Naushad and Mr. Mohammad Vatuvara, conducted the interview, and upon selecting me, the discussion turned to salary negotiations.

Mr. Vatuvara, a seasoned negotiator, initially offered me 800 AED per month. But I thought that amount was low for a draftsman and stood firm, insisting on 900 AED (USD 245). After a series of back-and-forth negotiations, Mr. Vatuwara finally relented, acknowledging my ability to secure the best deals for the company in future negotiations.

"All right, I'll agree to 900 AED," he conceded, his tone bright. "If you can negotiate this salary with me, I have no doubt you'll excel in bargaining with clients, securing the best deals for our company."

This was my first taste of negotiation, a skill I had yet to fully develop.

Basically, I believe that arguments over money are best avoided. But I argued over my proposed first salary in Dubai on the basis of the confidence afforded by study and experience. I was not worried of losing out even if it was a job in my dreamland.

Thankfully, things played out swimmingly. At the age of 21, I was about to have my dream fulfilled. Even at that young age, I was clear about my path and goals. The destination was clear before me. There was no confusion whatsoever.

I was lucky that Ahmed Bhai, the owner of Trust Travels Private Limited was the recruiting agent of UTCC Wade Adams Company for Bombay. He left a lasting impression on me. A native of Tirur, he surmounted his physical challenges with unbelievable self-confidence and dedication. Within his family, he was a hero adored by all. He embodied the belief that one's abilities far outweigh any shortcomings. His humility and genuine joy in celebrating the achievements of others taught me invaluable lessons.

Bombay to Kerala

As I prepared to bid farewell to my company in Bombay, a whirlwind of aspirations for Dubai filled my mind. The allure of a job in a multinational company beckoned me.

My bosses, Mr. Pandya and Mr. Harshad, expressed their sadness at my departure. With heartfelt farewells to my co-workers, I boarded the train bound for home. I particularly relished the professional association with Namrata Oza, a talented architect, and Neelima, the ever-reliable company secretary.

The news of my job offer in Dubai was met with jubilation by my family and friends.

They celebrated my success with heartfelt congratulations and genuine pride, their excitement mirroring my own aspirations. My parents, who had always supported my ambitions, beamed with joy, while my friends eagerly discussed my impending adventure, filling the air with plans and well-wishes. Their collective enthusiasm and belief in my potential further inspired my resolution, making the dream of starting anew in Dubai feel even more tangible and within reach.

Reflecting on my time in Bombay, I realised the impact it had on me. What did Bombay teach me? Beyond simply learning to speak Hindi, I had gained a newfound confidence in my abilities.

Navigating the city's fast-paced and competitive environment had honed my adaptability, teaching me to thrive under pressure and seize opportunities. The diverse community in Bombay exposed me to different cultures and perspectives, broadening my understanding of the world and enhancing my interpersonal skills. The challenges I faced and overcame there instilled in me a sense of self-reliance, reinforcing my belief that I could handle whatever obstacles came my way.

I boldly charted my own course. Quitting my government job and catching the train to Bombay was entirely my call. The same went for leaving Bombay when Dubai beckoned with opportunity. No outside pressure swayed me. My dreams were finally about to blossom, validating the choices I had made. I felt a deep sense of happiness, my face radiating with joy at the thought that my success was the result of my own decisions, free from any external pressure or coercion. I felt proud of myself.

An unexpected turn

Eagerly awaiting the arrival of my visa to Dubai, months passed by in hopeful anticipation. But then, like a bolt from the blue, news reached me that shattered my dreams into a million pieces. I couldn't believe it. All the hopes I had nurtured and the confidence I had built up were suddenly torn down, leaving me reeling in disbelief.

The devastating news came like a tidal wave — due to the Kuwait-Iraq war, the Wade Adams Company had ceased all new recruitment efforts, dashing any chance of me starting my new job in Dubai. My heart sank, and my mind spun with uncertainty, unsure of what to do next. How could I face my family and friends, who were eagerly awaiting my departure for Dubai?

In the aftermath of the devastating news, I found myself in a state of limbo, caught between the future I had envisioned and the stark reality before me. Each day felt like an uphill battle as

I tried to come to terms with the abrupt end of my plans. The sparkling dreams of Dubai, once so vivid, now seemed distant and unreachable. Sleepless nights became my new normal as I tossed and turned, my mind racing with unanswered questions and fears. I often found myself staring blankly at the ceiling, the weight of uncertainty pressing down on me.

The sense of loss was beyond words, almost suffocating. The future I had meticulously planned and the goals I had set for myself now seemed to crumble before my eyes, leaving a void that felt impossible to fill. Conversations with family and friends became painful reminders of what could have been, their well-meaning words of comfort only highlighting the gap between my aspirations and reality. I felt isolated in my anguish, unable to articulate the depth of my disappointment and confusion. Every decision I had made, every step I had taken, seemed to unravel, leaving me stranded at a crossroads with no clear direction. The thought of starting over was daunting, and yet, the idea of giving up was equally unbearable.

As I grappled with the wreckage of my shattered dreams, I felt a glimmer of hope flicker within me, urging me not to surrender to despair. Despite the overwhelming sadness and the whispers of doubt from those around me, I knew deep down that giving up was not an option.

I made the difficult decision to return to Bombay.

Challenging oneself while heartbroken

Before departing for Bombay, I knew I had to share one of the most pivotal decisions of my life with my father. I have two sisters Pushpa and Sajana, and a brother, Abhilash, who is 14 years younger to me.

As the patriarch of our family, Achan had provided for us well, with a comfortable bank balance and substantial assets. Yet, I felt compelled to make a choice that diverged from the path of inheritance.

"I don't seek any share of your property," I confessed to my father, bracing myself for his reaction. "Divide it amongst my siblings."

His surprise was palpable. "But what will you do?" he inquired.

"I will work and earn," I asserted confidently, though I lacked a job at the time. "I have plans in place."

It was a decision I made with a sense of liberation and contentment, unburdened by the weight of material possessions. Though my family questioned the timing of my choice, for me, it was a strategic move in facing the uncertainties of life.

It was a valuable lesson in crisis management for me. No crisis should deter one from one's principles.

As I stood at the railway station, preparing to set off on the journey back to Bombay, my closest friends, Pradeep, Prakash, Rajesh and Babu, gathered to bid me farewell. My outward demeanour of smiles masked a tumult of emotions inside me. With each hug and well-wish, the facade of strength crumbled, revealing the vulnerability hidden within.

I confided in Prakash, my voice trembling with emotion. "Nothing seems to be falling into place, my friend," I admitted, the weight of my dreams and struggles heavy in my words.

"It's going to be alright, Dileep," he reassured me. Tears flowed down his cheeks. He hugged me. I allowed myself to surrender to the rawness of my emotions, shedding tears in the presence of friends for the first time in my life. I was weeping like a child.

In Mumbai again

After a gruelling two-day train journey, I found myself back in Bombay once more. Making my way to the familiar room shared with old friends Sreeni, Anil and Gopi, I was met with surprise.

"Haven't you left?" they asked, their confusion evident.

"No, the job didn't pan out," I replied with a heavy heart.

Without hesitation, they welcomed me back into the fold.

The following day, I mustered the courage to return to my former company, where I met with the owners to discuss my abrupt departure and offer my sincerest apologies. To my relief, they accepted my apology and graciously allowed me to resume my old position.

Life in Bombay resumed its familiar rhythm — the cacophony of the local trains, the hurly-burly of the streets, the daily grind of work and chores.

A month later, in February 1991, the call I had been eagerly awaiting finally came. Ahmed Bhai, the owner of Trust Travels Private Limited, delivered the news I had been longing to hear — a job opportunity in Dubai awaited me, with the visa ready for my departure.

Ahmed Bhai called up and told my office, "Reach Dileep and tell him he's landed a good job in Dubai. He needs to prepare for departure soon."

Overwhelmed with joy, my dreams of Dubai reignited with newfound vigour. Yet, a nagging concern remained — how would Mr Pandya and Mr Harshad react to my departure once again?

Unable to face them, I made the difficult decision to leave without bidding them farewell, relying on my colleagues Namrata and Neelima to relay the news. As I made my way out of the company, the weight of my decision hung heavy upon me, overshadowed only by the sorrow of parting ways with Maniyettan, his family and my friends.

As I prepared to depart, Anil approached me.

"Dileep," he began, his voice tinged with earnestness, "when you reach a good position in Dubai, I want you to buy me a welding machine. I've always dreamed of starting a small welding company."

Caught off guard by his sincerity, I couldn't help but feel a surge of emotion. Despite the uncertainty of my own future, Anil's unwavering faith in my success filled me with a renewed sense of purpose.

"Of course, Anil," I replied, "I promise to make your dream a reality."

DUBAI, MY LOVE

4

To Dubai with $10

February 13, 1991, marked a pivotal moment in my life, despite the ominous connotations of the number 13. Who said 13 was an unlucky number? The number of the house we stayed in Butchammal Street, Chennai, was 13. It took me 22 years to realise 13 was indeed a lucky number as I prepared to leave for Dubai!

While a war raged between Iraq and Kuwait, I remained firm in my decision to pursue my dreams in Dubai, even in the face of objections from my family and friends. Accompanied by my friend Gopi, I made my way to Bombay Airport in a bus. He carried my suitcase. The presence of Surendran and Chandrettan (Chandran), my father's friend, at the airport made me happy. Surendran was one of my close friends.

"Don't fret, Dileep," Chandrettan reassured me. "Change can be daunting, no doubt. But remember, with every challenge comes growth. Stay steadfast, my friend. You've got this. Things will fall into place."

I waved to them and stepped into the airport for the first time, the thrill of anticipation coursing through me. I couldn't believe it. I was inside an airport! I felt proud.

With check-in complete, I headed to the currency exchange with the rupees in hand. Exchanging them, however, brought a sobering realisation. My stack of rupees yielded a meager $10 USD.

With only $10 in my pocket, I boarded the Emirates flight bound for Dubai — poor in cash, but rich in dreams. Deep inside I knew that I wouldn't be poor for long. Rows of well-padded seats, upholstered in earthy tones, lined the spacious cabin, offering ample legroom for passengers to stretch out. Soft ambient lighting illuminated the space.

As the engines roared to life and the plane began to taxi down the runway, a surge of adrenaline pulsed through my veins, matching the rhythmic thud of my heart. With every passing second, the anticipation built, like a crescendo in a symphony, as the aircraft gained momentum. The Emirates flight EK 503 lifted off the ground.

My heart filled with excitement and nerves as the aircraft flew 30,000 ft above the ground. However, I couldn't shake off the pang of guilt for not saying goodbye to Mr Pandya and Mr Harshad, my former employers. The weight of my decision to leave without informing them hung heavy on my conscience.

High above the clouds, as I flew towards my dreams, I made a solemn vow to never again hurt any employer. I always follow my conscience. Yet, I couldn't ignore the complexities of decision-making and the unintended consequences that may follow. Sometimes, pursuing our dreams requires tough choices.

Salutations, my beloved land

I gazed out the window of the plane, overawed by the view of Dubai. Landing on the tarmac, I felt a surge of emotion. I bowed down to Dubai, my dreamland. I touched the tarmac. A silent wave of gratitude washed over me, grounding me to this new land of opportunity. It was as if I was kissing the earth, mentally expressing my deep appreciation for the journey that led me here.

In 1991, Dubai Airport retained elements of its humble beginnings while hinting at the grandeur that would later define it. The terminal, though modern, still exuded a sense of intimacy, with low ceilings and simple yet functional architecture. As travellers walked along well-lit corridors, they were greeted by a blend of traditional Arabian motifs and contemporary touches, reflecting the city's evolving identity. Outside, the desert landscape stretched as far as the eye could see, a stark contrast to the burgeoning metropolis that Dubai would soon become.

Stepping off the airport bus, I went to the immigration and collected my luggage. I was greeted by my sister Pushpa's husband, Keshavettan (Keshavan), who had come to pick me up. His warm smile instantly put me at ease as he ushered me into the waiting vehicle. "I'll take care of the luggage," he assured me, his familiarity with the city evident.

As the luggage was carefully placed in the trunk of the car, memories flooded back. There it was, the same suitcase Keshavettan had gifted me during his visit to Kerala from Dubai. I couldn't help but recall the same suitcase Maniyetyan had clutched tightly when I first arrived in Bombay, guiding me through the busy streets. Now, as fate would have it, that very suitcase from Dubai had made its journey full circle, returning to the city where it originated.

The taxi was driven by a Pakistani driver.

We proceeded to Bur Dubai. The narrow streets were lined with bustling souks, where the aroma of exotic spices mingled with the sounds of haggling merchants and shoppers. Towering above the labyrinthine alleyways were the iconic wind towers and minarets of ancient mosques, adding to the area's cultural richness. I found a diverse array of restaurants, cafes and shops catering to locals and tourists alike.

Arriving at the residence of Haridasettan (Haridas) in Bur Dubai, I was met with warm hospitality. "You'll stay here tonight," Keshavettan insisted.

The following morning, I prepared to join UTCC Wade Adams, greeted by the sight of Shihabka (Shihabudeen), a seasoned Malayali driver, who arrived to collect me in a gleaming white pick-up truck. With meticulous care, I placed my suitcase beside me in the car. Shihabka abruptly snatched it up and flung it into the truck bed without a second thought. I felt sad. His rough handling of my favourite suitcase hurt me, but I chose to remain silent.

Meeting Mr Naushad and Mr Muhammad Vatuvara, I was filled with a sense of pride at the opportunity to work in such a prestigious multinational company.

For a newcomer like me, working in such a company, had many advantages. It would provide access to cutting-edge technologies, best practices and innovative strategies, promoting continuous learning and skill enhancement. I knew that the multicultural environment of multinational companies in Dubai cultivated a dynamic and inclusive workplace, where collaboration with colleagues from various backgrounds enriched perspectives. Moreover, Dubai's strategic location would offer exposure to a wide range of markets and business opportunities, providing newcomers with the chance to expand their horizons and advance their careers on a global scale.

For many of us, the Dubai we cherish today is a dazzling metropolis of futuristic skyscrapers, opulent shopping malls and awe-inspiring attractions. However, not too long ago, our beloved emirate existed in a vastly different state. Cast your mind back to 1991, and you'll find a Dubai that bears little resemblance to the imposing city we know today. Picture Sheikh Zayed Road as little more than a barren expanse, devoid of the iconic skyline that now defines it. Imagine a time when the Burj Khalifa was nothing but a distant dream, yet to materialise in the minds of visionary Sheikhs and architects.

On Valentine's Day

On February 14, 1991, I began my journey with UTCC Wade Adams, coincidentally on Valentine's Day. For me, it marked not just the start of a new job, but also the beginning of my love affair with the city of Dubai. However, I've always felt that love shouldn't be confined to a single day; it should be celebrated every moment.

Assigned as an Assistant Quantity Surveyor in the main office, I found myself under the guidance of Mr K. G. Nair, a veteran in the company who held the esteemed position of Chief Estimator. Our projects primarily revolved around government institutions like the Dubai Municipality and UAE Public Works Department, focussing on road and drainage construction.

In Mr John Andrew Papadouris (JAP), the general manager of our road and drainage construction division, I found a mentor and godfather. His journey from humble beginnings to professional success was truly inspiring. JAP was a forward-thinking visionary leader, while K G Nair represented the traditional management style.

After my first day at work, Shihabka dropped me off at my living quarters, which I had assumed would be nearby but turned out to be a 20-minute drive away. It was during this journey that I got my first glimpse of Dubai's sandy landscape, dotted with ongoing construction projects and bustling activity.

The golden sands shimmered under the tenacious Arabian sun. Occasionally, wisps of desert winds would stir up tiny whirlwinds, creating ephemeral patterns in the dunes that shifted with each passing breeze. Against this backdrop, the sporadic sight of construction projects rising like mirages punctuated the otherwise barren landscape.

Arriving at Al Awir via the Al Rashidiya-Al Awir Road, I noticed our company's asphalt and concrete batching plants, where damaged heavy machines were being repaired. The sight of small cabins scattered around struck me, later realising they were labour camps where multiple workers resided.

Sharing my cabin was Nair, the company's lab technician, whose warm personality and wealth of experience immediately put me at ease. As I settled in, the cool breeze from the window AC provided relief from Dubai's scorching heat, a luxury I had yet to experience back home but quickly came to appreciate in this new environment where AC was a necessity for comfort.

Life in a labour camp

Although my accommodation in the labour camp was a far cry from luxury, it was a significant improvement from my previous experience in Bombay. Sharing a room with just one other person and having access to clean toilets without any foul odours was a welcome change. The commute from work to the camp in a double-cabin pick-up truck felt like a luxury, especially compared to the overcrowded local trains I used to endure.

In the desert expanse of Al Awir, the labour camp, made of wooden portable cabins, seemed isolated from the city of Dubai. Surrounded by endless stretches of sand, it was a haven for labourers, drivers and newcomers like myself. I developed a strong rapport with fellow residents, particularly forming close bonds with Unni, Robin, Mathews, Joseph, Abraham, Salih, Noorudheen, Shamsukka, Sajimon, Khalid Abbasi, Murali, Venu, Fule Khan, Kamaruddinka (Kamaruddin) and Reji, many of whom had also journeyed from Bombay. I particularly became close to Unni later.

Night walks outside the camp held a special charm. In the distance, the Dubai-Al Ain road stretched out like a ribbon, its string of streetlights puncturing the vast darkness. Only the Dubai Trade Center pierced the night sky with its brilliance. Dubai back then was a far cry from the metropolis it is today.

Immersed in my work, I found myself captivated by the intricacies of international building designs and the precision of construction techniques. The heavy equipment I saw there was totally new to me.

Drawing upon my background in pencil drawings and craftsmanship, I quickly adapted to my new role and earned praise from higher officials.

Dubai was a classroom and every day brought a new lesson. My thirst for knowledge extended beyond the office walls. I devoured the city during my commutes, observing the streets and the quietude of the labour camp. Unlike my fellow commuters, lost in their personal worlds, I found myself actively seeking out knowledge. Their focus seemed on routine, while I craved understanding. Yet, a common thread did weave through our seemingly disparate experiences—a simple joy for life's little moments.

An insatiable thirst for understanding excites my fascination with human lives. I explore people's backgrounds and experiences, each encounter adding a new brushstroke to my own personal canvas.

With the job eventually shifting to Dubai Gold Souk, under the guidance of project manager Tariq Hidayat, a Syrian, I learned the value of punctuality and professionalism in the workplace, traits that would shape my approach to work and life.

I found many friends at the site and main office, including Najeeb, Zainudeen, Mathew, Shaji, Sugesh, Nasser, Vijayan, Edisson, Raghavan, Prathapan and Varghese. There were also others I met, like Abdul Rahim Sadeeq, Hisham Moqbel, Harris Constantino, Kyriacos, Imtiaz, Chandrasekhar, Mitzi, Ashok, Mike Tsialis, Kumar and Shooja. The list continues.

My first lesson learnt from Dubai Dubai was punctuality. Punctuality often goes unnoticed, treated as the bare minimum rather than a valuable virtue. Some even feel a strange emptiness upon arriving on time, as if something is amiss. Yet, for others, punctuality is a cornerstone of respect and efficiency. I've always admired those individuals who understand its power.

It's time to shift our perspective. By prioritising punctuality, we avoid wasting the precious time of ourselves and others. This extends beyond appointments—punctuality becomes a way of life, upholding respect for commitments and maximising productivity.

In awe of a golf club

During our daily commute, I couldn't help but notice the imposing construction projects lining the streets. "What's going on there?" I inquired of Shihabka one day, my curiosity piqued by the sight.

"That's the Dubai Creek Golf Club under construction," he replied, his tone matter-of-fact yet tinged with a hint of intrigue.

The mention of a major sports project immediately caught my attention, stirring my childhood love for sports. Though I had never played golf, I was captivated by the idea, especially as I watched the golf club take shape before my eyes with each passing day.

Standing on the picturesque banks of the historic Dubai Creek, the Dubai Creek Golf and Yacht Club has been built as an iconic landmark of leisure and luxury in the heart of the city.

Brian Johnson, the architect behind the famed Emirates Golf Club, envisioned the iconic clubhouse. Inspired by the billowing lateen sails of traditional dhows, Johnson's design incorporates similar graceful curves. To win the project, he took a strategic gamble. An eight-inch model, costing just £100, became his winning weapon. But Johnson's vision extended further. A brilliant suggestion from his business partner—a reflection pool surrounding the clubhouse—created the illusion of a building floating effortlessly. The Yacht Club itself takes a different design cue. Its silhouette evokes the prow of a luxurious cruise liner. Karl Litten, another key figure, designed the golf course. Given complete creative freedom, Litten crafted not only the main 18-hole course but also a dedicated Par-3 course and practice facilities, transforming the area into a golfer's paradise. Lars Waldenstrom (father-in-law of European Tour star Thomas Bjorn) and his company Swedish Design (now LW Design), designed the interiors.

The course's undulating fairways and meticulously manicured greens present a challenging yet rewarding terrain, while the meandering creek and lush foliage provide a serene backdrop for each swing. Fairways stretch out like emerald ribbons, bordered by swaying trees. Boasting panoramic views of Dubai's ever-evolving skyline, the clubhouse exude elegance and sophistication. As golfers traverse the greens, the gentle rustle of leaves and distant chirping of birds provide a sonata of Nature's soundtrack.

Eager for more information, I persisted in questioning Shihabka during our journeys. "How much does it cost to play there?" I pressed.

His response, delivered with a hint of annoyance, left me taken aback. "The annual membership costs AED 25,000."

Every time we passed through the golf club, I kept asking him questions. When my questions became persistent, he flew off the handle.

"Are you crazy? You'd need three years' worth of salary just to join and play there," he scoffed, his words punctuated by exasperation.

I decided that day. I'd never ask him about golf any more.

Retail windows and Walkman rhythms

During the one day off I had each week, I made it a point to reconnect with my loved ones by writing letters. In an era devoid of instant communication, letters were our lifeline, bridging the gap between distant friends and family in a world without mobile phones, WhatsApp or social media.

No matter how hectic life gets, I firmly believe in the importance of nurturing relationships regularly. Neglecting them can render them obsolete over time. By the time we realise we need to reconnect, our once high-spirited friendships and relationships may have dwindled beyond repair. Communication, whether through letters or other means, serves as the lifeblood of maintaining and strengthening these bonds. It's through consistent effort and genuine connection that we can sustain meaningful relationships for the long haul.

Every month, I dutifully sent a portion of my salary back home. I also fulfilled a promise to support an orphanage run by Fr Joseph, whom I had met during my journey to Bombay. It was a small gesture, but one that held great significance in my heart.

With my newfound financial stability, I indulged in long-awaited luxuries, treating myself to a music player and splurging on Nike shoes and a Lacoste T-shirt. Weekends were spent with friends at Al Ghurair Centre, the hub of activity in Dubai at the time, where we would window shop and dream of owning the latest fashions displayed behind glass.

Sometimes, I found myself browsing through shops just to gauge the prices of items I desired to own. It was a methodical approach—I gathered information, set a savings goal, and patiently waited until I've amassed the necessary funds. Once I reached my target amount, I made a deliberate decision to go for the purchase.

Dubai 92 FM became the soundtrack of my Dubai life, with Mariah Carey, Amy Grant, Bryan Adams, Luther Vandross, Whitney Houston and other iconic artists filling the airwaves. Inspired by the music, I invested in a Walkman, eager to enjoy my favourite tunes wherever I went, whether in my car or relaxing in my room during precious moments of downtime. The old Walkman, with its sleek design and simple controls, boasted a sturdy exterior adorned with the iconic 'Walkman' logo, its cassette player within a compact, portable casing. It was magic packed into a simple gadget. As I began achieving my small dreams, one by one, it opened the windows to even bigger aspirations.

Ashraf arrives in Dubai

As the Iraq-Kuwait war came to an end, Dubai buzzed with newfound energy and optimism, sparking a flurry of activity in construction, trade and tourism sectors.

My success has never been meant to be a solitary journey. Ever since arriving in Dubai, I've envisioned a future where I could share this prosperity with my loved ones back home in Kerala, particularly those who haven't been as fortunate. Now, with the conclusion of the war, Dubai's climate seemed especially favourable for new opportunities. This felt like the perfect moment to turn that vision into reality.

"It's heart-warming to see the city coming alive again after the war," I wrote to Ashraf, my friend at Polytechnic College.

"Yeah, good to know that you can feel the positive vibes everywhere," Ashraf replied, sharing the excitement of the city's revival.

With the opportunity ripe for stable employment, I wrote to Ashraf. "Hey, Ashraf, how about joining me in Dubai? There are plenty of opportunities here now," I suggested.

After a few weeks, I received his reply. "That sounds like a great idea! I'm in," he exclaimed, his family overjoyed at the news of his upcoming adventure.

At that time, none of my other friends were particularly enthusiastic about coming to Dubai for work.

I had an additional reason for inviting Ashraf to Dubai. Back when I found myself in a moment of despair, stranded in Edappal without the job I had hoped for, I sought solace at his home in Kuttipuram. With a heavy heart, I poured out my troubles to Ashraf, hoping for a word of comfort. In his gentle and reassuring manner, he listened attentively and offered words of encouragement.

"Dileep, never lose heart or despair. Brighter days lie ahead for you. Trust that everything will work out in the end," he assured me.

His comforting words, filled with genuine care and love, brought a sense of tranquility to my troubled soul that day. They were a balm to my wounds.

As I extended the invitation to Ashraf to come over to Dubai, I saw it as an opportunity to repay his kindness and support, knowing that I could offer him a glimpse of the same peace and encouragement he had once bestowed upon me.

Guided by the efforts of Mr. Naushad, Ashraf secured a position at Wade Adams, the same company where I was employed. "Thanks for this opportunity, Dileep. I can't wait to start this new chapter," Ashraf expressed his gratitude, ready to start his Dubai journey under the mentorship of Mr K. G. Nair.

The aura of holy places

Working tirelessly for Wade Adams, I poured my heart and soul into maximising profits for the company. But I had a nagging feeling that I was not paid enough.

I worked hard, even dedicating my precious Fridays, the only day off in Dubai.

Traditionally, Friday served as the public holiday in Dubai, aligning with the Islamic holy day of Jum'ah prayer. This day holds immense significance for Muslims, who gather for congregational prayers at mosques. To facilitate participation in Jum'ah prayer, most institutions, shops and businesses would naturally close on Fridays.

"It's amazing how Friday prayers unite the community," I mused to a colleague, reflecting on the significance of the public holiday.

In recent years, however, the public holiday in Dubai has shifted to Sunday.

Talking about Friday prayers, I'm reminded of my admiration for religious architecture, with mosques, churches and temples alike captivating my imagination. There's something truly special about the design and ambiance of places of worship.

During our commute to the labour camp, the driver would often pause near the Al Rashidiya Mosque. Every time, I couldn't help but be captivated by its magnificence. And as the evening descended, transforming the sky into a canvas of hues, the mosque would come alive, bathed in the warm glow of decorative lamps, casting a spellbinding aura.

I respect all religions. It runs deep, stemming from a childhood spent observing the rituals of various faiths. Religious diversity is a reflection of the richness of human experience.

During my time at the convent school in Ponnani, I vividly remember joining my classmates in prayer at the church before embarking on an excursion. I've had the privilege of offering prayers in various temples throughout my life. Each religious place holds a unique energy for me, revitalising my spirit and creating a sense of peace and connection with something greater than myself.

In Malappuram, my native place, love and friendship transcend religious boundaries. I cherish bonds forged with friends of diverse backgrounds. I believe in the power of love to bridge divides.

Al Rashidiya Mosque

As we neared the Al Rashidiya Mosque, Shihabka turned to me and said, "Wait here for a bit. I'll be back." With a nod, I stepped out of the vehicle, my gaze drawn to the activity of the faithful gathering for the Maghrib prayer.

Inside the mosque, a sea of worshippers bowed in prayer. As I observed the serene scene before me, my mind drifted to the challenges I faced. Months had passed since my arrival in Dubai, yet my salary remained meagre; the accommodation was sparse in terms of amenities. I wondered: how would my dreams be fulfilled?

As the visitors prayed with closed eyes, I too sought refuge in silent supplication, pouring out my hopes and fears to the divine.

Tears welled in my eyes as I pleaded, “Help me achieve my dreams and aspirations. I’ll give my all, but please don’t abandon me.”

I lingered outside the mosque until the worshippers emerged from prayer, their faces aglow with inner peace.

For me, prayer had always been a source of comfort, a lesson instilled by my grandmother at a young age. “Pray before bed and upon waking,” she’d said, and I’d carried that habit with me ever since.

Regardless of religion or deity, prayers offered a space where troubles could be set aside, if only for a moment, in deference to a higher power.

Even after three decades have passed, the memory of that prayer offered at Al Rashidiya Mosque remains vividly in my mind as I pen these words. In that moment, I felt a deep sense of hope and tears welled up in my eyes.

My persistence in advocating for a raise finally bore fruit. The company acknowledged my efforts, offering a modest salary increase. While it wasn’t a windfall, it was a significant validation for a 22-year-old me. Sure, part of the raise likely reflected their appreciation for my work ethic. But even a small victory felt monumental at that stage in my career.

John Papadouris and A R Shaji

One of the biggest influences on my journey to success was meeting Mr John Andrew Papadouris, the General Manager of our company, hailing from Cyprus.

Whenever I crossed paths with him, whether in the office corridors or the parking lot, I’d initially keep quiet, waiting for him to initiate conversation. But once he started sharing snippets of his life story, I couldn’t help but be drawn in. His journey mirrored mine in many ways—starting from nothing and achieving success through sheer resoluteness and hard work. His life became a blueprint for me to follow, and even after 33 years, he remains a role model and one of my dearest friends.

Mr K. G. Nair also left a lasting impact on my life. While both he and Mr John influenced me greatly, they did so in different ways. Mr Nair embodied the wisdom of the old guard, while Mr John adopted innovative management practices.

I consider Mr Nair more than just a role model—he's like a guru to me. As for Mr John, he was instrumental in securing a salary increase for me and arranging for better accommodation. He promised to move me to an apartment near Sharjah Corniche. His swift action not only benefited me but also led to a pay rise for others in the company.

Moving to a new apartment meant leaving behind friends from the labour camp, like my dear friends Unni and A. R Shaji. I particularly missed A. R. Shaji. We used to spend countless hours together, sharing stories and admiring the starry night sky. We had nothing else to do. At night, we would walk near the asphalt plant of the labour camp we were allotted. Time would stand still.

A. R. Shaji's dedication to hard work, even in the sweltering summer heat, left a lasting impression on me.

In my new apartment, furnished with all the modern conveniences, memories of our makeshift refrigerator made from a window AC often come to mind.

We used to hang bottles of non-alcoholic beer and other soft drinks on the air conditioner using a belt. After a while, the AC would chill the drinks perfectly, and we would savour them cold. This simple pleasure was one of the joys of living with modest means.

Some of my friends advise me not to remember the hardships of the past, but I can't help it. These memories are an integral part of my life. They encompass both the good and the bad—tears, smiles, laughter, pain and joy. These experiences shape who I am today. Our life experiences and memories are our greatest teachers, providing invaluable lessons and shaping our identities.

Home, sweet home

After two long years in Dubai, the prospect of returning home filled me with excitement and anticipation. The thought of seeing my loved ones, especially my parents, after overcoming numerous challenges and securing a good job, was a moment I had longed for.

In the days leading up to my departure, I busied myself with buying gifts for my family and friends. Each gift held a piece of my heart.

Finally, the day arrived, and as I set foot on familiar soil, I felt a wave of nostalgia and warmth engulf me.

I could see the pride gleaming in my parents' eyes, and the excitement on the faces of my siblings and friends such as Prakash, Babu, Pradeep and Rajesh.

But there was one unfinished business—my friend Hari. Despite our past differences, I knew I needed to mend our friendship before returning to Dubai.

With a smile on my face and an open heart, I approached Hari, ready to bury the hatchet.

"If there is any problem between us, I have come to settle it."

"What problem? I forgot all that. After all, there could be some minor alterations between friends. Leave it there," he said.

"I wanted to talk to you before I left for Dubai."

"It's okay, Dileep," he said. "We're still friends."

Our conversation flowed naturally, easing any tension that had existed between us. It was a relief to reconnect with Hari.

Life isn't a constant melody, but an overture with moments of dissonance. Disagreements and conflicts are natural parts of human interaction. However, these don't have to be permanent. Just as a song's beauty lies in its contrasting notes, resolving conflict can strengthen relationships.

The brevity of life compels us to cherish connection. Holding grudges or harbouring negativity steals precious time from enjoying love and understanding. Forgiveness and reconciliation pave the way for a more fulfilling existence. My guiding principle has been to strive for harmony whenever possible.

As I dipped into the sights, sounds and flavours of my homeland, I relished every moment, from the lush greenery of the countryside to the sacred temples I visited.

I was determined to make the most of my two-month leave, making up for the years I had spent away from my native place. I relished the joy and beauty of my village, which I had missed over the past two years. I visited temples and wandered freely. I also made it a point to seek out and help friends and relatives in need. We are happy only when people around us are.

But I'm sure that not everyone around me was. Some, perhaps conditioned by stereotypes of the regular Malayali worker in the Gulf, might have secretly wished for me to be back home jobless. Little did they know the fire that burned within me, the drive that set me apart.

Dwelling on negativity can be draining. While the sting of their judgment continues, I choose not to let it define me. Years may have passed, but the memory remains. Back then, a seed was planted—the seed of a desire to prove not just to them, but to myself, that I could carve my own path to a fulfilling life.

I had long leave but my mother's no-nonsense demeanour served as a gentle reminder that my time at home was limited.

"Aren't you going back to Dubai?" she asked.

"Amma, I have 60 days leave. It's only been a week now."

"Leave is enough for two weeks, hurry back to Dubai and start your work. Duty comes first."

"I know, Amma," I said, smiling.

I thought she was worried whether I would not go back to Dubai.

Duty calls

I decided to cut my leave short to 15 days and proceeded to Dubai.

As I journeyed back, after meeting a friend in New Delhi, my thoughts naturally drifted towards self-reflection and planning. It's in my nature to meticulously consider every aspect of my life, especially when it comes to progress and growth. I firmly believe that by scrutinising our path and strategising, we pave the way for new opportunities to emerge.

Before beginning any endeavour, it's crucial to pose questions to ourselves and find their answers. Through this process of inquiry and analysis, we gain valuable insights that illuminate the path forward.

This introspective practice allows us to identify our strengths and weaknesses, enabling us to make informed decisions and avoid potential pitfalls. By thoroughly understanding our motivations, we create a roadmap that guides us through the complexities of our journey. This self-reflection creates strength, as we are better prepared to adapt to challenges and seize opportunities as they arise. Ultimately, asking the right questions and seeking honest answers empowers us.

While I take pride in my current standard of living, I'm driven by the pursuit of improvement. I understand that achieving excellence demands continuous effort and dedication. Every moment of spare time presents an opportunity to advance towards my goals, and I'm committed to making the most of it.

I actively seek out new knowledge and skills to enhance my personal and professional development. I strive to broaden my horizons and stay ahead of the curve. By setting ambitious yet achievable goals, I maintain a clear direction and purpose in all my endeavours. This proactive approach not only generates my motivation but also ensures that I am always moving forward, continuously refining my abilities and expanding my potential. I always look up to Nature for guidance and knowledge. You can learn everything from Nature. This helped me become a different person. This improved my confidence and eventuality changed my life completely.

I decided to abbreviate my leave and return to Dubai promptly.

Credit to cruise

As I journeyed back, after meeting a friend in New Delhi, I was on a mission to make my next big dream a reality: owning a car. Saving up from two years' worth of salary seemed like a daunting task, so I decided to explore other options. That's when I headed to the bank and sorted out a car loan. Once the paperwork was squared away, I wasted no time in snagging a golden-coloured Ford Tempo.

This car was Ford's pride and joy from '84 to '94, taking over the reins from the Fairmont. It was all about downsizing and embracing that sweet, sweet front-wheel drive action.

With my shiny new ride parked outside my new apartment, life was looking up. But I wasn't just about cruising the streets — I had my eye on getting back into sports, specifically tennis. Armed with a racket and some basic skills picked up from watching matches on TV, I hit up Safa Park for some court action. Consistency was key and I made the trek from Sharjah to Safa Park every single day.

Six months later, reality hit me hard. It felt that the car wasn't really mine as it was all tied up in that pesky loan and the monthly payments were starting to weigh me down. With a heavy heart, I had to bid farewell to my golden beauty.

On certain days, when the urge to drive became irresistible, I rented a car and navigated the city streets. I rent my favourite cars, celebrating the thrill of the journey in this coruscating metropolis.

But where there's a will, there's a way. Thanks to some serious hustle from Mr. John at work, the company hooked me up with a sleek Daihatsu Feroza SUV. This one was a compact beast, ready to take on anything from city streets to off-road adventures. It had a robust and boxy design, featuring a compact body with pronounced wheel arches, a distinctive front grille and round headlights that emphasised its rugged, off-road capability.

Needless to say, I was stoked. Not only did I score a sweet new set of wheels, but it felt awesome to be recognised by the company. It was a win-win all around.

Fresh insight, new motivation

True success extends beyond financial gain. While financial security is important, it's not the sole measure of a well-lived life. Inner peace, strong family bonds and overall health and happiness are equally crucial. It's about finding meaning and fulfillment beyond wealth, power or position. Just like money can't buy happiness, happiness is rarely fleeting and superficial.

My approach to weekends in Dubai might have differed from others. While I certainly enjoyed music and sports, I also dedicated time to planning for the future. This wasn't about neglecting leisure; it was about prioritising building a strong foundation. Just as a building needs a sturdy framework before adding decorative elements, a balanced life requires laying the groundwork for long-term success. Prioritising planning allowed me to approach leisure activities with a clear conscience, knowing my future was secure.

Living in Dubai for two years was a game-changer for me. It was like my whole perspective got a major upgrade. Working alongside both senior and junior management teams in a multinational company gave me this fresh burst of energy in both my thoughts and my work. Formal education lays the groundwork, but real-world experiences and guidance from seasoned professionals can be equally, if not more, valuable in shaping us. Suddenly, I saw this fire inside me that I never knew was there before. It was pretty cool to witness my own transformation unfolding right before my eyes.

One big factor in this change was landing the post of Senior Quantity Surveyor on some pretty massive projects. Now, back home in Kerala, the role of a quantity surveyor isn't exactly common knowledge. Quantity surveyor are the unsung heroes of the construction world. They've got their hands in everything, from finances to materials to the actual building process itself. They're basically the backbone of any construction company, reporting directly to the big bosses.

I was the person in charge of keeping tabs on project costs. I worked hard. Demonstrating my commitment, I regularly put in an extra few hours on Fridays, even when it was a holiday. It was my responsibility to make sure we were staying on budget and not overspending. And it was not just number-crunching from behind a desk. I was out there on-site, making sure every brick, every beam, heck, even every nail was up to snuff. Because at the end of the day, it was all about delivering top-notch quality, maximising value for our clients and making more profit for my company. And that was where my hustle came in handy.

Fortune and cross-cultural friendships

Dubai isn't just a hotspot for living large and making bank; it's also a melting pot of international friendships. Here, there's no distinction between men and women when it comes to camaraderie. It doesn't matter where you're from or what faith you follow; friendships here flourish based solely on mutual respect and human connection. Some friendships are like sturdy trees, providing shade for a lifetime, while others bloom like seasonal flowers, bringing joy before gracefully fading away.

Both types of friendships hold unique value and meaning in our lives. The enduring ones, like solid trees, offer constant support and reliability, becoming an integral part of our existence through thick and thin. On the other hand, the fleeting friendships, like seasonal flowers, enrich our lives with their vital presence and leave us with warmmemories, even as they naturally drift away. Appreciating the beauty and significance of each type helps us understand the different roles people play in our personal growth and emotional well-being, reminding us to treasure every connection, no matter how long it lasts.

I had friends from all corners of the globe, including many amazing women. We shared laughs, stories and experiences, but I always kept things purely friendly. Back then, I had this nagging fear that getting too close to someone from a different culture might lead to heartbreak. My female friends were great people, but I couldn't see a long-term connection because our mindsets didn't quite sync up.

5

Finding my bride

One Friday, I was flipping through the classifieds in *Gulf News*, on the hunt for a new car. As I skimmed through the car sale ads, something unexpected caught my eye: matrimonial ads. Yes, right there in the newspaper. It struck me as kind of funny at first, but I couldn't resist giving them a read.

I stumbled upon an ad that seemed promising. It had a landline number listed, so after some internal debate, I decided to take the plunge and give it a ring.

When I dialled the number, they wasted no time in inviting me over. "Come on over," they said. "We can chat once you've seen the girl." I agreed and hung up the phone, but the whole scene felt oddly familiar, like being in a car showroom and picking out your dream ride.

In India, they call this setup arranged marriages, where families do the matchmaking based on tradition and elder advice. I decided to give it a shot, in line with tradition and all.

Since none of my family was around in Dubai, I enlisted the help of my friends—Ravi and his wife Kavita, Vimal and his wife Suchi, and my cousin Arvind. Together, we headed to Karama, where the girl's family lived, and parked outside a sports shop.

As we got out of the car, I briefed my friends: "All we got to do is confirm the number from the advertisement and then roll on in." They were onboard with the plan, but just as I went to grab the paper with the number, I realised I'd forgotten it.

My friends couldn't resist teasing me as I blushed in embarrassment. "What's up, Dileep?" they chuckled.

But no worries—I had that six-digit phone number stored in my brain. I thought: if the number was wrong, if I could not recall it, we'd drop our plan and return home; if it is right, we meet the girl.

As Google Map or similar facilities were not around, the only option was to call up and check.

I gave it a shot. Was this good luck or bad luck? The number was spot on. They answered, gave us directions, and wouldn't you know it, their place was right next to where we parked.

Found each other's gaze

We pulled up to the girl's house exactly as her family had directed us. Her father and sister were there, and I learned that her mom had passed away when she was just 21.

As we chatted about family stuff, she suddenly appeared in the living room, like a flash. We were all eager to meet her. Now, back home, it's customary for the girl to serve tea when you're meeting for an arranged marriage. But here? It was a total reversal. Tea and sweets were already set out on the table when we arrived, so there was no grand entrance with the tea tray.

When she walked in, smiling, my friend Vimal's wife, Suji, shot me this look of surprise. I totally got what she was getting at—this girl was stunning. But I played it cool, took my seat without making a big fuss. Couldn't let them read my mind. Inside, though, I was feeling kind of nervous. Seeing a girl like this in the arranged marriage scene, or as we call it in Malayalam, 'Pennu Kanal,' was a whole new experience for me.

"I'll get back to you on my decision," I told them when it was time to leave. We said our goodbyes and exchanged numbers. Her name? R. And we started talking after that.

Now, here was where it got tricky. We exchanged our horoscopes. According to Hindu customs, the horoscopes are checked to find if they match. They didn't match up. She was rather let down when she found out. But despite that, we didn't want to call it off.

I wasn't entirely sure if I was in love with her, but we kept spending time together and started to feel a sense of familiarity between us.

Honestly, I still don't get this whole horoscope thing. Is there any real science behind it? Beats me.

We've seen incompatible horoscope pairings lead to happy marriages and vice versa. We decided compatibility shouldn't be a dealbreaker.

I've my doubts about horoscope accuracy.

People manipulate compatibility readings to avoid marriages they don't want. It becomes a tool—for some to escape unwanted proposals, for others to pressure acceptance. Compatibility issues post-marriage might be blamed on ignoring horoscopes, while happy unions get no credit for skipping them.

So, we decided to go ahead with the marriage, the horoscope be darned.

We went ahead and had our engagement in Dubai, keeping it simple and sweet.

Relationship nuances

Within days of our engagement, we started noticing some small differences between us. What started as minor disagreements quickly escalated into full-blown arguments. We'd go back and forth for hours, sometimes arguing on the phone till the early hours of the morning.

As the arguments dragged on, it became clear to me that our marriage might not work out. If we couldn't handle these issues now, how would we manage when we actually lived together? I found myself unable to tolerate her behaviour and I questioned the point of continuing the relationship. I thought: it was fortunate that we recognised the discomfort between us early on. After marriage, it could have become much harder to address, impacting the entire family.

I made a tough call and reached out to her uncle. "I don't think we can make this work," I told him honestly. "It's better for both of us to call it quits."

I told him this with a good intention.

But instead of supporting my decision, I thought he was kind of justifying her. He tried to reassure me. "Hey, these are just initial hiccups. Once you two start living together, things will smooth out," he said.

Though I had an inkling about her nature, I took his words to heart as he was an elder and convinced myself that I needed to give it another shot. I resolved to put an end to the arguments and give her time to adjust. Maybe, just maybe, things would improve, and we could salvage the relationship.

I decided to take a step back and give myself some breathing room. Maybe, being quiet could give me some peace of mind.

I still doubted whether I was mature enough to make such a significant decision about marriage at the age of 27.

When I initially thought about marriage, I had all these dreams and aspirations. I thought: marriage was a journey of shared experiences—joy, work and even finances.

I believed in building a partnership, not separate accounts. I envisioned a family life where everything was enjoyed together. Two people working as a team could achieve far more than one alone.

In marriage, I was looking for a partner who valued cooperation and mutual love in all aspects of life.

As our plans progressed, we decided to find a place to call home after marriage. Luckily, we stumbled upon a lovely apartment through Al Nabooda Real Estate in Abu Hail and decided to rent for our future together. It was peaceful, quiet and a place we truly adored.

Sealed: our destined union

Our wedding went down on April 20, 1997, back in Kerala. It was a full-house affair with all our family and friends gathered to celebrate.

You've probably heard the whole spiel about Indian weddings being these extravagant affairs. Some folks even call them the "big, fat, Indian wedding." It's true, we Indians tend to go all out, sometimes seeing it as a chance to flaunt our wealth and status. Especially up north—those weddings can get wild, lasting for days with stadiums, airplanes and even submarines thrown into the mix.

But compared to our Western counterparts, who usually keep things low-key with private ceremonies attended by just close family and friends, we do tend to amp it up a notch here in Kerala too.

To each their own! Weddings are deeply personal celebrations and everyone has the right to express themselves in a way that feels meaningful.

Let me tell you about the bride. Picture this: most of our guests were taken aback when they first saw her. She was taller than me, fairer than your average Keralite, and with these striking features that could easily pass for someone from Lebanon or Spain. Her hair had this beautiful sun-kissed hue and she had this air of mystery about her—friendly yet distant, with a tough exterior.

Yes, she wasn't one to chat up a storm or mingle too much with the crowd, but that was just her nature. She didn't interact much with my family and friends. It didn't mean she wasn't affectionate. But she remained aloof.

I've encountered people who come across as arrogant based on their demeanour and communication style. However, beneath the surface, they might simply lack social skills.

Misunderstandings often arise because people judge solely on outward appearances—behaviour, mannerisms and speech. Moreover, these individuals might not prioritise the opinions of others.

Beyond movie fantasies

My wife had this idea that our life together should mirror the romance and passion we see in movies. You know, those lovey-dovey scenes between the hero and heroine? Some people are like that, they want a fairytale love story in real life.

But I wasn't buying it. I told her straight up, "Movies are just fantasy. Real life isn't scripted or rehearsed. It's messy, with ups and downs, joys and sorrows. We got to deal with it all, not just the highlights. A movie is just for two hours, but life is to be lived for decades."

No matter how much I tried to explain, we just couldn't see eye to eye on this.

Our first two years of marriage were eye-opening. I quickly learned that marriage isn't always rainbows and butterflies—it's hard work. We faced our fair share of challenges.

From financial pressures to communication breakdowns, we faced our fair share of obstacles that tested our commitment to each other. Each hurdle seemed like a mountain to climb, and there were moments when it felt like we were barely hanging on.

Luckily, my wife was working as an office administrator in Dubai, pitching in with the monthly expenses. Her contribution was a huge help, especially since my salary alone couldn't cover everything. It was a relief to have her support during those early days of marriage.

My first business investment

I had this nagging feeling that no matter how many years I spent grinding away at my job, I wouldn't be any closer to achieving my dreams. Working for someone else just wasn't cutting it for me anymore.

Three times in six years, I had handed in my resignation. I had tempting offers from European companies, and each time I was ready to jump ship, Mr. John swooped in, offering me more money and perks to stay put. Plus, there was that sense of loyalty to the company that gave me my start in Dubai.

But deep down, I knew I needed more. I started thinking about starting my own part-time work on the side, something to give me that extra boost. I splurged on a fax machine and a new mobile phone with a sim card, investing my first chunk of capital in 1998 when I was 28. I bought these for AED 950, my first investment in business. My wife gave me money from her savings for developing my part-time business and this led to my eventual growth.

As word got out, friends and small companies started throwing work my way, and before I knew it, I was working overtime like there was no tomorrow. And just when I thought things couldn't get any busier, I got promoted to Senior Quantity Surveyor with the company, with a sweet bonus equivalent to the salary for two months thrown in.

Juggling multiple projects simultaneously became my new reality. Increased responsibilities at work demanded most of my attention, leaving little free time.

Despite the pressure, I remained focussed on my long-term goals. My approach has always been to chip away at them, one by one.

My mind was fixated on one thing: a new car. I had my eye on a slick SUV, but when I brought it up to Mr John, he gave me the runaround. Sure, he listened to me and nodded along, but when it came down to it, he wasn't willing to fight for me.

"If I give you a new car, the other Indians in the same post you're in will raise similar demands. It's not practical for the company to fulfil all these," he said.

Despite my self-pep talk—"Everyone is unique, just like five fingers on a hand. We might judge them all the same at first glance, but each finger serves a different purpose"—I remained unconvinced Mr John would approve my request for a new car.

That's when it hit me—I couldn't rely on this job to get me where I wanted to go. If I wanted to make my dreams a reality, I had to take matters into my own hands. It was time to say goodbye to the company grind and hello to my own business venture. Only then could I carve out the life I wanted for myself.

A novice's adventure on the green

One day, I mentioned to my colleague Alex, who's a golf enthusiast from Cyprus, that I had a hankering to learn the game. The problem was, I didn't have the cash to splash on a fancy golf set. Alex, being the helpful guy he is, came through with a genius suggestion.

He told me about how used golf sets often pop up for sale in the classifieds. I figured, why not give it a shot? I didn't need brand new gear to start learning, and my wallet definitely agreed.

Sure enough, after scouring the classifieds, I stumbled upon an ad for an old golf set going for 1,000 AED. I gave the seller a ring and soon enough, I was the proud owner of my very own set of clubs.

In 1999, in my thirties, I dipped my toes into the world of golf, using that trusty old set. Alex even took me under his wing, showing me the ropes at the Dubai Creek Golf and Yacht Club after work. From the driving range to the practice green, he taught me everything I needed to know to get started.

Golf isn't as easy as it looks. It takes skill, precision and a whole lot of practice. But as I spent more time on the course, I found myself falling in love with the game. There's something about the strategic thinking and concentration it requires that just hooks you in.

Golf stands apart from most ball games due to its lack of a standardised playing area. Instead, players navigate varied terrains across courses, presenting a unique challenge with each round. Courses typically feature either nine or 18 holes, each with its own cup—the target for the ball.

Starting from designated teeing grounds, players work their way through a variety of terrains, including the fairway, rough (tall grass) and hazards like water, rocks or sand-filled bunkers, before reaching the putting green with the cup.

For novice golf players, mastering the fundamentals of the swing, achieving consistency in ball striking, understanding course management, honing the short game, developing mental toughness, and learning golf etiquette and rules pose significant challenges. Overcoming these obstacles requires dedication, practice, and a willingness to learn, gradually building skill and confidence on the course.

I should confess: golf stole my heart. I couldn't afford full-time membership at the club, but that didn't stop me from playing whenever I could. I'd hit the practice area (Par 3 course) a few times a week, paying 20 AED for the privilege. This continued for four or five years. And on special occasions, I'd treat myself to a round of 18 holes, though I was not trained in this format.

To master the full 18-hole game, I focussed heavily on honing my short game. The beauty of chipping and putting is that they can be practised even while playing a shortened version of the course. By maximising my playing area with this strategy, I ensured ample opportunity to refine my short game skills.

The value of friendship

Meanwhile, two of my close friends from back home came to the UAE. Prakash was in Ras Al Khaimah hunting for a job, arranged by his uncle. With a diploma in electrical engineering, he landed a job at a ceramic company. Whenever we got together, whether at my place in Sharjah or his in Ras Al Khaimah, our conversations inevitably drifted back to our childhood memories. One of my best friends, he saw me off at the Kutippuram railway station for my Bombay train. Prakash, coming from a big family, wasn't one for grand ambitions like me. He was fluent in English. Back when they lived in Ooty before settling in Edappal, he introduced us to cricket, igniting our passion for the game. I saw a cricket bat for the first time thanks to him. His love for cricket was contagious and kickstarted our cricketing adventures back home.

I also lent a hand to my friend Pradeep's journey to Dubai. Thanks again to Mr Naushad from Wade Adams Company, he landed a job and visa with our assistance. He always wanted to come to Dubai and used to persistently tell me about whenever we met or spoke over telephone. When he arrived for the first time, Prakash and I were there to pick him up from the airport. But Pradeep was cut from a different cloth than Prakash. He was bursting with dreams and aspirations, his energy seemingly measureless.

Then there's Pramod, my childhood friend from school. We lost touch for years until I made it a mission to find him. Thanks to Hari, another friend of mine who later became my manager, we tracked down Pramod's family in Ponnani. Sadly, they revealed he had left home due to financial woes. He remained elusive, preferring to stay off the grid. He kept a distance from his friends, I gathered.

The first vacation

Just like we can't forget our first girlfriend, we can't forget our first trip either. It was back in 1999 when I finally took my first holiday in my late twenties it was unforgettable. My wife and I went on a journey to Bangkok, Singapore, Mumbai and Dubai, and it was a whirlwind adventure from start to finish.

Bangkok was our first stop and it was an eye-opener. From its ornate temples and bustling markets to its lively nightlife and delectable street food, Bangkok captivated with its cultural richness and urban dynamism. We were both so excited to explore new places together and even though we had to be careful with our spending, we had an amazing time.

But it was Singapore that stole my heart. Ever since I saw it in Malayalam movies like 'Love in Singapore', I'd been dreaming of visiting. And it didn't disappoint. The urban beauty and cleanliness of the city were beyond impressive. Everywhere we looked, there were trees and plants lining the streets, making it a green paradise. We mostly relied on public transport, as car journeys were expensive. The public transport was top-notch and contributed to the city's low smog levels.

As a civil engineer, I couldn't help but marvel at the construction and cleanliness of the roads and buildings. Skyscrapers and massive shopping malls seemed to be around every corner, giving the city a futuristic vibe.

But it wasn't just about the sights. It was about the lessons I learned from observing people's lives in these countries. I realised the value of hard-earned money and the importance of enjoying life while we can. Travelling opened my mind to new perspectives and broadened my horizons in ways I never imagined.

And there was something special. The date of our return, 9-9-1999. Not only is it a beautifully arranged number, but it also holds the memory of us enjoying breakfast in Singapore, lunch in Mumbai and dinner back home in Dubai, all in one day. It's a day I'll never forget.

Travels and lessons learned

Setting foot beyond my familiar borders wasn't merely about sightseeing—it sparked an unbelievable transformation in my perspective, reshaping the very essence of how I viewed the world. I found myself in a rich array of experiences that transcended mere tourism. Each encounter with noisy markets, historic landmarks and the daily rhythms of life in foreign lands left a deep mark on my consciousness, offering valuable insights into the essence of humanity itself.

As I traversed unknown terrain and engaged with people from diverse backgrounds, I came to appreciate the true value of earned currency. No longer was money just a means of transaction—it became a conduit for realising dreams, pursuing aspirations and cherishing life's experiences. In moments of quiet reflection, as I surveyed the serene landscapes and crowded cityscapes, I contemplated the fleeting nature of existence and the importance of seizing the present moment.

Seeing life's brevity, I resolved to use my hard-earned savings to fulfil my dreams and desires. After all, we have one precious life, a fleeting experience. Delaying enjoyment until after work and responsibilities is a gamble; our prime years might be gone. Travel, as I discovered on my first holiday, is a transformative force. It shatters narrow perspectives, opening our minds to a vast, global view. It was this journey that truly matured me, from a provincial Edappal resident to a citizen of the world. It was a journey not just of physical exploration but of personal growth and enlightenment. With each step taken on foreign soil, I went on a voyage of self-discovery, uncovering new perspectives and embracing the diversity of the world around me. And as I returned home, my heart brimming with memories and my mind enriched by the experiences, I knew that this journey had forever altered the course of my life, igniting within me a passion for exploration and a deeper appreciation for the beauty of the world.

Ending my days as an employee

Improving my earnings became my goal. My paycheck was steady, but my dreams were bigger than what my current job could offer. I wanted a nice car and a golf club membership—things I couldn't afford on my current salary.

But just as I was gearing up to leave, the company decided to shake things up. They brought in a new project manager from the Abu Dhabi branch, and suddenly, everything changed. I had less say in things, and the new manager was making decisions that didn't sit right with me. It became clear that sticking around wasn't an option anymore.

I decided to hand in my resignation. It was a tough call, considering I'd spent nine years with the company. But sometimes, you just got to take a leap of faith. They accepted my resignation, but asked me to stick around for three more months to tie up loose ends.

Leaving was bittersweet. I was proud of the work I'd done there and the relationships I'd built, but it was time for a new chapter. I couldn't help but feel a pang of sadness as I walked out of the door for the last time.

But every ending is just a new beginning. Year 2000 stood as a nexus, a point where the world teetered on the cusp of a new century and my own life took a dramatic turn. Witnessing this collective transition was a privilege few could experience. Just as the world flipped the calendar, I flipped the script on my career, leaving my employee days behind and venturing into a new world of entrepreneurship. It felt like the numbers on a car's speedometer rapidly ticking over—a clear marker of the new direction my life was taking. With the new millennium upon us, it felt like the perfect time to start fresh. Who knows what the future holds?

Confidence surged through me, a constant companion even during those early, hand-to-mouth days in Kerala and Mumbai.

After all, if I could navigate those scrappy beginnings, what could possibly hold me back now? In that exhilarating moment, an intense thought struck me: how incredibly lucky were we to witness this pivotal shift? How many could claim the fortune of experiencing a new century dawning?

A failed partnership

When I left my job and was gearing up to launch my own business, a friend swooped in with an offer: "Invest in my construction equipment rental venture," he said. "You'll rake in a cut of the profits each month."

Intrigued by the potential learning experience and perhaps a touch of friendly persuasion, I decided to take the plunge. "Why not?" I figured. "It could be a good learning curve before I dive into my own thing."

Unfortunately, the venture floundered faster than a faulty elevator. Within a year, we were drowning in losses. My friend, facing a serious financial crunch, couldn't keep the business afloat. Here's where things took an unexpected turn. He did something extraordinary. Despite the mess, he returned my entire investment—all of it. This stash was my hard-earned savings, built up over nine years of blood, sweat and tears at my job and countless part-time projects.

This setback, though painful, became a crucial turning point. While the business failed, my friend's gesture was a powerful reminder of genuine goodwill. Not everyone would do that, I realised. Some wouldn't even share profits during prosperous times, let alone when the ship is sinking.

This experience hammered home a crucial lesson: never toss your savings into someone else's business. It's a gamble with potentially devastating consequences. That day, I made a pact with myself: no more throwing my money into other people's ventures or running a business on borrowed funds. Lessons like these sting, but they shape you. It was a real eye-opener, a baptism by fire.

Tiger arrives

Back in 2002, while we were still living in the apartment, my wife surprised me with a tiny ball of fluff—a Persian kitten. Despite not being a huge pet person, this little charmer, with fur as soft as silk and eyes that sparkled like emeralds, quickly won me over. He looked like a creature straight out of a storybook. We christened him Tiger and it wasn't long before he stole a permanent place in our hearts. As he grew, Tiger showered us with affection, his playful antics and unexpected snuggles a constant source of delight.

Like all Persian cats, Tiger boasted a luxurious coat and captivating eyes. Their history, shrouded in a touch of mystery, stretches back to the 1600s. While some believe they originated in Mesopotamia, the region once known as Persia (modern-day Iran)—hence the name—others point to genetic similarities with cats from Western Europe. This intriguing twist adds another layer to their fascinating story.

Tiger, with his carefree spirit, seemed to embody this rich heritage with effortless grace. Fast forward a few years and we found ourselves living in a villa of our own. Feeling Tiger might enjoy some company, we brought home a queen we named Snow. They became an inseparable pair, but sadly, none of their litters survived.

Tiger is much more than just a pet to me. He holds a special place in our family. Some people might find his name a bit unconventional, but for me, he's always been a tiny tiger cub at heart. It's all about perspective. After all, big cats and small cats—they're all part of the same magnificent feline family.

6

Birth of Heilbronn

My friend's failed business venture only solidified my resolve to carve my own path. I decided I'd never be a partner in someone else's business. February 2, 2002, became an auspicious date marked in my memory. It was the day Heilbronn Construction LLC, with me at the helm, was born. I was 33 years old while starting my own company.

A touch of serendipity surrounded the date itself: 02-02-02. When you add the digits together, you get six, a number that seemed to hold a strange significance for me. It was my high school registration number and back in Mumbai, six of us shared a living space. Could number six be my lucky charm? Perhaps.

Those initial days at Heilbronn were a one-man odyssey. I juggled every role imaginable—writer, director and the star of the show. Running the entire office solo for months was a demanding but rewarding experience.

There's a powerful truth to the idea that everything in life is interconnected. When we dig deeper, we often discover surprising links and influences.

A close friend in Bengaluru, a man with significant financial muscle and business savvy, approached me about a partnership. While the offer was enticing, it didn't align with my vision for the future. For me, starting my own venture held an irresistible allure: the immense freedom it offered. As the sole owner, I wouldn't be answerable to anyone, free from the need to persuade others or navigate the intricacies of shared profits and losses. More importantly, I yearned for the experience of constructing a business from its foundation. My dream wasn't to command a colossal entity, but rather to create a company that thrived on efficiency and minimised the potential for roadblocks and complications.

The name, 'Heilbronn', often sparks curiosity. People want to know its origin. Let me take you on a trip down memory lane to my childhood. It all started with a simple pencil. Cheriyachan gifted me a pencil from Bahrain, proudly proclaiming it was 'Made in Germany'. That pencil and the charm of the country it came from sparked a fascination within me. Years later, when it came to naming my company, Heilbronn, a quaint town in Germany, felt like the perfect fit. It evoked an international vibe, something that would stand out. Just like the town itself, I envisioned my company to be small but beautiful.

Yet, the name was just one piece of the puzzle. My true desire was for Heilbronn to stand for something bigger. Client satisfaction and service were paramount. When I started Heilbronn, I wanted to keep my clients happy and cultivate long-term relationships with them. Profits, I knew, would eventually follow.

Companies that prioritise customer satisfaction build a loyal customer base, which acts as a springboard for long-term profitability. Focussing solely on profits risks short-circuiting value creation by neglecting customer needs. By actively listening to feedback, addressing concerns, and elevating the customer experience, businesses engender trust.

One thing was clear: I didn't want to be known as a contractor when Heilbronn was launched. Because I knew what was happening around. Projects would start with smiles and promises, only to devolve into nitpicking and disputes once completed. These undesirable developments often resulted in clients finding excuses to reduce or withhold payments. I had seen many such instances during my nine-year work in the industry. I vowed to break the cycle. Heilbronn's initial decision was to provide the manpower and machinery for construction jobs, offering daily services with a focus on transparency and exceptional customer service. My motto became clear: client satisfaction mattered far more than a quick buck.

Wings of growth

A few months into Heilbronn's journey, my phone rang. It was a friend from Emirates Airlines. They needed a contractor to build a temporary access road for their prestigious Al Maha resort. My initial instinct was to politely decline. Building a peaceful, stress-free business was my ultimate goal and this project seemed to radiate potential headaches.

But my friend was persistent. He emphasised the positive impact a successful project could have on Heilbronn's reputation, especially considering the client—a giant like Emirates. "Payments won't be an issue," he assured me. "It's a chance to build a strong relationship with a major player."

"I know Emirates is good for payments," I conceded, "but taking on a contract feels overwhelming right now. Peace of mind is important to me."

I told him I was not interested in being a contractor.

The pressure of a contract wasn't appealing. Yet, loyalty and trust mattered. My friend, new to his position at Emirates, was also eager to establish himself. Ultimately, a combination of factors swayed me: his firm support, the potential for a major client relationship and the chance to prove myself. With a deep breath, I decided to take a chance and submit a tender.

The wisdom of my old bosses, Mr K. G. Nair and Mr Vatuvara, echoed in my mind. They were firm believers in client satisfaction, always striving to offer favourable and competitive rates. Their philosophy—that a company thrives on the support of its clients—struck a chord with me.

I submitted a modest bid: AED 150,000. It felt like a significant sum for me at the time, but lower than what the other contractors quoted.

To my surprise, my proposal emerged victorious. In a surge of resolve, I delivered the project on time and without complications. The success was a game-changer, injecting a powerful dose of confidence into my vision for Heilbronn.

This contract became a turning point. It not only opened doors but also forged a valuable connection with Emirates Airlines, a major player in the UAE market. The project I initially avoided became my springboard to success. Thereafter, Emirates awarded many projects to Heilbronn. It was a powerful reminder that sometimes, the universe has a plan, even when it doesn't match our own. The key is to be open to the possibilities and roll with the punches. Everything happens for a reason. God has specific plans for each of us.

The million dollar achievement

Dubai's transformation into a global metropolis mirrored Heilbronn's own rapid growth. Just a year after starting the company, by the time I turned 34 in 2003, we had reached the coveted million-dollar mark.

Dubai's transformation in the early 2000s was a remarkable phenomenon, driven by a confluence of advantageous factors. Soaring oil prices provided a massive financial boost, acting as the engine for the city's ambitious projects. This windfall empowered the visionary government to invest heavily in infrastructure, constructing a network of new roads, bridges and airports.

However, Dubai's growth wasn't just about financial resources. It was about strategic vision. The government implemented a series of bold initiatives, like establishing free trade zones and developing luxurious resorts. These projects proved to be a magnet, attracting foreign investment and businesses to Dubai.

Dubai's strategic location also played a crucial role. Situated at a crossroads between Asia, Africa and Europe, the city boasts a prime position for trade and logistics. Recognising this advantage, the government poured resources into developing its ports and airports, further enhancing Dubai's position as a global hub.

Riding this wave of development, Heilbronn thrived alongside it.

While success felt sweet, I never allowed pride to cloud my judgment. The support from mentors, friends, and most importantly, our clients, was instrumental in our achievements.

Joining the One Million Dollar Club was a surreal experience. It's a select group, and to be a part of it through sheer hard work and talent was incredibly humbling. Only those who've achieved it will know this.

For someone from a simple village in Kerala, achieving millionaire status within a year of launching a business in Dubai was a significant milestone. It shows the power of hard work, regardless of your background.

Each accomplishment feels like a movie reel playing in my mind— family, friends, teachers, past bosses, and yes, even those who doubted me.

While I hold no grudges, there have certainly been doubters throughout my life. Their negativity, in a strange way, powered me. As a young person, I faced criticism from some adults, but I never let their words define me. I possessed a clear vision and the confidence to pursue it. There have also been instances where people questioned the value of my friendships. They have criticised us for being friends. These experiences can be hurtful, but I've chosen to focus on the positive impact these relationships have on my life. There's a natural desire to prove my doubters wrong, but it's more about showing myself that I've achieved what I set out to do, regardless of their dismissal.

I don't feel the need to flaunt my achievements, not even within my close circle of family and friends. My happiness comes from living a fulfilling life inside this circle, surrounded by loved ones.

Success is a motivator, but it's not the sole driver. The journey itself holds immense value. Every challenge overcome, every obstacle hurdled, becomes a stepping stone to the next peak. These victories, big and small, incite my desire to keep growing, to keep pushing the boundaries of what I thought possible. That's the fire that burns within—a sustained pursuit of improvement, a dedication to becoming the best version of myself.

Building dreams in Dubai

Year 2003 was a turning point. At 34, I made a move from my apartment to a villa in Mirdif, a reflection of the growing success of Heilbronn. My trusty Mercedes E-class and old BMW 3-series were traded in for a sleek BMW X5, a well-deserved reward for all the hard work. After all, we work hard to build the life we dream of and I was determined to make those dreams a reality.

Heilbronn started as a small company, but its growth trajectory was impressive. Till 2007, we were a thriving medium-sized business. We were ready to level up again, venturing into the exciting world of property with the birth of Heilbronn Properties. Our focus? Snagging plots and properties across Dubai, with a vision to transform them into modern-style villas and apartment complexes.

Ambition, however, was tempered by a growing environmental awareness. As I began acquiring land in India for potential projects, a realisation struck me. The thought of clearing trees to make way for buildings became unbearable. Trees are the lungs of our planet, providing the very oxygen we breathe and cool shade. It was a wake-up call and I made a difficult but important decision—any projects requiring deforestation were shelved. In Dubai, thankfully, development largely arose from the desert sands, leaving the natural world untouched.

The creative spark within me has always been bright. From a young age, I've been drawn to artistic expression. Whether through painting, crafting intricate handicrafts, or shaping clay into unique creations, this artistic inclination laid the foundation for my future career path. Though a diploma in civil engineering was all my family's resources allowed, my passion for design couldn't be contained. Independent study became my classroom, stirred by a constant thirst for knowledge in design and architecture. I meticulously observed the world's most innovative building plans and modern architectural trends, honing my own design sensibility. This dedication to artistic exploration has translated beautifully into my work as the lead designer for Heilbronn Properties. Here, I get to translate my vision into reality, designing luxury villas, apartments and entire complexes in my signature style.

Achan and Amma—a photograph taken by me

Another day in the life of a Quantity Surveyor—while I was working at the UTCC Wade Adams Contracting LLC in Dubai

With Amma

With sisters Pushpa and Sajana,
and brother Abhilash—in 1989

The house built by Cheriyachan in Edappal for our family

My sister Pushpa and her husband Kesavettan (Kesavan). He received me at the Dubai airport when I landed there first on February 13, 1991

Cheriyachan,
my childhood hero,
and Cheriyamma at
my Edappal home

Ford Tempo, the first car I bought in Dubai in 1994

My sister Sajana, her husband Dinesh, their kids, along with Amma and Achan

Drawn from memory: this is my depiction of our family's 1970s home in Edappal, Kerala, with a thatched roof. It was later rebuilt by Cheriyachan

An old photo of Achan on his way to the agricultural fields. He is flanked by my friends Saibu, Ali and Razaq

With Parutty Chechi

Achan A V Narayanan and Amma Sarojini on their wedding day in 1967

Generations of love! I captured this precious moment of Achan with my son Gautam

Achan, Amma and brother Abhilash—a 1989 photograph

Posing with my trusty Tata Sierra and childhood friends, Rajesh and Pradeep, back in 1997

Maniyettan and his wife Sudha Chechi call on me in Dubai. So grateful for his help in finding accommodation when I first arrived in Mumbai

Cheriyachan A V Balakrishnan
in my Dubai home

My friend Prakash and his sister

More than just luggage - this suitcase, a thoughtful gift from my brother-in-law Kesavettan, has been my first travel companion to Mumbai and Dubai. Still a cherished souvenir!

With Haridasettan.
I started my journey in Dubai in 1991 with the kindness of Haridasettan, who hosted me on my first day

My dear friend Babu. On his scooter, Babu ferried me to Kuttipuram station for my Bombay train in 1991. Forever grateful!

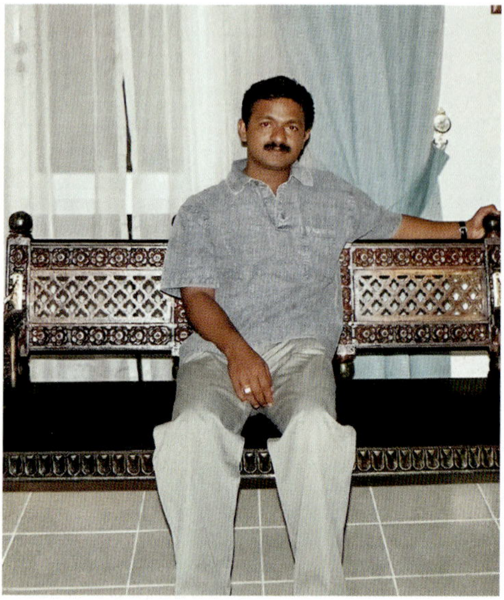

My friend A R Shaji at my Meadows-9 residence in Dubai

That's me, second from left, hanging out with friends Rajesh, Giri, and Hari in Edappal. Always a good time

Catching up with Kuttettan, my former roommate in Mumbai, after 30 years when I re-visited the city

With my former classmates at SSM Polytechnic College

Old friends. new memories! Enjoying a reunion with my former classmates of SSM Polytechnic College in beautiful Tirur

With Suresh, my former school-mate

Mumbai wouldn't have been the same without Surendrettan's kindness. He opened his living quarter and his heart when finding accommodation was tough!

Friends from high school days—Viswan, Sasi, Nandan, Ramachandran and Sajeev—visiting my Dubai office

These faces may have aged a bit, but the friendships are as strong as ever! So grateful for this reunion with my SSM Polytechnic College class-mates in our old classroom

1991—new city, new job, new me! Excited to join UTCC Wade Adams in Dubai

High school friends who shared a bench reunited! Sasi, Ramachandran and me—years later

A new chapter begins—standing proud with my first Mercedes Benz in front of the Heilbronn office at the stunning Emirates Tower in Dubai. My friend Bhasiyettan (cine actor Ramu) took this photograph

His Highness Sheikh Mohammed Bin Rashid Al Maktoum, Vice President and Prime Minister of the UAE and Ruler of Dubai (left) and His Highness Sheikh Mohamed Bin Zayed Al Nahyan, President of the UAE

His Highness the late Sheikh Zayed Bin Sultan Al Nahyan, the architect of the UAE, and His Highness the late Sheikh Rashid bin Saeed Al Maktoum, who was largely responsible for creating the modern emirate of Dubai and a co-founder (1971) of the UAE

Bathed in blue, the majestic Dubai skyline rises from the desert sands. A truly awe-inspiring sight

A 2011 photograph of our first residence in Emirates Hills—E183

Starting my car collection strong with a Lamborghini and Ferrari—in 2008

Heilbronn's work in progress for a project of Emirates Airlines

The logo of Heilbronn

My first business investment, in 1997—a fax machine—still preserved in my home office

Photographs taken in 2023 of
some of the cars in my collection

Our residence—HT-15—in Emirates Hills, after renovation

Taking Gautam to his first day of school in 2007. Around 30 million people watched a reel capturing this moment that went viral on Instagram

Proof that hard work pays off! My first Ferrari, a symbol of the dreams Dubai helped me achieve

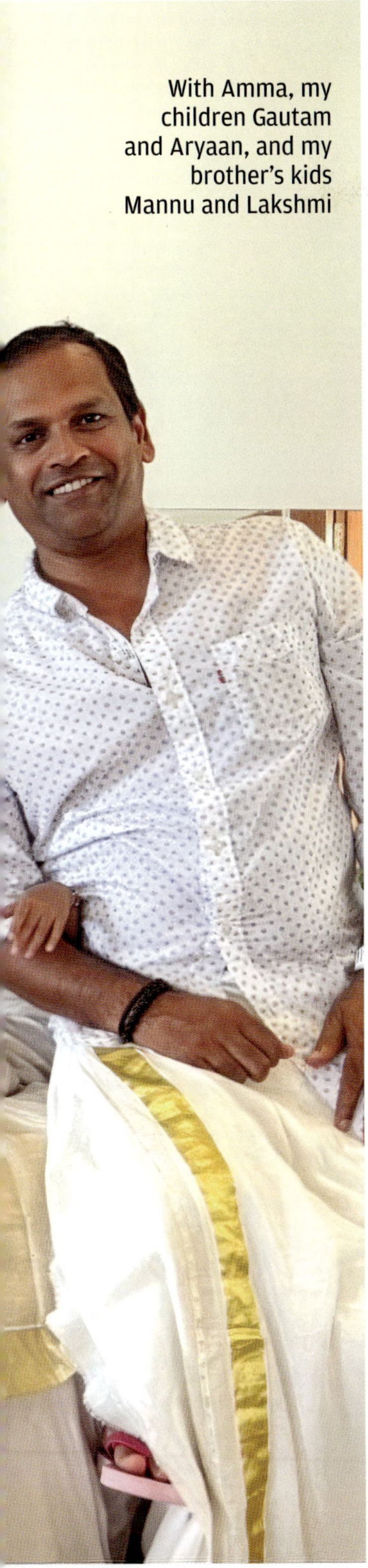

With Amma, my children Gautam and Aryaan, and my brother's kids Mannu and Lakshmi

With my driving guru Kuttettan and his wife

Our pet cat Tiger

MJ and I
on a golf course
during our travels

MJ and I at Taj Mahal,
an eternal monument of love

MJ and I in Kerala

At son Gautam's convocation

7

The happiest day of my life

May 26, 2004, is a date forever inscribed in my memory as the happiest day of my life. I woke up that morning on cloud nine, a feeling of pure anticipation buzzing through me. At precisely 6 a.m., witness a miracle unfold—my wife bringing our little bundle of joy, Gautam, into the world. Pure bliss! I never knew a single moment could hold such overwhelming ecstasy. They say true happiness keeps you up at night, and that morning, sleep was the furthest thing from my mind.

However, our journey to parenthood wasn't your typical one. My wife and I had been married for seven years before Gautam arrived. Yes, it took us longer than some, but as the saying goes, good things come to those who wait. We made a conscious decision, together, to delay parenthood. We wanted to build a solid foundation, achieve financial stability and create a secure environment to welcome a child.

Such a decision, however, wasn't met with universal understanding, especially back in India. Traditional societal norms often dictate a specific timeline for marriage and family. The absence of children after marriage often invites a barrage of intrusive questions and unwanted scrutiny. Thankfully, relocating to Dubai offered some reprieve from this pressure, although not entirely. The questions persisted, a constant reminder of the societal pressure to conform, often disregarding individual choices and circumstances. "Why no children?" or "Haven't found the right partner yet?"—such inquiries, often insensitive and intrusive, highlight the expectation to adhere to conventional norms.

But on that beautiful May morning, none of it mattered. As we held our precious Gautam for the first time, our hearts overflowed with a love and joy that transcended everything else.

Looking into his tiny, sparkling eyes, I whispered, "Welcome to the world, my dearest."

Teeing off

For years, I didn't ask Shihabka anything related to golf. But I learnt a lot about it through different sources.

The Dubai Creek Golf and Yacht Club opened in 1993. It quickly became a symbol of Dubai's burgeoning golf culture. Its charm, however, remained out of reach for me as I watched from the sidelines. It wasn't until 14 years later that I finally attained a full-time membership, a feat that felt like the culmination of a lifelong dream. The cost of entry, a hefty AED 30,000, was a testament not just to financial success, but to personal achievement.

Reflecting on my journey, I recall Shihabka's remark about needing three years' salary to afford such a membership. Back then, the idea seemed as distant as the lush greens of the club. Yet through perseverance and hard work, I turned that dream into reality.

Now, I proudly carry my membership, reserved for celebrities, social icons and business leaders, like a badge of honour. It fills me with immense pride and joy. Every chance I get, I'm out there practising, honing my skills. It's a world away from my childhood in Edappal, where I whacked a cricket ball with a makeshift stick. Golf was not even in my distant dream.

There's a common misconception that golf is a breeze—easy to learn and effortless to play. Watching professionals on TV can definitely create that impression. But trust me, the reality on the course is a different story.

There's a truth to the saying, "don't judge a book by its cover." The same applies to golf. From the outside, golf can appear elitist, even boring. Take me, for instance. As a youngster, the image of golf was far removed from my world. Ironically, the neat and tidy attire held a certain appeal, even if the game itself didn't.

However, these perceptions often crumble upon closer examination. Statistics show that around 70% of beginners abandon the sport. It's a demanding game, requiring both mental focus and consistent practice. But for those who persevere, the rewards are immense.

My own journey to golf started with initial skepticism. However, the very first time I connected with the ball and sent it sailing, I knew I was hooked. Golf is a game of control and accuracy, constantly challenging you to improve. It requires dedication, but the satisfaction of mastering a shot or sinking a putt is unparalleled.

American golfer Arnold Palmer's words ring true: "Golf is deceptively simple and endlessly complicated; it satisfies the soul and frustrates the intellect. It is at the same time rewarding and maddening—and it is without a doubt the greatest game mankind has ever invented."

Now, a serious golfer myself, I occasionally catch glimpses of curious faces peering through the gates of golf courses. Perhaps, in their eyes, I see a reflection of my younger self— a wide-eyed observer yearning to be part of this exclusive world. The game itself continues to surprise me. There's a hidden elegance in the effortless swing of a pro, a humbling reminder that mastery takes a lifetime.

Lessons from the fairways

Indeed, golf mirrors life in its highs and lows, its lessons echoing beyond the fairways. It demands discipline and the ability to bounce back from setbacks—qualities essential both on the course and in life's journey.

It is a game of strategy and precision, where each shot requires careful calculation and execution—a metaphor for the deliberate choices we make in handling life's challenges. In the pursuit of mastery, golf demands not only physical skill but also mental fortitude, teaching us the importance of focus, patience and perseverance in the face of adversity. Just as a golfer must weather the unpredictable elements and unforeseen obstacles on the course, so too must we confront the uncertainties and trials that arise in our personal and professional lives. Ultimately, golf is more than a sport—it is a metaphor for the human experience, reminding us that success is not determined solely by our wins or losses, but by our commitment to the journey.

Just like achieving milestones in life elevates our standing, so too does success in golf. Each conquered hole and well-placed shot brings with it a surge of pride and accomplishment. Beyond the scorecard, golf offers surprising health benefits. Playing a full round can translate to walking up to 11 kilometres, a fantastic way to burn roughly 2,000 calories.

But the true magic of golf lies in the connections created on the course. It's a chance to meet and network with people from diverse backgrounds, many of whom may be highly successful in their own right. While explicit business deals might not be struck on the fairway, the conversations and camaraderie can cultivate valuable relationships and offer unexpected life lessons.

I played with over two dozen European and American professional golfers in Pro-Am tournaments.

Through golf, I've forged connections with fellow enthusiasts, from everyday players to celebrities. I've had the privilege of teeing off with a diverse array of sports and entertainment personalities, including Indian cricket legend Kapil Dev, alongside Indian cricketers Yuvraj Singh, Sreesanth and Sanju Samson. Joining us on the course was also South African-born English cricketer Nick Compton, Bollywood star R. Madhavan, and Cheyenne Nicole Woods, the niece of the renowned golfer Tiger Woods. These encounters, far from the boardroom, have offered invaluable lessons and camaraderie.

And while golf may not be for everyone, its appeal lies not in exclusivity but in its timeless charm. For me, it sparked not only a passion but also the drive to pursue entrepreneurship, intertwining with my love for cars to shape my path forward.

A dream home in my dreamland

India, the land of my birth, will always hold a special place in my heart. Yet, Dubai has blossomed into my dreamland, a city where I've built a life and found endless opportunity.

I trust Dubai. In 2005, at the age of 36, I decided to settle here. I consider it my wisest decision in life.

I longed for a place of my own in Dubai. Nothing can match the ease and comfort of returning to one's own home from work. Here, I could nurture my thoughts and ideas amidst lush greenery, free from the uncertainty of yearly rent hikes.

When I stumbled upon a spacious 3,800 square feet villa in Meadows-9, I knew it was the perfect place I had envisioned. However, the hefty price tag of AED 1,450,000 seemed daunting. Undeterred, I took a bold step and secured a loan of AED 1 million from the bank, determined to make this dream a reality. I could put together the remaining AED 450,000.

In 2005, I bought this new villa and relocated from my rented place. In those days, people who bought villas and apartments in Dubai were few. Everyone thought: was it wise to invest in property in Dubai?

Despite prevailing doubts about Dubai's property market, my faith in the city remained unshaken. For me, Dubai was more than just a destination—it was a place of inexhaustible opportunity. And in return for my loyalty, Dubai bestowed upon me countless blessings and achievements.

For the same reason, I wanted to live in Dubai for the rest of my life. As I settled into my new villa in 2005, I became an advocate for homeownership among my peers. While some did, others hesitated, plagued by uncertainties.

I still remain steadfast in my belief that no other place in the world offers unparalleled safety and prosperity as Dubai does. Making Dubai, a true heaven on earth, my permanent home was a decision I'll always cherish.

Double joy: our second little prince

The anticipation for February 15, 2007, was palpable—it marked the arrival of the second most beautiful day of my life. That day, our family welcomed a new addition, our son Aryaan, joining his elder brother Gautam, who had blessed our lives in 2004. These two milestones, written in golden letters in the diary of my existence, brought immeasurable joy and purpose to our family.

Both Gautam and Aryaan took their first breaths at Al Wasl Hospital in Dubai. I remember bringing both of them home in my BMW car.

My wife possessed a natural knack for nurturing, showering our children with abundant love and care. Her culinary skills ensured that our home was always filled with delicious meals, crafted with love for our little ones.

Yet, beneath the surface, subtle fissures began to emerge in our relationship. Despite our differences, I chose to turn a blind eye to the discord, opting instead to shield our children from the spectre of conflict. People point to our astrological mismatch, with her being a Taurus and I an Aquarian. Did it compound the divide? I do not know.

While my wife was not inherently malevolent, our souls seemed to occupy distant realms, our connection strained by unvoiced grievances and unaddressed rifts. The facade of marital harmony we presented to the world masked the underlying truth of our emotional detachment.

Our situation mirrored that of countless couples worldwide, navigating the delicate dance of maintaining appearances while grappling with internal turmoil. I, like many others, chose the path of silent resignation, unwilling to disrupt the fragile equilibrium of our family dynamic.

Yet, I am acutely aware of the dissonance between outward affection and inner discord, the disingenuousness inherent in wearing a mask of marital contentment. But in the absence of viable alternatives, I found myself compelled to perpetuate the charade. Maintaining appearances wasn't ideal, but for the time being, it offered a semblance of stability.

The Malabari who bought a Ferrari

Owning a Ferrari was more than just a fascination for me—it was the ultimate symbol of success. It was a dream come true. With each milestone in my business, thoughts of that iconic red Ferrari danced in my mind. The Ferrari poster that once adorned my childhood bedroom wall in Edappal had transformed into a gleaming reality parked in my Dubai home.

When the day finally came to bring that Ferrari home, it was a moment of triumph celebrated by family, friends and colleagues alike. Its sleek design, powerful engine and dazzling red hue stood as a proof of my hard work.

The emblem of the Prancing Horse epitomises exclusivity and quality on a global scale. Ferrari's reputation is forged through decades of athletic triumphs and the incomparable elegance of the vehicles, distinguished by their pioneering innovation, cutting-edge technology and unsurpassed driving experience.

Every morning, as I gazed upon my Ferrari parked proudly in the driveway, it remind me of how far I'd come. For a farmer's son from Edappal who arrived at the labour camp and worked for AED 900, the journey was nothing short of fulfilling.

My love for sports cars extended beyond mere aesthetics. Sports cars are the thoroughbreds of the automotive world, engineered for exhilarating performance and head-turning design. They boast powerful engines that deliver thrilling acceleration, hugging corners with precision handling. Beyond the raw power, their sleek, aerodynamic designs are a statement in themselves, crafted with cutting-edge technology for a matchless driving experience.

Back in 2007, owning a Ferrari was a rarity in Dubai. As I cruised down Sheikh Zayed Road, heads turned and eyes lingered—a far cry from these days when such cars aren't a rare sight.

The Ferrari F430 wasn't just a car; it was a symbol of possibility, a proof to the belief that with dedication, anything is attainable. And while I've added other luxury vehicles to my collection over the years, the Ferrari F430 holds a special place in my heart, much like a first love. The joy and self-confidence I felt the day I owned it are beyond words. The car conveyed a message that hard work would truly pave the way. Every time I drive it, I'm filled with gratitude for all those who supported me on this journey. As a token of thanks for the blessings received, I park the Ferrari in front of Rashidiya Masjid.

This love for cars extends to my family. I've passed down my craze for cars to my children. Watching them marvel at the beauty of these machines, lending a hand in their care, fills me with pride.

In our household, cars serve as more than just vehicles—they're family, an integral part of our lives. They're also a means for our children to earn pocket money. Through performing small tasks like helping us wash the cars, they receive wages, which we uphold as their pocket money. It's a rule we stand by: car washes warrant payment.

I recall acquiring the Ferrari in 2007 for AED 1,000,000 at a time when my 3,800 square feet villa was valued at AED 1,450,000. Despite facing ridicule from some who questioned the prudence of such a purchase, I remained firm in my pursuit of dreams. For me, ambitions know no bounds, and I am resolute in following my desires regardless of external opinions.

The journey didn't end there. With a yellow convertible Lamborghini joining the ranks in 2008, our driveway has become a showcase of automotive excellence. Alongside the Lamborghini, my collection boasts a Jaguar, a Mercedes-Benz, and a BMW X-5, each representing a unique blend of style and performance. But this isn't the finishing line, it's just the beginning.

Heilbronn grows as Dubai soars

My journey with Heilbronn has been an extraordinary one, marked by significant growth and notable achievements. Founded in 2002, Heilbronn quickly established itself as a reputable brand in Dubai.

During this period of expansion, Dubai was experiencing unprecedented development, with the real estate sector booming and opportunities abound. Everyone was talking about profits. There was intense competition in the business world to excel. Along with Dubai, the other emirates too prospered.

As our projects multiplied, Heilbronn invested in state-of-the-art technology and equipment, reinforcing our commitment to quality and innovation.

My fascination with Dubai began in 1980, during my childhood, upon hearing descriptions of a remarkably modern Arabian city unlike any other in the Gulf. Its allure was undeniable, igniting a desire within me to one day call Dubai home. Over the years, the UAE has emerged as the top destination for job seekers from India, with many of them considering it the epitome of satisfaction in terms of living and working abroad. Today, the UAE stands as a paragon of excellence across various sectors, boasting a knowledge-based economy, a world-class healthcare system, and innovative educational initiatives. Its commitment to integrated infrastructure development and promoting a conducive environment for growth has propelled it far ahead of its regional counterparts. The UAE leads the Arab region in empowering women and youth, cultivating a diversified economy and achieving milestones such as space missions and the establishment of the first nuclear power plant.

Dubai is a city that never ceases to amaze. Here are just a few of the things you can experience in this dynamic metropolis: The Office of the Future, not science fiction but reality! Dubai boasts the world's first fully functional 3D-printed building, built in less than a month in 2016. Imagine a 250-square-metre building with innovative working spaces, meeting rooms, a lounge and a cafe, all constructed using 3D printing technology—that's The Office of the Future . Expo 2020 Dubai wasn't just a six-month celebration; it made history as the first World Expo ever held in the Middle East, Africa and South Asia region. The Expo welcomed visitors from 192 countries and featured global superstars like Coldplay, Alicia Keys, Cristiano Ronaldo and Lewis Hamilton. The futuristic Expo City Dubai continues its rich legacy. Need to travel anywhere? Look no further than Dubai International Airport (DXB), one of the busiest airports in the world, handling over 90 million passengers annually. With over 6,500 flights a week operated by more than 140 airlines, you can travel to over 270 destinations worldwide from Dubai. Terminal 3 at DXB is also eco-conscious, boasting the largest solar energy system in the Middle East, reducing its energy consumption by almost 30 per cent. And if you're looking for record-breaking sights, Dubai has you covered! In addition to the world's tallest building, the Burj Khalifa, Dubai holds Guinness World Records for the world's deepest swimming pool at Deep Dive Dubai, measuring an astonishing 60.02 metres deep, and the world's tallest landmark sign in Hatta, which stands at an impressive 19.28 metres, even taller than the Hollywood sign in Los Angeles!

As the UAE continues its trajectory of growth, rivaling even the wealthiest Western nations, the government's strategic plans for the next 50 years promise unprecedented advancements and prosperity in the development industry.

The visionary leadership of Dubai and the UAE, led by His Highness Sheikh Mohamed Bin Zayed Al Nahyan and His Highness Sheikh Mohammed Bin Rashid Al Maktoum, has been instrumental in shaping the region's success story. Their dedication to progress has set the stage for UAE's transformation into a global hub of commerce and innovation.

I write this with heartfelt gratitude and enormous respect for the visionary rulers who have guided its remarkable journey. They are models for rulers and heads of States elsewhere. Every time I land here, it's like returning to a sanctuary, a land that has embraced not just me, but millions of families like mine. Dubai is a place where dreams take root and flourish, nourishing not just its own people, but countless others around the world. Both Dubai and UAE feel almost divinely blessed, where even the harshest desert sands seem infused with a touch of God's favour.

Back in 1991, even before Dubai's meteoric rise, I was captivated by its potential. It was like fertile ground, waiting for seeds to be sown. And haven't they sprouted! Dubai's growth has been nothing short of miraculous, exceeding even the wildest imaginations. Today, over 10 million people call the UAE home, living safe and secure. But the impact extends far beyond borders. Another 30 million lives, families across the globe, are woven into the framework of this nation, their livelihoods and well-being inextricably linked to

Dubai's success. It's a land marked not just in their memories, but in their daily prayers.

Brand of authenticity

Day by day, Heilbronn's business continued to expand. It became a major brand in construction and architectural design. At the heart of Heilbronn's success lies our dedication to client satisfaction and fair business practices. Timely payment of employees and subcontractors has been a cornerstone of our ethos. When payments for employees are delayed, we do injustice to them. When workers are happy, they sincerely work for the company's progress.

In my entrepreneurial journey, I've learned that true success transcends monetary gains. Instead, it's found in the happiness derived from our endeavours. For me, business success is synonymous with the reputation of our company, the respect it garners and the confidence stemming from our commitment to our vision and meticulous planning. This philosophy has guided my approach, where prioritising integrity and passion over mere pursuit of profit has been paramount. About 98 per cent of people in the world senselessly chase money. That is why, only the remaining 2 per cent succeed.

I've never shied away from sacrifice in pursuit of excellence. Whether toiling under scorching sunrays on outdoor sites during blistering summers, in 45 degree Celsius, or overcoming adversities, my dedication to delivering quality work on time has remained unwavering. I've a no-compromise attitude to work. I'm ready for no adjustments in this. Passion can't be stopped by rain or roadblocks. Challenges are merely opportunities to showcase our resolve and with a steadfast mindset focused on our goals, no obstacle is insurmountable. Like a determined sprinter hurdling towards the finish line, I've remained focussed on the long-term vision for my business, understanding that enduring success requires patience, perseverance and a firm commitment to our unique path. My business strategy aimed to establish a resilient business model through steady profits, ensuring long-term viability.

Rather than emulate others, I've forged my own distinct path, recognising that each individual's journey is inherently unique. While we can draw inspiration from others, true fulfillment lies in embracing our own strengths, capabilities and resources. By eschewing comparisons and upholding our individuality, we liberate ourselves from the shackles of self-doubt and pave the way for authentic success and fulfillment.

The past, present and future are interwoven strands in the narrative of my life. I cherish the memories and wisdom gleaned from yesterday. Embracing the present, I actively stitch my goals and aspirations, grounded in reality and empowered by my skills and resources. True success flourishes from this harmonious interplay of past knowledge, present action and future vision. To disregard the lessons of the past is like building on unstable ground; a prosperous future demands a foundation constructed from the strengths of all three.

Emirates and Heilbronn

Heilbronn's combination of professionalism and competitive pricing set us apart from many multinational companies. This earned us numerous projects from Emirates, the world's leading airlines. Our strong relationship with its senior management, coupled with our commitment to top-quality work and timely delivery, promoted a two-decade partnership built on continuous projects.

As Heilbronn gained recognition for its efficiency, transparency and adaptability in construction operations, renowned companies sought to collabourate with us. Projects were awarded by leading entities in the UAE such as Khansaheb, BESIX, Emirates SkyCargo, Emirates Flight Training Academy, Emirates Aviation College and Spinneys, further solidifying our reputation in the industry.

Heilbronn's portfolio boasts prestigious projects in Dubai's most coveted locales, including Palm Islands, Jumeirah Beach, Emirates Hills and Nad Al Sheba. From luxurious villas to high-rise buildings and apartments, our commitment to excellence shines through in every endeavour.

Our involvement in notable projects such as the Mall of the Emirates, Madinat Jumeirah and the Headquarters Building of Emirates Airlines underscores Heilbronn's role in shaping Dubai's skyline. We've also contributed to critical infrastructure projects like the Chilled Water Pipeline to Burj Khalifa District and earthworks for the Airbus A380 Hangar for Emirates, highlighting our versatility. Heilbronn landed projects one after the other.

It's the fire of passion that's always burned within me. The hobby I started at the age of five, I still do. The materials may have changed—from childhood clay and crafts to the concrete and steel we shape today—but the thrill of creation remains constant. That's the driving force behind Heilbronn's success.

Sure, I'm building world-class structures in iconic locations—that's the adult me, the professional. But the spark that ignited my passion in childhood still burns brightly. The unbridled enthusiasm of those clay-house days powers my approach to every project, keeping curiosity alive and pushing boundaries.

One of Heilbronn's most significant milestones was the roads, pitches and other infrastructure work for Sevens, a purpose-built rugby sevens stadium and cricket ground owned by Emirates Airlines. The 200-acre development took Heilbronn to another level.

The stadium hosted the 2008 Rugby Sevens World Series.

Surmounting obstacles

Business isn't just about the highs; it's about handling the lows too. Every setback, every crisis, is a lesson waiting to be learned. I've had my fair share of challenges in my entrepreneurial journey, but I never let them defeat me. Instead, I considered each hurdle as an opportunity to grow and evolve.

Running a business is like sailing a ship in stormy seas. The waves of adversity will test our resolve, threatening to capsize us at every turn. But true success lies in our ability to weather the storm, to steer our ship safely to shore despite the tempest raging around us. It's during the toughest times that we discover our true strength.

When faced with problems, I've learned to stay calm and composed. Instead of panicking, I take the time to analyse the situation, to understand the root cause of the issue. What are the real problems? What are the reasons? What are the motives? I try to find out. Sometimes, I've waited for days for the answers. Sometimes, the solution reveals itself when we least expect it. Nature has a way of soothing our troubled minds, offering clarity and perspective. I've often found joy in the simple beauty of a sunrise, knowing that with each new day comes renewed hope and possibility.

I firmly believe that every problem has a solution; we just need to have the patience and perseverance to find it. Nature has all the answers to your questions. Observe closely and you will know. Mother Nature has been my silent teacher, her every season and storm whispering wisdom that has shaped me. From her, I've learned the importance of adaptation and the power of quiet strength.

Teamwork pays

Our success is a result of the hard work and dedication of each and every member of our team. From our skilled craftsmen to our trusted advisors, each individual plays a vital role in our journey towards greatness.

Through Heilbronn's pioneering projects that have transformed Dubai's landscape, I've gleaned invaluable lessons in managing multifaceted endeavours and exploring diversity in construction and design. Central to my approach has been the ethos of inclusivity, where I've prioritised providing opportunities to my old friends and family members. Whether through employment in my own company or facilitating roles in other organisations, I've strived to extend a helping hand to those dear to me. Witnessing their joy in collaborating with me or benefiting from opportunities in Dubai has been immensely gratifying, reinforcing the importance of leveraging success to uplift others.

I've always believed in leading by example, in promoting a culture of teamwork and collaboration. Heilbronn's success is a collective effort, driven by the passion and dedication of every person involved. History teaches us that no leader single-handedly wins battles. Victories are achieved through the combined efforts of courageous troops, brilliant strategists and extensive support from the home front. I believe in the power of encouragement. A kind word or gesture can have a significant impact on a teammate's motivation and morale, often exceeding the value of a paycheck. Unfortunately, many talented people lack the inspiration and appreciation they deserve.

I constantly advocate for turning work into a passion. Approaching each day with enthusiasm allows us to truly invest ourselves in what we do. Ideally, work shouldn't be something we're forced to leave behind at the end of the day.

There's a difference between pursuing your passion and external pressures. Many things in life are not in our control: our names, religion and the like. Some of these were forced on us when we were babies. However, our preferences are in our control. We can choose our work and business paths. Choosing a career that aligns with our interests leads to greater happiness and fulfillment, both at work and at home. Following someone else's dream or succumbing to external pressure will ultimately lead to dissatisfaction.

In 2002, Heilbronn started as a one-man operation in the Emirates Towers building. Since then, countless companies and people have contributed to our growth and profitability.

First and foremost, I acknowledge the role of our clients. Their trust and willingness to entrust us with their projects are the real foundation of our success.

But above all, I owe our success to the dynamic team at Heilbronn—the unsung heroes—Shaiju Komban, Vinod, Maria, Kelvin, Rachappa, Manoj Mathew, Mathews, Sudhakaran, Sujith, Salih, Imran, Harris, Rento, Anwar, Ibrahim, Shamsir, Ashokettan (Ashokan), Krishnanettan (Krishnan), Mohan, Marwan, Fatima, Layla, Ann, Christie, Aroop, Shoib, Rabbani, Rajeeve, Sanjay, Leann King, Benson, Hazel, Varghese, Aneesh, Hasna, Sachin and many others.

Their hard work and dedication inspire me every day.

8

Heart-rending times

Life is like a rollercoaster ride, full of unexpected twists and turns. Just when you think everything is going smoothly, something comes along to shake things up. It's the ebb and flow of life, the ups and downs, that make it so unpredictable.

There were moments of deep sadness that cast a shadow over my happiness. The strain in my relationship with my wife weighed heavily on my heart, like a dark cloud looming over me. Perhaps it was the postpartum blues or maybe just the natural course of married life taking its toll. Either way, I found myself grappling with feelings of confinement and uncertainty.

But the pain ran deeper still with the disappearance of my dear friend, Pramod. The uncertainty of his whereabouts and well-being gnawed at me. And then there was Prakash, my closest confidante, whose untimely passing left a gaping hole in my heart. His words of encouragement and unwavering support had always been a light in my darkest moments. I can still recall the consoling words he said to me as I wept at the Kuttipuram railway station, just as I was about to board a train to Mumbai.

I remember the last time I saw Prakash, his infectious smile masking the turmoil within. He spoke of life with carefree abandon, urging me to take in each moment with joy and laughter. Little did I know that his own struggles would eventually overwhelm him, leading him down a path of despair from which he could not return.

He once cryptically warned me of some impending news, leaving me puzzled and apprehensive. "Don't be shocked by the news, Dileep," he told me.

Little did I anticipate that the news would shatter my world—a month later, I learned of his tragic decision to end his own life within the confines of the factory where he toiled. Prakash wasn't just a friend; he was a brother, whose absence still leaves an unfillable void in my life. If God appears before me and grants me a single boon, I'll ask. "Bring my dear Prakash back to life—at least for a day."

The news of his passing shook me to the core, leaving me grappling with unanswered questions and an unbearable sense of loss. Why did he choose to end his life? What demons was he battling that drove him to such a drastic decision? The pain of not knowing haunts me to this day, a constant reminder of the fragility of life and the fleeting nature of happiness.

Prakash, your absence echoes in every milestone achieved, every triumph celebrated. I can only hope that your spirit gazes upon my accomplishments from the realms above.

As I sit here, penning down these words, my heart aches with grief and sorrow. The memories of Prakash flood my mind. I long to hear his voice, to feel his reassuring presence by my side. But all I'm left with are tears and unanswered prayers.

I struggle to find the words to capture the depth of my emotions, to do justice to the memory of a friend who meant the world to me. So, for now, I'll let my tears speak for me. Till we meet again, my friend, may you find peace in the arms of eternity.

Story of a friendship

Two distinguished guests graced our Meadows Villa one day back in 2006. Among them were the renowned Malayalam cinema figures, actor, director, and screenwriter Sreenivasan, and a prominent producer from the Malayalam film industry.

Sreenivasan is a true powerhouse in Malayalam cinema. Not only has he starred in countless films, but he's also a gifted screenwriter who has penned the scripts for numerous Malayalam hits.

Few writers and directors can dissect the Malayali psyche with the same incisiveness as Sreenivasan. His sharp wit and social commentary, often delivered through blistering satire, expose the pretentiousness that can sometimes mask Malayali behaviour.

His collaborations with top directors produced gems like 'Gandhinagar Second Street', 'Sanmanassullavarkku Samadhanam' and T.P. Balagopalan M.A.', films that explore the struggles and anxieties of the Malayali middle class.

Sreenivasan is a master of self-deprecating humour, a talent he brings to life in films like 'Vadakkunokkiyanthram' and 'Chinthavishtayaya Shyamala', both of which he not only wrote but also directed.

For Malayalis living and working in the Gulf, 'Nadodikkattu' is a movie that brings back warm memories. The film follows Dasan and Vijayan, two unemployed men chasing their dreams of a brighter future in the Gulf. Their journey, filled with hope, challenges and a hilarious twist of fate in Chennai, captures the mix of aspirations and realities familiar to many Malayali expatriates.

The day Sreenivasan arrived at my home, I had hoped to welcome a prominent screenwriter and homoeopathy physician from a village near my native place. But alas, he couldn't find his way to my home in those pre-Google Map days. However, I had the pleasure of crossing paths with him recently at an Iftar hosted by my friend Siddique. The screenwriter clearly remembered the day he couldn't make it to my home.

I vividly recall the light-hearted banter initiated by Sreenivasan upon entering my house. Upon hearing my wife's preference for only two actors—Shahrukh Khan and him—he quipped with his trademark humour, "The only thing common between those two names is beauty!"

As we dined together and engaged in conversation, I couldn't help but reminisce about my dear friend. Pramod and our unbreakable bond. Tears welled up in my eyes as I shared the story of our friendship and my persistent efforts to reconnect with him.

Opening up about my quest to find Pramod, I expressed my dismay at his reluctance to reach out.

"He probably believes that I wouldn't accept him now, given how my lifestyle and status have evolved. But he's mistaken," I said.

Sreenivasan, ever the sage, offered his perspective, urging me to let go and focus on the present.

"Let it be. If he doesn't show interest, let him be. You've got your own life to focus on, don't you? Keep moving forward."

I fell silent.

"True friends are the ones from our childhood. They didn't befriend us for our wealth or success, only for our genuine affection. All they want is our love and time."

As I uttered these words, Srinivasan lapsed into silence.

Telling a tale

'Katha Parayumbol,' penned by Sreenivasan, caught my eye.

I watched a CD of the movie. My manager Hari had given me a set of CDs for watching and this one was in it. In those days, I also used to collect CDs of Malayalam movies whenever I went to Kerala. As I have told you, I love films. From my school days, watching Malayalam films has been a deep influence, shaping my perspectives and evoking deep emotions. It was through these movies that I first encountered the enchantment of romance. Since then, I've come to understand that a heart filled with love can enrich life in ways nothing else can. Upon settling in Dubai, my cinematic preferences evolved, leaning towards English movies. Icons like Sean

Penn, Susan Sarandon, Cuba Gooding Jr, Clint Eastwood, Meryl Streep, Will Smith, Morgan Freeman, Robin Williams, Al Pacino, Julia Roberts, Jack Nicholson and Tom Hanks captivate me with their performances. And films like 'The Pursuit of Happiness' and 'Pretty Woman' have become perennial favourites. I find solace and joy in revisiting these movies repeatedly.

As I watched 'Katha Parayumbol', I was struck by the poignant line at the climax, rendered by a superstar of Malayalam cinema, "True friends are the ones from our childhood." It resonated deeply with me, echoing the sentiment I had shared with Sreenivasan during his visit to my home in 2006. I had uttered the same line to him at the dinner table.

I had shared the complete story of Pramod with Sreenivasan. Despite achieving entrepreneurial success in Dubai, my quest to find Pramod remained a constant thread in my life, I told Sreenivasan. I had recounted my entire life story, emphasising the enduring nature of this search. Sreenivasan had listened to this story intently.

Witnessing the genius of Sreenivasan unfold on screen, in 'Katha Parayumbol', left me in awe. His portrayal of a barber, akin to my friend Pramod's background as a blacksmith, showcased his storytelling prowess. The lead character of the movie had found success in the world of cinema as an actor–like I did in business.

I have deeply admired Sreenivasan's work such as 'Nadodikkattu.' This man has prodigious talent.

Later, I learned that 'Katha Parayumbol' had been remade in Tamil as 'Kuselan', in Telugu as 'Kathanayakudu' and in Hindi as 'Billu Barber,' all garnering immense success. While I rejoiced in the filmmakers' accomplishments, my heart still ached for Pramod as he was still indigent and struggling in life to make ends meet.

I reached out to congratulate Sreenivasan on 'Katha Parayumbol.' Unfortunately, he did not take my call. Nor did he return the call. Twenty years have elapsed and I never got the chance to speak with him thereafter.

Remembrances of things past

My reflection on the past is deep; it's evident that my memories hold significant meaning for me. So it is for every person.

The past has constituted my character and filled me, I believe, with simplicity and humility. My past and my heritage are a source of strength and clarity to me. If at all I've reached anywhere in life, the credit goes to the paths travelled.

I recall Bob Dylan's lyrics:

How many roads must a man walk down
Before you call him a man?
How many seas must a white dove sail
Before she sleeps in the sand?
Yes, and how many times must the cannonballs fly
Before they're forever banned?
The answer, my friend, is blowin' in the wind
The answer is blowin' in the wind

Recalling moments with friends, like A. R.Shaji and Shihabka, brings back a blend of nostalgia and gratitude for the journey I've traversed. When I open the refrigerator in my villa, I remember A. R. Shaji and the times we chilled drinks on window ACs. When I cruise in luxury cars, I remember Shihabka and the cramped rides from the labour camp.

Each memory seems to carry its own lesson or sentiment.

The past is a treasure trove of lessons learned, the present an ongoing exploration and the future a fiery horizon brimming with dreams and hope. These elements propel my journey forward.

I cherish the friendships forged in Bombay and Dubai, acknowledging the impact they've had on shaping my life.

Ravi and Vimal have been steadfast friends since my arrival in Dubai and their friendship remains as strong as ever. Ravi's wife, Kavita, holds a special place in our circle; she happens to be the daughter of the esteemed Malayalam lyricist and film director, Sreekumaran Thampi. Likewise, Vimal's wife, Suchi, is equally dignified and graceful.

Even with luxury surrounding us, the urge to squeeze the last drop from a toothpaste tube persists. Like a stubborn echo from the past, this simple act reminds us of our resourceful beginnings.

The vestiges of the past, like roots anchoring a tree, are a permanent part of who we are. Simple things like the childhood shirt, shoes, pants, and study materials my father bought me are fresh in my memories. They're not just objects; they're tangible reminders of adored memories and life experiences.

This appreciation extends beyond the physical. I believe there's valuable knowledge to be gleaned from everyone, even a young child.

The story of Lake View Home, my dream residence in my hometown, is woven from the threads of unexpected encounters. The inspiration for this haven came from the most unexpected source—a simple comment by a labourer.

One day, while I was still living in my road-side house, a labourer remarked on the noise and pollution of city life. His words struck a chord—why indeed should I spend my days surrounded by the city's din and smog? The idea of a peaceful, lake-side escape began to take root.

Years later, when I crossed paths with the same labourer again, I felt compelled to express my gratitude. I presented him with a cheque, a token of appreciation for the spark that ignited the idea of my dream home.

Here's where the story took a turn. The man was genuinely surprised and confused by the gesture. He repeatedly questioned the purpose of the cheque, and I haven't revealed the reason behind it yet.

What a blessing to have so many such people light up my life!

Emirates Hills: my new abode

We must not allow the clock and the calendar to blind us to the fact that each moment of life is a miracle and mystery, as H. G. Wells states.

And indeed, my life was about to unfold a series of miracles, one after another. It all started back in 2008 when, at the age of 39, I found myself acquiring a piece of property in Emirates Hills, the epitome of luxury living in Dubai, reserved only for the elite.

Imagine this: at the entrance of Emirates Hills, where every square metre costs a fortune, I secured a prime plot spanning 60 cents, overlooking the lush greenery of the golf course. This bold move made me the first young Indian to own property in this prestigious enclave.

But let me tell you, behind this groundbreaking achievement lay an unflagging single-mindedness to defy the odds. I'm here to tell you that nothing, absolutely nothing, is beyond reach when you set your mind to it. Dreams are meant to be realised, not relegated to the realm of wishful thinking forever.

I took matters into my own hands, meticulously crafting plans and designs for the villa that would soon grace this coveted address. And with my company, Heilbronn, at the helm, we brought this vision to life—a stunning 25,000 sq.ft masterpiece that flawlessly melds opulence with functionality. From its inception in 2008 to its completion in 2010, the journey was nothing short of exhilarating.

The construction of my villa not only put me on the map but also garnered attention for my work. Its strategic location, impeccable design and flawless execution left spectators in awe. Imagine a vision in white, reminiscent of a grand Parisian palace, adorned with majestic pillars—it's a sight to behold.

Of course, as with any significant achievement, there were naysayers in my circle. Some questioned my decision to invest in Emirates Hills, while others couldn't resist the urge to criticise. But, of course, some celebrated my triumph with genuine happiness.

Burj Khalifa: my second home

Months later, another stroke of luck graced my life. I made the decision to invest in not just one, but two apartments in the iconic Burj Khalifa, standing tall as the world's tallest building. These luxurious spaces weren't just for me—they were meant to host my guests and friends, providing them with a taste of Dubai's finest hospitality.

From the moment I acquired the keys in 2009, these apartments became a sign of prestige. It made me the first Malayali to secure a residence in this iconic symbol of luxury.

Let me tell you, this skyscraper isn't just tall—it's a marvel of modern engineering, boasting a plethora of records and accolades.

Think about it: tallest building in the world, highest number of stories, highest occupied floor—the list goes on. Its architectural prowess, inspired by the elegant Hymenocallis flower, is a tribute to human ingenuity and creativity. Designed by the renowned Skidmore, Owings and Merrill (SOM), the same minds behind iconic structures like the Willis Tower and One World Trade Center, the Burj Khalifa stands as a symbol of architectural innovation.

Living in the Burj Khalifa is an experience like no other. The panoramic views from the swimming pool are breathtaking, casting the bustling streets of Dubai and the vast desert landscape below as if they were mere miniatures. And let's not forget about the interiors—luxury abounds, with glass, stainless steel, and polished stones adorning every corner. It's a display of refined taste and opulence.

The allure of showcasing my exclusive abode to the world notwithstanding, I initially hesitated. However, after some persuasion from a leading Malayalam media house, I relented. Their argument—that many back home dreamt of glimpsing the interiors of the Burj Khalifa—made sense, prompting me to open my doors to the public eye.

Sure, maintaining these apartments comes at a hefty price, with yearly payments to Emaar Properties rivalling the cost of purchasing properties elsewhere in Dubai. But for me, it's more than just bricks and mortar—it's about owning a piece of history, a slice of the Dubai skyline that I proudly call home.

BMW World Amateur Championship

Life continued to surprise me. If the wonders in Emirates Hills and Burj Khalifa came through my earnings, the new marvel came through my pet game: golf. I was on cloud nine when I qualified to represent the UAE in the World Amateur Golf Tournament. At the 2006 BMW World Amateur Golf Cup Final in South Africa, there I was, feeling like a champ as I sank the eight-foot putt and watched the UAE flag flutter against the backdrop of the sky.

I thought about the irony: amid thunderous applause from thousands, a person of Indian origin was representing UAE at the tournament, rubbing shoulders with golf giants from the rest of the world.

A golfer in a tournament faces several challenges. First, the mental pressure of competing at a high level is intense, requiring focus. Weather conditions, such as wind, rain or extreme heat, can significantly impact performance. Moreover, the golfer must adapt to the specific layout and conditions of the course, which may differ greatly from their usual practice environment. Managing fatigue over several days of play and maintaining consistency across multiple rounds also present significant hurdles. Lastly, the competitive nature of the field means that even small mistakes can be costly, adding to the overall pressure to perform well.

That day in South Africa will forever be imprinted in my memory. Something else made it even more special. Meeting Walid Alattar, an Emirati national who turned out to be more than just a fellow golfer—he became like a brother to me.

After the tournament, Walid and I bonded even more. Along with his wife, Aziza, we spent a week in South Africa, soaking in the golfing vibes. It all started with a two-day qualifying round at Emirates Golf Club and Dubai Creek Golf Club, and before we knew it, we were representing UAE on the world stage.

The images of the past flashed through my mind. It all started in 1991 with a Malayali youth's fleeting desire to play the game while passing by a golf club in Dubai. A brief glimpse of the golf course triggered it. Back then, the idea of having a membership in a golf club seemed out of reach. He left his job, started his own business, earned and secured a membership. He mastered golf through constant practice. Standing on the very same course where he once yearned for entry in 1991, he now conquered the qualifying rounds of this prestigious international contest.

And here he was representing the UAE in a golf tournament.

What further marvels are there to be found? God is great!

9

Thirteen, my lucky number: parting ways

After 13 years of marriage, we decided to part ways. In 2010, when I was 41, we mutually agreed to approach the Dubai court and end the marriage. It wasn't a decision made in haste, but rather after acknowledging the discomforts and disagreements that had crept into our relationship. Despite the challenges, we approached the divorce with mutual respect and understanding.

I won't say our marriage was all bad—far from it. But sometimes, two people realise they're better off apart. We both knew that continuing down the same path would only lead to more strife and affect our children's well-being.

We arrived at the decision fairly quickly. Thankfully, our separation wasn't marked by bitter fights or animosity—unlike what we see around usually. We parted ways amicably, with each of us choosing our own path. And I consider it a blessing that she entrusted our two children to my care. She knew I'd do everything in my power to raise them right.

There may have been complaints on both sides, but one thing was never in doubt: my commitment as a father. Our kids, bless their hearts, handled the situation with remarkable maturity, despite their tender ages of four and seven. Although there was no outward conflict, the children picked up on the underlying tension. They knew their mother was departing, but displayed remarkable emotional intelligence by remaining calm and respectful. They ensured that I came across no difficulty.

Thirteen years may seem like a long time, but it was destiny. I've always considered 13 my lucky number and perhaps it was fate that our marriage ended after that exact span.

All my assets were held in joint ownership by both of us. I went for joint registration of assets, recognising her role as the mother of my children. Before the divorce, she transferred to me all the assets registered in her name. Greed was not her thing. We were similar in this respect. I gave her the assets she desired, a house and a car.

How could I not help her when she had given me AED 50,000 for my business expenses? It was all of her savings of AED 50,000 that enabled me to start Heilbronn.

Greed had no place in our parting.

But there's one unforgettable moment from that time. As we sat in her lawyer's office, ready to sign the divorce papers, she asked if she could have the kids with her for two days a week. I agreed, but I wanted her to know she had more flexibility.

"You're their mom," I said. "If you want them longer, just say the word."

After 13 years together and with her being the mother of our kids, I felt it was the least I could offer. "I won't forget this," I said sincerely. "Despite our changing circumstances, my respect and consideration for you as the mother of my children will never diminish. Thank you for everything. Also, you may contact me for anything except living under the same roof."

Then, out of nowhere, her lawyer butted in. "Don't believe a word he says," she warned. "Men never keep their promises after a divorce."

I was taken aback.

I couldn't help but speak up. "Look," I told her, "you've known me for 13 years. You decide whether to trust me or some lawyer you just met."

The lawyer got the message loud and clear and backed off.

In the end, we signed the papers in silence. And ironically enough, that lawyer who doubted me later became a friend. Life's full of unexpected twists, isn't it?

Thank you, always

Saying goodbye to her after 13 years wasn't easy. I thanked her for all the love and support she gave to me and our kids throughout those years. Even though neither of us was thrilled about the idea of divorce, cent percent, we knew it was the right move for our own peace of mind. Staying together just for appearances wasn't an option for us. Disagreements happened, but we kept them respectful and private, ensuring a peaceful home environment. Unlike many estranged couples keeping appearances— we never lived in separate rooms and houses in all those years of marriage. Ultimately, our happiness wasn't contingent on external validation. We didn't feel the need to portray a perfect image for others—the health of our relationship was a personal matter.

When the Dubai court finally issued the order in June 2011, her voice on the phone still rings in my mind. I could hear the sadness in her trembling voice as she talked about our separation. It was clear that despite everything, there was still love and tenderness in her heart. But certain things in life proved too difficult for her to adapt to.

For me, it was the end of a chapter. I wanted a new life.

Life inevitably throws challenges our way and sometimes we have to make difficult choices.

Divorce was tough, probably the hardest thing I've ever had to go through. But I knew I had to keep moving forward, especially for my two kids who trusted me wholeheartedly. They had dreams, aspirations, and I was determined to make sure they reached them, no matter what.

I made it clear that I valued her role as a mother to our children. The friendship we built would also have a place. I committed to offering support, including financial assistance, if needed. Ironically, we perhaps began to understand each other after the breakup.

Moving into our spacious 25,000 sq. ft villa in Emirates Hills after the divorce felt different. It was just the three of us now, under that big roof, feeling like we were the only ones in the world. I couldn't shake off the feeling that the amenities I had arranged for my ex-wife and kids were silently mocking me. But I refused to let my children see my pain or feel like they were missing out on having a mother.

We parted at a difficult time. My children were at an age when they craved their mother's love and affection the most. It tore at me—they shouldn't feel the absence of a mother in their formative years.

Determined to provide a stable environment, I decided on a fresh start. We'd build a new life together, a new home. The past, with its problems and the isolation of divorce, would be left behind. I wouldn't let it cast a shadow on their future.

My goal was clear: to raise them in a loving, nurturing environment, free from deprivation and the sense of loss that often came with a broken family. I looked forward to starting a new life in the new home. I longed to leave the past behind and move on. I wanted the dreams and aspirations of my children to flourish, to see them grow into well-rounded individuals, even surpassing my own achievements.

Thankfully, my children shared my resolve. They trusted me to provide them with the security they needed and they willingly joined me on this new chapter.

The nonstop cycle of time spins on. Summer surrenders to the crisp chill of autumn, then winter's frosted grip, before spring awakens with stimulating life. Rain cleanses, nourishes, and gives way to sunshine's warmth. All these elements, in their constant dance, are ultimately swept away by the ever-flowing river of time.

Yet, within this impermanence lies a comforting truth: time heals. Like the earth renewed by each season's transformation, our wounds too can mend with the passage of time.

A successful marriage, a respectful farewell

In the background of our divorce, rumours about us spread like wildfire, both in Dubai and back home in Kerala. Some people were blissfully behind this. For some, it hurts to see others suffer. These rumour-mongers enjoy our failures. Our sorrows are entertainment for them. But I guess that's just how some people are—they thrive on others' misfortunes. Like Shakespeare mused: "As flies to wanton boys are we to the gods; They kill us for their sport."

These gossip gods mock us for kicks.

Humans are complex creatures and our fascination with negative stories can sometimes be perplexing. Consider the popularity of and rating for news reports on disasters or reality shows featuring personal struggles.

For me, our marriage wasn't a failure. Viewing it from the life we led after parting ways, it was a success. And it was brief—lasting 13 years.

But we were just two people who weren't meant to be together in the long run.

Our time together taught us valuable lessons about ourselves and what we need in a partner. In the end, our separation allowed us to grow individually and find paths that were better suited to each of us.

Competition never found a place in our marriage. My ex-wife, a loving person at heart, grappled with personal challenges. She admitted to me many times that she had a lot of worries. Perhaps influenced by envious friends, her path diverged from mine.

Life, like any story, unravels with purpose. While our reasons for parting ways emerged, it didn't diminish the 13 years we shared. We built a foundation of friendship, weathered storms together, and provided each other with both security and companionship. We built a life together, shared a lot of travelling experiences, and, more importantly, were blessed with two lovely children.

These experiences enriched us and the lessons learned remain valuable.

Even the end held a sense of peace. We defied the astrologers' prediction of a short-lived marriage, lasting a remarkable 13 years. For this, I'm eternally grateful. The greatest gift of our union—our two wonderful children—will forever connect us. For anything she needs, her children and their father will be around.

Just as fate brought us together, it led us on separate paths when our children were young. Not long before we had the kids, we were on the brink of separation. Neither of us can be held responsible for the turn of events. It's fate. Our marriage, in its entirety, was a success. We fulfilled the vows we took, sharing joys, sorrows and responsibilities. Our marriage ended after achieving the milestone of having children together. The accusations of failure sting, but they don't reflect reality.

Divorce is undoubtedly a difficult experience. However, darkness can often lead to light. As an optimist, I believe everything—past, present and future—contributes to a deeper understanding and seeing the light of life. Perhaps by now, my ex-wife will have recognised that sad truth: the kind of partner she walked away from. Maybe, it will haunt her all her life. The wounds may continue to hurt her.

Boys' group: in new home

Closing the door on both happy and sad memories, my two kids and I bid farewell to Meadows-9 Villa. Destiny had something new in store for us—a lavish villa in Emirates Hills, a fresh start for the three of us. In June 2011, we stepped into our new abode, accompanied by our trusty helpers: cook Subhash, Deepa Nanny (Deepa), house manager Sujith and driver Sudhakaran. Our pets Tiger, Sweetie and Rocky also joined us in our new home.

Living in Emirates Hills meant being neighbours with administrators from around the world, renowned celebrities and titans of industry.

On our first day there, I sat the kids down and had a heart-to-heart. "You should never feel sad because your mother isn't here," I told them. "Life doesn't always give us what we want, but we have to look ahead. Trust that everything happens for a reason and focus on making the future the best it can be. No one gets everything in life. Though created equal by God, people develop distinct qualities. They have different characters and abilities. Observe others closely and find out what you lack. It will reveal to you what you should set out to achieve."

I made a promise to myself to spend more time with my children, to fill the void left by their mother's absence. It is the right of children to live with their parents. Divorce wasn't their fault and they deserved the best care from their father.

I remember the overwhelming emotions that flooded me that first day in the villa. A swarm of thoughts buzzed through my head like agitated wasps. This villa, my dream realised through years of dedicated work, was meant to be a haven for my family. We envisioned laughter echoing through these halls, a life built together. But fate, it seems, had other plans. Instead of a triumphant homecoming with my family, I stand here alone, the woman who anchored our home absent.

Perhaps it wasn't meant to be, or maybe she wasn't meant to be here. Whatever the reason, I hold onto the belief that everything happens for a reason. While happiness for everyone was my only wish, the current reality hurt me.

Unlike many, I keep my sorrows close, a burden I carry alone. Yet, the weight of this solitude, of myself and the children facing this emptiness, was undeniable.

After a bath, I found solace in the prayer room, pouring out my heart to God. Tears streamed down my face as I untangled the knots of sorrow within me. It was a rare moment of vulnerability for me who usually keeps my emotions bottled up.

Deepa Nanny caught sight of my tear-streaked face when I emerged from the prayer room and her own eyes welled up in response. We stood in silence for a moment before the kids came running to me. Determined not to let them see my tears, I discreetly wiped my eyes. Never again should they see my tears. Never again should they witness the storm within me. They had come here for a fresh start, and I was resolved to ensure they saw nothing but happiness in their new life.

Sunshine and sprinkles

The kids were thrilled with our new home. They couldn't get enough of the theatre, playroom, spacious dining area and the swimming pool. Slowly but surely, they started to adjust to life without a mom around. I made a point to spend more quality time with them—playing games, watching movies and dining out. I took them to the malls and food joints in malls. I even started coming home for lunch just to sit down and eat with them.

Mornings were all about getting them ready for school and evenings were dedicated to playing and storytelling until they drifted off to sleep. Just like my paternal grandmother, I filled our home with stories. A flood of childhood stories surged back: spooky whispers that sent shivers down my spine, fantastical tales that ignited my imagination, myths that resonated with grandeur, and stories of bravery and compassion that shaped my heart.

Once the children were in bed, I took care of whatever needed doing around the house before finally hitting the sack myself around 10.30 p.m.

This routine became our new normal, with kids visiting their mom twice a week as per the court's orders. After the initial adjustments, our home became an oasis of peace and joy. No more arguments or tense atmosphere—just pure bliss.

As time passed, our house started buzzing with activity again. Guests came over, parties were thrown and laughter filled the air. It felt like we were rediscovering the joy of family all over again.

I couldn't help but think of a book Cheriyachan gave me ages ago, with a picture of Korea on the cover. Korea symbolised peace and tranquility to me, and after 13 years, our home felt just like that serene green place.

Thirteen unrelenting summers had baked the house, but a gentle spring had finally bloomed within those walls. The thunderous storms of sadness had subsided, leaving a verdant landscape of happiness in their wake. Every room vibrated with a newfound vitality, a mesmerising green that whispered of hope and renewal. Laughter filled the halls, like the joyous chirping of birds returning after a long winter. I saw it reflected in my children's eyes—the way they gathered colourful blooms, their innocent joy adorning the house with their love.

Deciding to amp up our health game, I hired a gym trainer to come to our place. Subair, a professional trainer, started whipping us into shape bright and early every morning.

Before the divorce, hitting the gym used to trigger a barrage of questions from my ex-wife. "Why now?" she'd ask, laced with suspicion. "Thinking of a new marriage?"

Post-divorce atmosphere, I didn't face any such question.As my focus on health and well-being improved my mood and energy levels, it had a ripple effect. The children, sensing the positive shift, became happier, more playful, and more engaged with life.

Our new life offered a fresh start: a new house, a new neighbourhood and a new environment. The impressive Emirates Hills villa attracted a steady stream of visitors. The daily parade of guests became overwhelming. Back then, villa prices in Emirates Hills ranged from 45,000,000 to 100,000,000 AED. Today, those prices have more than doubled, with location and size playing a big role. While we initially welcomed everyone with open arms, the constant influx started to raise concerns.As the saying goes, "a big house comes with big problems". We worried that the endless stream of visitors might disrupt the children's privacy and our sense of normality. This realisation led us to find a way to limit viewings of the villa.

Home-bound

We decided to take a trip back to Kerala during the kids' school break. They were eager to experience life with our extended family and I wanted them to understand that they were surrounded by love and support, no matter where they were. After all, family is the cornerstone of our lives, whether we're talking about human beings, animals or any other living beings.

As soon as we reached Kerala, they hit it off with my mother, sisters, brother and the rest of the family. Everyone was introduced and they were welcomed with open arms.

The journey from Dubai to the lush greenery of Kerala was a real eye-opener for them. I made sure to enrol them in the local school so they could soak up the values and lessons that only our hometown can teach. Because the best university is often right in our backyard, surrounded by our own people and our roots.

Schools in Kerala have a unique ambience and culture. They carry an egalitarian spirit. Unlike any other part of India, Kerala is known for its unique social capital. Here, cultures co-exist happily. At least, in its educational institutions. As kids, we were never bothered about our caste or creed. At least, my generation was so. Kerala still nurtures this spirit of togetherness and equality. And that makes this place unique. While Kerala's verdant beauty is undeniable, it's the State's progressive social values that truly draws visitors in.

Once my kids started school in Kerala, their minds seemed to lighten up. They quickly found their groove, making new friends and immersing themselves in games and activities. The rustic charm of Kerala seeped into their souls, washing away any persisting sadness from the divorce.

It was heartwarming to see them not just forget about their mom's absence, but actually feel happy and content surrounded by relatives and friends. The Kerala trip provided a much-needed break after the challenges of our divorce. It was a chance for the kids to transition to a more normal life.

10

My father departs, like the fall of a flower

One day, while I was in the middle of something at the office, my manager Hari called me, his voice trembling. I could sense something wasn't right. "Your father is no more," he said, his words hitting me like a ton of bricks.

Achan had passed away in 2008 at the age of 75. About 30 minutes before Hari's call, I had spoken to Achan on the phone, unaware that it would be our last conversation. He had been battling cardiac issues for two decades. His illness took a turn for the worse, leading to a hospital stay. Once he was back home, I reached out and we had a long conversation. We made plans for a visit, a chance for me and the children to see him again and spend time with him. Sadly, he left before we could get to him.

We wasted no time. As soon as we received the news, we booked a flight and headed home to Kerala. Arriving in the early hours of the morning, we were greeted by a sea of people—relatives, friends, neighbours—all gathered to offer their support. It was a proof of Kerala's warmth and community spirit.

My brother and I took charge of the funeral arrangements and I remained in Kerala for 15 days to complete all the necessary rituals.

I heard about Achan's last moments with tears in my eyes. After talking to me on the phone, Achan went to bed and asked his grandchildren to massage his feet. One granddaughter, who was massaging his right leg, was a bit chubby, while the other, rubbing his left leg, was thin. With a gentle smile, my father said, "I don't feel the massage on the left leg." Everyone laughed softly, cherishing the tender moment. Then, he closed his eyes, never to open them again.

Before he passed, Achan had been joking with his grandchildren as they massaged his feet.

Little did we know it would be his final moment of levity before he peacefully slipped away.

His death was as graceful as the life he had led. He perhaps earned it with his good deeds. I could see the delicate beauty of life's end.

I've heard people in the neighbourhood say, "Narayanettan was a kindly soul. Lucky! What a peaceful death he had!"

In India, we believe that people should earn peace in their last days. This concept is deeply rooted in our cultural and spiritual traditions, which highlight the importance of leading a virtuous life, even in the face of adversity, and the rewards that await those who uphold righteousness till their last breath.

Reflecting on Achan's passing, I couldn't help but admire the grace with which he left this world—surrounded by love, laughter and the innocence of his grandchildren. He only saw the good in my life, never witnessing the challenges that followed, like the recession of 2009 or the divorce in 2011.

Many people die, writhing in pain. But Achan passed away with a smile, after a joke. Look at the beauty of it!

I'd like to have a death like my father did—leave the world with a smile. If it happens, it will be a blessing.

Even in death, Achan offered solace to those around who witnessed the transition. In his final act, he bestowed a precious gift upon his loved ones, showing them that even in the face of death, it is possible to face the reality with equanimity and poise.

Achan was more than just a father; he was a role model—a hard worker who provided for his family and instilled in us the value of dreaming big. He had a quick temper, it always came from a place of wanting things to be done right. He harboured no grudges and was always honest, even if it meant speaking his mind.

From his humble beginnings to his eventual success, Achan led a life of dedication and integrity. But perhaps his greatest lesson was his compassion for others, regardless of their background or beliefs.

Achan was a strong-willed man with a clear vision for what he wanted to achieve. His honesty and bluntness were evident in his actions. His greatest strength was his unwavering work ethic, which he applied to everything he did. His love and care knew no bounds, sometimes even bordering on self-sacrifice.

Every Onam and Eid, Achan brought more than just food kits to our neighbours. He delivered a message of unity. For years, he practised the very essence of what all religions teach: the importance of living together as one human family, transcending the divisions of religion, caste and politics. This act of kindness wasn't just about food; it was a powerful lesson. Achan's compassion expounded the truth of our oneness as human beings.

Achan, I miss you. I miss all those moments we shared. I miss the time we walked to the agricultural fields, toiling for the family. I fondly recall the precious days in Edappal, when you, Amma, my siblings, and I formed a perfect, blissful family portrait. Looking back, each of those moments were precious — every word spoken, every tear, every smile, every hug. None of it will ever come back. Each moment is frozen in time. Each second has been transformed into a memory. And these cluster of memories power my existence, my present life.

I strive to emulate his qualities every day. People say that I'm his updated version. He continues to live through me.

Amma, my beacon

There is one person back home who rejoice the most whenever I pen down tales of my conquests in the metropolis of Dubai—my mother. Without her support and insistence, my achievements would have felt incomplete. I It was her constant push that urged me to venture beyond the borders of India and explore the realm of business. She did this overcoming her desire to have me, her eldest son, near her always. If not for her persistent encouragement, I might have still been rooted in Edappal.

My mother epitomised the essence of hard work, embodying it as a way of life until she was confined to a wheelchair three years ago. For close to 60 years, she dedicated herself to her children and her husband, leaving a permanent impression on our lives. Among the women who left the greatest impact on me, my mother stands tall.

Managing everything single-handedly at home, my mother ensured the well-being of both her children and my father. From her, I inherited the ability to navigate through life independently. She has been a good wife, mother and grandmother. Though she projects a stern exterior, her heart overflows with love and affection for everyone.

Her knack for understanding people with lightning speed is a trait I've inherited. This ability to see through others has been a guiding light in my interactions. And it's not just me; my siblings also cherish the pride of being born to such a remarkable mother.

My mother's compassion for the less fortunate is unparalleled. She would often share stories of those in need within our family, inspiring me to extend a helping hand whenever possible.

My mother instilled in me the value of measured kindness. "Don't blindly help everyone," she'd advise. "Be reasonable and practical. When you actually need help, there may be no one around."

I'd acknowledge her wisdom. "That's good advice, Amma," I'd say. "Maybe, you speak from experience."

"She'd always smile and reply, "You're right, son. It comes from the lessons I've learned in life.

Ever the advocate for staying active and energised, my mother detested idleness and led by example through her own industrious life.

I've requested her several times to live with me in Dubai, but she has turned it down always. She remains rooted in her beloved home in the Kerala countryside, visiting Dubai only twice after much persuasion.

I'll never forget her words after witnessing the splendours of Dubai: "Dubai is truly heaven on earth."

Everyone who visits Dubai feels so.

When some of my relatives relocated to Kerala, she exclaimed, "How could they leave such as wonderful place like Dubai behind?"

Her observations about Dubai surprised me. Such precise views coming from her, who hasn't visited any other country, astonished me.

Even now, my mother serves as my greatest motivation to return home to Kerala every two months. Spending time with her, away from the chaos of life, is a pet ritual that I hold dear. I spent many days with her after my father's death.

Her greatest joy is being surrounded by her children and she showers my own kids with boundless affection. Witnessing the love between grandmother and grandchildren fills my heart with warmth.

No words can adequately convey my gratitude for all the love, guidance, and inspiration my mother has bestowed upon me.

Can any child, nurtured by its mother, ever truly repay the depths of her love? Her every touch, every whispered lullaby, every sacrifice made in the quiet hours of night, carve into our souls a love so overpowering that it transcends words. We carry her heartbeat in ours, her dreams in our aspirations, her tenacity in our struggles. She is the quiet strength that steadies us in life's tempests, the gentle voice that whispers courage into our doubts. Yet, in the vast expanse of gratitude, we find ourselves humbled by the enormity of her love, a love that asks for nothing in return but our happiness. And so, we strive not to repay, but to honour, to cherish, to hold her essence close in the silent depths of our hearts, forever guiding our steps with her tacit wisdom and limitless love.

I'm reminded of the verses in Adi Shankaracharya's 'Mathru Panchakam', beginning with 'Aastham Thavaddeyam', in which he pours out his love for his mother and the respect for all mothers in the world:

> *Oh, my dearest mother,*
> *With gritted teeth,*
> *you endured the excruciating pain of childbirth,*
> *Welcoming me into this world,*
> *You shared your bed, soiled by my infancy,*
> *For a year, you cradled me in your arms, comforting my cries,*
> *Throughout those nine months of carrying me,*
> *Your body grew weary, your strength tested,*
> *For all this, my beloved mother,*
> *I can never repay,*
> *Even in my greatest achievements.*

Amma, thank you for being the guiding light in my darkest hours, for instilling in me the courage to face adversity and for shaping me into the person I am today. The light will shine inside me till I leave this world. I know that no amount of thanks will ever suffice. I know that no deed will ever repay what she has done to me. Love you, love you, my beloved Amma!

An independent life, a happy life

Living a life free from scrutiny or judgment has always been my goal. There's something liberating about being able to live on our own terms, without the constant pressure of others' expectations.

Even in pursuit of this freedom, I never neglect my responsibilities. Whether it's towards my children, friends, family or work, fulfilling my duties remains paramount.

Contemplating life's purpose is something I often find myself doing. For me, it boils down to simple yet deep pursuits—love, happiness, peace, health and a fulfilling family life. These are the things that truly matter to me.

I've come to realise that contentment and the rat race are incompatible. The constant pursuit of success at the expense of inner peace is a trade-off I'm not willing to make. Instead of competing with others, I choose to compete with myself. Every day is an opportunity to improve upon yesterday's achievements.

In my journey, I've learned that true success isn't solely measured by wealth or material possessions. While money is undoubtedly important, it's not the ultimate marker of success. Mental satisfaction, peace of mind and good health are invaluable treasures that money alone can't buy.

This perspective guides my approach to life and business. I don't feel the need to prove my worth to anyone or outshine others. My only competition is with myself, and my definition of success is centred around personal growth and fulfillment.

In addition to personal growth, I prioritise making meaningful contributions to my community and society at large. Success, to me, encompasses leaving a positive impact on the world around me, whether through acts of kindness, philanthropy or advocacy for important causes. By aligning my actions with my values and striving to make a difference in the lives of others, I find fulfillment that transcends mere material achievements. This holistic approach to success not only enriches my own life but also creates a ripple effect of positivity and inspiration in the world.

In short, my life philosophy revolves around embracing simplicity, prioritising inner peace and striving for continuous self-improvement. There is more to life than wealth.

THE HEART MATTERS

11

Seoulful journey

It's been 35 years since Cheriyachan gave me that book with the beautiful scenery of Korea on the cover page. The image is still vivid in my mind, kindling my desire to finally visit South Korea.

I booked a ticket to Seoul, albeit traveling alone this time, as my children were with their mother. Despite being independent, solo travel doesn't excite me much, unlike the adventures I had with my ex-wife exploring cities like London, Thailand, Singapore, Athens, Munich, Heilbronn and Rome.

Flying with Emirates Airlines, my preferred choice for its comfort and my professional ties, the journey from Dubai to Seoul took about eight and a half hours. Arriving in May 2011, I was greeted by Seoul's flamboyant energy as I stepped off the plane. The airport buzzed with travellers from all over the world, and the modern and efficient terminal of Incheon International Airport hinted at the city's dynamic atmosphere. The bustling scene reflected Seoul's status as a major global hub, with sleek architecture and state-of-the-art facilities.

As I made my way through the terminal, a mix of languages filled the air. Outside, the city skyline stretched out before me, a captivating blend of traditional hanbok-clad locals and sleek, futuristic buildings. Neon lights illuminated the streets, where vendors offered a tempting array of both traditional Korean delicacies and international cuisine.

On the way from Incheon International Airport to the hotel, I couldn't help but notice the impressive cityscape. One standout feature was the 21.38 km long Incheon Grand Bridge connecting Seoul and the airport over the sea, known as one of Korea's longest and one of the world's longest cable-stayed bridges. Constructed at a cost of ₩2.45 trillion, it highlights South Korea's dedication to crucial infrastructure development for the Northeast Asian economy. The bridge appeared as an extraordinary achievement in civil engineering. My car journey took about an hour, eventually leading me to the hotel.

My accommodation at the Grand Hyatt Hotel was luxurious, conveniently located near downtown Seoul, offering breathtaking views of Han River and Mount Namsan. The professionalism of the reception staff left a lasting impression. My luxurious hotel room in South Korea impressed with its attractive interiors. A subtle yet delightful Korean influence permeated the design, creating a unique and welcoming atmosphere. The amenities were equally impressive, offering everything I needed for a comfortable stay.

The five-hour time difference between South Korea and Dubai meant adjusting my watch upon arrival. A consistent routine is vital for me when travelling. Knowing the exact time allows me to plan my day effectively, from the invigorating morning routine of waking up early, hitting the gym or going for a walk, to enjoying breakfast and tackling other activities. Packing workout clothes is a must for every trip—maintaining a healthy routine is important to me, no matter where I am in the world

13 glorious hours of sleep

After a refreshing bath, the fatigue of travel melted away, and I indulged in a delicious meal featuring Galbi, a Korean specialty bursting with savoury flavours.

Galbi, also known as kalbi, is a type of grilled meat in Korean cuisine, typically marinated with soy sauce, garlic, sesame oil and sugar. The dish is a delightful fusion of savoury, sweet and slightly tangy flavors, perfectly complemented by a side of lettuce leaves for wrapping and accompanied by rice and various banchan (side dishes).

The meal wasn't just flavoursome, it was a captivating introduction to Korean flavours. It hinted at the culinary adventures that awaited, a tasty promise for the days to come.

Throughout my travels, I prioritise experiencing local cuisine and exploring beyond tourist hotspots, getting in touch with rural life. Villages offer a glimpse into a country's soul. Here, you'll witness traditional ways of life, experience local customs firsthand and connect with the genuine warmth of rural communities.

Like me, most Malayalis love exploring other cultures. They are renowned for their adventurous spirit and global presence. This is evident in the vast Malayali diaspora, a community of emigrants who have made their mark in all corners of the world. Education is a major driver of this outward migration, with a significant number of Kerala students seeking opportunities and diverse learning environments abroad. The trend has only accelerated post-pandemic, with an exponential increase in student mobility.

This adaptability extends beyond education. Malayalis are known for their ease of acclimating to new environments and cultures. They integrate harmoniously into their adopted countries, working efficiently, adhering to local laws and achieving success in their chosen fields. This industriousness is reflected in the high concentration of wealthy and accomplished Malayalis abroad, a fact I've personally witnessed in my travels.

Kerala boasts the highest passport penetration rate in India, with an estimated 32% of its population holding passports compared to the national average of 7%.

One unexpected surprise during my travel this time was a blissful 13 hours of uninterrupted sleep. Collapsing onto the bed, I drifted into a deep sleep. There's a certain tranquility in South Korea that perhaps allows for deeper slumber, something I haven't necessarily found in every country I've visited.

Even while travelling, I find time to check in on my business affairs. Discipline and meticulous planning are key to achieving this balance. As the saying goes, success begins with small acts of discipline, like making your bed each morning.

A Korean beauty

As I boarded the plane to Korea, my biggest wish was to see the natural beauty depicted in the book Cheriyachan had gifted me. The very next day, I stumbled upon a place filled with pine trees, just like the ones in the picture. It was a breathtaking sight. Koreans call these majestic trees 'sonamu', meaning 'supreme tree,' and they hold a special place in the country's culture, even being mentioned in the national anthem. Rows of these pine trees grace many places in Korea.

Venturing into the busy Shinsegae Department Store at Yeongdeungpo in southwest Seoul, I was struck by the glamour and elegance of Korean fashion. Korea's department stores have three major players—Lotte, Hyundai and Shinsegae, the most glamorous of the lot. Shinsegae had its roots in the Samsung Group but branched off in the 1990s.

Among the designer bags and clothes at the Shinsegae Department Store, I couldn't help but notice the impeccable style of Korean women. Maybe, it's the combination of good food and fair weather that adds to their beauty.

I was captivated by the beauty of a woman named Song Lee I saw in the store selling skincare products. Attempting to strike up a conversation, I asked for her number, but she politely declined, offering her email instead. Much to my relief, she spoke English.

She stood tall beside me. Her fairness was luminous, her skin as smooth as satin.

Wasting no time, I hurried back to the hotel and flung open my laptop. My fingers flew across the keyboard as I dashed off an email to her. Anticipation thrummed through me as I refreshed my inbox, hoping for a reply. Disappointment settled in my chest as my inbox remained stubbornly empty.

The next day, when I returned to the store, Song Lee was nowhere to be found.

"Excuse me, do you know where I can find Song Lee?" I asked a sales clerk.

"She's not an employee here, Sir. She's a client. She might come to pick her order after 2 p.m.," the clerk replied with a polite smile.

As I waited, 2 p.m. rolled around, and there she was, accompanied by an older woman who looked to be around 50. Initially, I assumed it was her mother, but it turned out to be her friend.

I tried to engage Song Lee in conversation several times, but she seemed uninterested in talking to me. That's when her older friend stepped in, her tone wary. "What are you doing? What exactly do you want from her?" she asked, her gaze piercing.

I wanted to say this: "Let her talk to me. I'll let her know when my intentions are." But I didn't.

Feeling the need to softly explain myself, I replied, "I'm an entrepreneur from Dubai, here on a trip. I simply wanted to invite her for coffee, so she could get to know me better."

Skeptical, the older woman retorted, "We can't just take your word for it. You'll need to prove what you're saying before we make any decisions."

Internally, I couldn't help but wonder, 'What kind of country requires evidence of who you are just to have coffee?' However, I quickly retrieved my cellphone and showed them photos of my life back in Dubai—my office, my family, my cars and my various activities.

"I'm not lying," I insisted, frustration creeping into my voice. "Why would I lie to you?"

Their expressions softened as they studied the photos, the tension in the air easing. Warmth flickered in their eyes, reflected in the subtle curve of their lips.

"I admit, I had my doubts at first. You see, I'm old," the older woman said. "But I suppose you've proven yourself enough. I'll convey to Song Lee all that you said. I'll make her agree to meet you at the coffee shop tomorrow at 4 p.m."

A serendipitous introduction

By then, my mind was consumed with anticipation, much like a lover eagerly awaiting a first meeting. The hours leading up to 4 o'clock the next day felt like an eternity, filled with racing thoughts and unanswered questions. It was my first experience.

When the time finally arrived, I made my way to the coffee shop as instructed. Each passing minute only intensified my heartbeat, a sensation I had never experienced before. I recognised the pang of longing, a sharp reminder of what it felt like to yearn for someone.

Would she show up? Was it all just a joke? Did the older woman take me for a ride? Would she disappoint me? If she'd come, how should I begin the conversation? What should I tell her? What would be her response? Many questions buzzed in my mind.

I reminded myself not to jump to conclusions. I tried to calm my nerves, reminding myself to approach the situation with an open mind. My mind found out answers and calmed itself. Why should I doubt them? When the time was up, she would arrive and talk. I told myself: never look at things with a provincial attitude. After all, I was in a foreign land called South Korea. I shouldn't forget that.

And then, right on time, she appeared before me, her smile lighting up the room. At only 26 years old, she exuded a beauty and radiance unlike any I had seen before. Till then, I hadn't met such a beautiful woman. I was taken aback when she revealed she didn't have a boyfriend. She was only interested in a serious relationship leading to marriage.

Our initial 20-minute chat stretched into a captivating two-hour conversation covering everything from history and culture to love and business. I learned that she was the only child of her parents, from Ansan, 45 km from Seoul. Educated and articulate, her simplicity belied a deep understanding of Korean literature and heritage.

I wanted her to know that I was being completely honest and genuine with her.

She chuckled as she shared the tale of a Korean emperor marrying an Indian queen 2,000 years ago, a story entirely new to me, one I had never heard before. I didn't understand why she told the story.

As our familiarity grew, we made plans to explore Seoul together the following day. Excited, she readily agreed to take leave for our getaway together. I felt a playful urge to showcase my best self. I spared no expense, renting a limousine with a chauffeur to whisk her away for a day of adventure. I headed to place to pick her up. With her as my guide, we traversed the city, indulging in a variety of Korean cuisines and soaking in the rich history and culture at every turn.

Through her stories, I discovered striking similarities between Korea and my homeland of Kerala, from traditional ways of life to the importance of family, agriculture and food.

South Korea's history is marked by a journey from colonial occupation and war to rapid industrialisation and modernisation, overcoming adversities to become a leading global economy and democracy. As the 20th century dawned, Japan, China and Russia engaged in a power struggle for dominance over the Korean Peninsula. Ultimately, Japan emerged victorious, seizing control of the peninsula in 1905 following the Russo-Japanese War and formally annexing it five years later. During the ensuing 35 years of colonial rule, Korea experienced rapid industrialisation under Japanese control. However, this period was marred by brutal repression as the Japanese attempted to erase Korea's unique language and cultural identity, coercing Koreans to assimilate into Japanese culture.

Despite its size, Korea stands tall on the global stage, boasting top-tier infrastructure. South Korean passports soared to second place in the 2024 global passport power rankings, climbing a spot from third place the year before. This impressive rise means Korean passport holders now enjoy visa-free entry to a whopping 193 countries, tying them with Finland and Sweden for the runner-up position according to the World Passport Index.

The names of its iconic brands like Kia, LG, Lotte, Samsung and Hyundai reveal South Korea's presence in the global market.

For me, the trip to South Korea was unforgettable. Great seasons, historical wonders, delicious cuisine and a fantastic travel partner elevated my experience.

A vow to return

In just a few days, I found myself not only falling for my South Korean friend, but also for her country. I usually don't spend more than 10 days in any one place. My trips are usually just a week long. But Korea was different. It hooked me with its experiences, knowledge, sights, tastes and most importantly, with a friend who showered me so much love.

Saying goodbye to South Korea was tough. I wasn't ready to leave behind all the memories and the friendship I had formed.

"I'll come back to you soon," I told her.

I saw tears welling up in her eyes. She tried to hide them, but I knew they were real. I recognised that she liked me. It hit me then how much she cared and maybe how much I cared too. It was like we had a connection that went beyond this lifetime. Our souls must have been bound together in some distant 'janma' or lifetime.

As I headed back to the airport, words seemed unnecessary between us. Her gaze held mine, a question lingering in its depths. Our silence spoke volumes, conveying emotions that words couldn't capture. And as I boarded the plane, I couldn't shake off the feeling of longing for Korea and for her.

Eight days ago, I landed at the airport all alone. Now, a dear friend was seeing me off. The surprises life throws at us can be astonishing. I wondered what more Korea had in store for me. I had come to Korea to see the scenery depicted in the book Cheriyachan had gifted me and I was leaving with a full heart, having found a great friend. Everything in life is connected.

I found someone to share all the joys and sorrows of life with—a friend who truly understood me and my feelings. This was the moment I waited for all my life. I had been looking for someone like that and now it felt real. My mind told me that she could be a great life partner. And believe it or not, I was her first boyfriend. At the age of 26, she had never had one until then.

Inside the flight, I couldn't stop thinking about South Korea and my friend. Every moment we spent together replayed in my mind like scenes from a movie. I thanked Korea for all those fine moments, for giving me the best friend I've ever met. How true it is that our destiny and deeds are written long before we are born! I mulled over the chance encounters that led me to these inevitable happenings.

If you look at the happenings in your life, you can see the inevitability behind them. Inexplicably miraculous encounters lead you to these events. Nature and the world seem to conspire to propel you to these happenings. The certainty is mind-blowing.

And I couldn't wait to share it all with my kids. They were eager to hear about my adventures in South Korea and meeting their future friend. I promised them we'd go back together and have even more fun, maybe even play in the snow. It was a plan I couldn't wait to put into action.

I had a plan to take them on a world tour.

Master of multitasking

At first, raising my kids alone after the divorce was incredibly tough. I never imagined I'd be in this situation, handling parenthood without their mother by my side. But life throws unexpected things and I was determined to face them head-on. It wasn't easy, especially in the beginning when I was figuring things out on my own. But I tackled the challenges one by one.

My two boys, Gautam and Aryaan, needed me more than ever and I was there for them every step of the way. From school drop-offs to doctor's visits, I took on everything that came our way. Juggling work, parenting, household duties, sports and my personal life was a constant act of balance. Yet, seeing the joy on my children's faces made it all worthwhile. I made sure to create moments of happiness for them. Whether it was taking them to school or spending quality time together, I prioritised their well-being above all else. And I started getting used to this whole parenting thing. Multi-tasking became second nature and I found a rhythm that worked for us.

There were days when I felt overwhelmed, but I never let it show. I wanted to set an example for my kids, showing them that no matter what life throwed at us, we could handle it with grace and strength. And as they grew older, they started understanding and pitching in, especially Gautam, who stepped up as a big brother.

With the support of family and friends, I managed the ups and downs of single parenthood. People were amazed at how I juggled it all, but for me, it was just part of being a dad. Of course, I dreamt of finding a loving partner to share this journey with, but until then, I'd continue being the best father and mother I could be for my boys.

Shining stars, our mothers

In the journey of life post-divorce, I've come to appreciate the fabulous role of mothers even more. Taking on the responsibilities of both a father and a mother, I've gained a whole new perspective on the immense dedication and sacrifice mothers put into running a household.

Every day, as I handle the chores and care for my children solo, I'm reminded of the superhuman strength and grace my own mother possessed. From managing the household to nurturing her children, she truly was a multi-star performer.

It's easy to fall into the misconception that men contribute more to the family by earning a living. But through my own experiences, I've learned that the loving atmosphere and life lessons imparted to children are equally, if not more, important. Women bring that special touch to the home.

Stepping into the shoes of a mother after my divorce has given me a newfound respect for the skills and qualities women possess. While it's challenging for men to balance household chores and childcare, I've realised the innate gift that women have for nurturing. And I've worked hard to embody those qualities.

Here's to all the mothers out there—your tireless dedication and hard work are the foundation of every happy home. You are the true lights that brighten our lives, and for that, we are forever grateful. Your strength, compassion and unconditional love guide us through thick and thin, shaping us into the people we are today. Thank you for everything, you precious mothers!

Korea-bound, love awaits

After two months, I made good on my promise to my girlfriend and headed back to Korea. This time, she was waiting for me at the airport, ready to welcome me with open arms.

As we drove through the city, catching up on lost time and sharing stories, it was clear that our bond had only grown stronger during my absence. She appreciated that I kept my word and returned and I admired her for understanding and valuing sincerity.

Our relationship was a bit unconventional for Koreans, who typically preferred to partner with fellow Koreans. But despite our age gap and differences in culture, language and background, we found a deep connection rooted in genuine affection and understanding.

After my divorce, she became an anchor in my life. A confidante with whom I could share anything, without judgment. Our bond went beyond friendship; she found a sense of security in my presence, a feeling I reciprocated. An undeniable connection pulsed between us, a silent language that transcended spoken words. It felt as though our souls somehow connected at a deeper level, a harmony that defied explanation. Perhaps it was shared experiences in this life or maybe a deeper connection formed in a past life.

We spent the days exploring Korea together, laughing, joking and knowing each other's worlds. She introduced me to san-nakji, a raw octopus dish that was a first for me–and it was as adventurous as it sounds! It was nothing short of eating live, chopped octopus.

Tasting san-nakji is an exhilarating rush of sensations as the tender, slippery tentacles glide across the palate, followed by a burst of briny sea flavours that awaken the senses with each bite.

Her knowledge of me ran deep. From the details of my business to the intricacies of my past divorce and even my children's lives, she knew everything. This complete transparency strengthened her firm belief in the sincerity of my love.

As we cruised through the city streets, our conversation flowed effortlessly, touching on topics ranging from world politics to Korean culture. I marvelled at her depth of knowledge.

I couldn't resist asking, "How did you become so well-versed in everything?"

With a smile that lit up her eyes, she recounted, "As a child, when I'd cry, my mother turned on the news instead of cartoons. Eventually, I found myself drawn to the stories and information, and before long, I couldn't get enough."

We were best friends, confidants and partners in adventure. We learnt much from each other. I made clumsy attempts to learn Korean. She described the specialty of Korean dishes as we ordered them. And waxed eloquent about Korean history and culture.

One day, over a meal of traditional Korean dishes, she casually mentioned a surprising piece of information—sushi, that ubiquitous Japanese delicacy, actually originated in Korea. My mind reeled with this revelation.

Korean-Malabari love moments

There's a general tendency for Koreans, Chinese, and Japanese to gravitate towards their compatriots. This can be attributed to the richness and distinctiveness of their respective languages and cultures. These cultures have endured for centuries, shaped by unique histories and instilled a deep sense of national pride.

Despite these cultural differences, my experience with Song Lee was extraordinary. Her beauty was captivating and even more surprising was the discovery that I was her first boyfriend. This revelation highlighted the strength of our connection, a bond that transcended the barriers of language, culture and lifestyle.

She confessed, "I'm amazed by how quickly you've captured my heart. I never expected a Malayali to steal my attention away from my own people."

I chuckled at her disbelief, insisting, "I'm just being myself. I've never been one to hide my feelings or thoughts. I don't like to confuse people. I'm direct."

Her laughter filled the air, a sweet melody that touched my soul. "And that's precisely why I'm drawn to you," she confessed, her gaze locking with mine. "Your confidence, your honesty...."

In a playful jab, she teased me about our height difference, "My height is 173 cm, yours is 170 cm."

But I brushed it off with a jest of my own, "Intelligence more than makes up for a few centimetres, don't you think?"

Her laughter bubbled forth. In that moment, encircled by the twinkling city lights and the soft hum of the night, I realised that I had found my home—in her laughter, in her smile, in her love.

Seven days in South Korea flew by and it was time to return to Dubai. This trip left me feeling far happier than my first. Song Lee filled my week with unforgettable moments and joyful experiences. Before I left, I extended an invitation for her to visit Dubai. I wanted her to experience my city, see my business and meet my children. She expressed a tentative interest, promising, "I'll talk to my parents about it."

When I met Song Lee's mother, a wonderfully warm woman who spoke only Korean, I understood the potential communication barrier. Indeed, her mother filled two whole pages with handwritten Korean, all that she wanted to tell me, for Song Lee to translate. I did not meet her father. He was not keen on our relationship. Understandably so, given the complexities of our situation—a divorced man with two children, a significant age gap and living in a different country. It was a lot for them to wrap their heads around and I respected their concerns, even if it meant facing opposition. As an only child, the thought of her leaving for a place as distant as Dubai was a heart-wrenching prospect for her father.

Despite the obstacles, our love remained steadfast. As I bid farewell to Korea once again, I left with a heart full of memories and a promise to return. Our story was far from over and I was determined to see where it would lead us next.

Live life fully

It had been two years since my divorce, and my kids and I were loving our new life in our new home. We weren't doing it for anyone else or to impress society.

I looked around and saw so many people living just to please others. Trying to constantly convince society that you're doing the right thing. But life is too short for that. We have to live for ourselves.

My perspective brings joy through simple things. Life is not always full of problems and as complicated as we often think. It responds to us the way we approach it. Our judgment shapes our experience. By adopting simplicity, we can create beauty without undue burden.

I learnt to find joy in little things. Like chatting with my kids, sharing meals, playing games and even sleeping together. Sometimes they'd wander into my room in the middle of the night and I loved it. Every time I walked in the door, I made a point to check in with my children. The practice continued even after they became big boys. No matter how late I was, I'd head to their room, even for a short while, and cuddle up with them before returning to my own space. They were my priority, always.

And then there was travel, which stemmed from my desire to celebrate every moment. Every trip was like a breath of fresh air for me. Exploring new places, meeting new people, trying new food—it was invigorating. Travelling has changed me, and shaped my thoughts and desires.

But in our busy life, we often forget ourselves, burying our dreams and joys just to please others. The truth is: we can't please everyone. We have to focus on our loved ones and ourselves. And ignore validation from others.

After my divorce, it was tough at first. But I decided to focus on the positive. Now, my kids and I had this beautiful, peaceful life together. I missed having a partner to share the joys and challenges of raising children. Ideally, I'd love to create a nurturing home with someone who can be a loving parent alongside me. In the meantime, I was fully committed to providing for my children's needs, fulfilling both parental roles as best I could. And I did hope to find love again someday, someone who would fulfil a mother's role at home.

12

In the lap of semi-retirement

When you go to those business parties with all the big shots and celebrities, the first question you always get hit with is, “What are you up to now?” That question used to bug me. I started giving different answers just to escape from the intrusion. “Oh, me? I’m leading a semi-retired life,” I’d say with a smirk.

Even though I joked about semi-retirement, it was a decision I made after a lot of careful thought. I’m ready to hustle hard till the end, but I needed a break from the crazy business rush. It wasn’t an easy choice, though. I had to weigh the pros and cons, and think about how it would affect my future, my family and my business.

Semi-retirement isn’t about sitting back and doing nothing. It’s about finding a balance between work and life. I’ve seen too many people get swallowed up by their careers, chasing money and success but never finding true happiness. I’ve seen people crying over situations where their hard-earned wealth came to no use. The wads of currency did not come in handy. They couldn’t even buy anything with their earnings. That’s not the life I want. I don’t seek excessive wealth or profits that surpass others.

I believe there are things money can't buy—like happiness, peace, love, health, friends and family.

For the same reason, I moved to a semi-retirement that balanced work and life. It's easy to preach about success in life and the ways to achieve it. Social media is flooded with motivational speakers preaching about happiness and success. But often, their pronouncements lack real-world application. True inspiration comes from those who've 'walked the talk', achieving success while living by the principles they advocate. Success mantras aren't found online; they're created in the fires of experience. Preaching is easy, but implementation is the true test.

In 2012, I made the bold move to step into semi-retirement. I know that it's a decision that still surprises people. It's a step people are afraid of taking.

But I went ahead and implemented it in 2012.

The most important decision

It was one of the major decisions I made since I moved to Dubai in 1991. I followed my semi-retirement plan perfectly.

I repaid all loans. I stopped chasing every client and started being selective. Only those who aligned with my values and ethics made the cut. And I made some changes in the office too. I hired senior and experienced managers to handle the day-to-day operations, giving them the authority to make decisions. A construction manager, a finance manager and a property manager joined the team. Delegating tasks and responsibilities to them proved to be a successful move. They were given the authority to make independent decisions and oversee the company's daily functions. With increased independence, they began to leverage their experience to make sound decisions. This shift led to a stronger sense of ownership within the company, resulting in a more responsible and engaged team.

While I empowered them, I haven't been idle. I still dedicate five or six hours daily to managing the team's workflow. This includes providing clear instructions, evaluating daily activities, and setting guidelines for the following day. On some days, I wouldn't visit the office.

This change freed up a ton of time for me. I maintained a healthy balance. Playtime, exercise sessions, yoga and gym time all remained a priority. Suddenly, I had time to travel, visit my mother, hang out with friends, spend quality time with my kids and even see my girlfriend. I got to live life on my terms while still maintaining my routines like playing sports, hitting the gym and doing yoga.

Maybe I could've made more money if I'd stuck to the old grind. But money isn't everything. Remember that you are born out of dust and to dust you shall return. Life is short, and when we're gone, we're not going to take any of our wealth with us. In death we cease to be owners of our wealth. After our death, nobody is going to care how much we earned. They'll remember *how* we lived. And I refuse to sacrifice my health and happiness for a bigger bank account. Why should I burn my life over wealth that's going to be someone else's after my last breath?

That's why I'm all about living for today.

Love life, live fully, and enjoy the fruits of your labour. But remember, wealth is a responsibility, not just a possession. We are fortunate stewards, not the sole inheritors. Sharing with those in need honors this responsibility.

True help is timely and discreet. Offer assistance when it's truly needed, without seeking recognition.Focus on helping the living. The greatest impact comes from those who work quietly behind the scenes, leaving a trail of uplifted lives. A silent hand extended in a moment of darkness can illuminate a path forward. Remember, the ripples of kindness can reach far beyond what we see.

The good we do today brings satisfaction, both to ourselves and those we help. That's why I believe in supporting those in need while they can still benefit. That's what I do.

Benefits of semi-retirement

Semi-retirement has brought a greater peace and happiness than I ever anticipated. It's not just about reclaiming time for old hobbies, but also discovering new joys that were out of reach before.

A shift in priorities, valuing life over wealth, is truly powerful. Instead of viewing the world solely through a businessman's lens, you rediscover your authentic self, unburdened by material pursuits.

The things we chase can be surprisingly different from what truly matters. Sometimes, what others see as grand achievements hold little meaning for us, while the simple pleasures might bring immense joy.

At their core, most religions share values like compassion, kindness and justice.

The Quran teaches, "Life is a test to see who will be 'best in deeds.'" This gives us a higher purpose for living. Doing good deeds naturally feels good too. The Bible says, "'For what shall it profit a man, if he shall gain the whole world, and lose his own soul? Or what shall a man give in exchange for his soul?" Lord Krishna says in the Bhagavad Gita, "'What is yours today, belonged to someone else yesterday, and will belong to someone else the day after tomorrow. You are mistakenly enjoying the thought that this is yours. It is this false happiness that is the cause of your sorrows."

Let me paint you a picture of my semi-retired life.

As I sat amid a crucial meeting at the office, discussing a prime property deal in Dubai with my team, a buzz from my phone interrupted the proceedings. Ignoring it momentarily, I focussed on the negotiations at hand, Europeans on one side, Indians on the other, haggling over the property price.

Then, my secretary Maria discreetly slipped me a note. It was from my friend Rafeeq, urging me to check my WhatsApp.

"Excuse me," I interjected, after checking Rafeeq's message. "I need to attend to an urgent matter. Carry on with the discussion and let me know the outcome."

Summoning my driver Parminder Singh, I hurriedly made my way to the location Rafeeq had mentioned. Arriving in Karama, I stepped out of my Rolls Royce and instructed Parminder to await my call.

Inside the restaurant, Rafeeq greeted me with a grin. "Aren't you eager for some piping hot parotta and beef?"

Steam rose from the soft, flaky Kerala parotta, enveloping the air with its inviting aroma. Adjacent, the Kerala beef fry sizzled enticingly, its rich spices glistening under the warm glow of the restaurant lights.

As we savoured the flavours of Kerala, laughter and banter flowed freely. At that moment, the weight of business negotiations faded into insignificance.

It was a photo of Kerala parotta-and-beef that Rafeeq had sent me on WhatsApp.

Business goes on, as do the meetings, but moments of true happiness like these are irreplaceable. No meeting could replace the joy of sharing parotta and beef with Rafeeq that day. Such are the benefits of semi-retirement.

No matter how far ahead we may go, we can never recapture the happiness of the present moment.

Semi-retirement is a deeply personal choice for me. While I'm sharing the positive impact it's had on my life, I recognise that others may find fulfillment in different paths. Some may thrive on a career-driven lifestyle and that's fine! Happiness isn't a one-size-fits-all proposition. What brings me joy might not work for you and vice versa.

As I often say, there comes a point where money takes a backseat. Our priorities naturally evolve throughout life, and financial gain may not hold the same weight it once did. By semi-retiring, you create a fertile ground for aspiring competitors to launch and contribute their fresh ideas to the marketplace. Their success becomes a sign of the vibrant ecosystem you helped nurture.

Do you read mail on your phone?

Believe it or not, I've never checked my email on my phone. It's true. I prefer to wait until I get to the office and open my laptop. That's how I want it to stay for the rest of my life. The key to my happiness is keeping business separate from personal joys.

Work can wait, but every moment missed is a moment lost to happiness. That's why I decided to only check my email at the office—And when I travel, I don't use even my cellphone to check e-mail. It's a choice I've made for life. Give it a try. Anyone can live like this.

I don't waste any time on Facebook. I created an account once, but a few months later, I realised it was sucking away my precious time, so I deleted it. It's saved me years of my life. I stayed away from all social media until I finally joined Instagram in 2022. Ever wonder how many hours you waste on social media every day? At least two to four hours? Maybe, more. Unless you leverage social media for specific goals, like influencing or blogging, it can easily consume significant chunks of your day.

These social media giants are all about profit. They connect people but only see us through their profit-driven eyes. It baffles me why the new generation is so hooked on social media.

Social media has its positives, but it's also flooded with fake news—90% of it, according to surveys. The new generation blindly likes, comments, and shares without realising it's all fake.

There's a flip side to everything. The new generation needs to learn to see the positive in social media and steer clear of the negative. It can be a great tool for studies, careers, work and business if used wisely. But mindlessly scrolling for hours? Not so much. How many hours are we wasting when we could be doing something more creative or spending time with loved ones?

Social media is seriously addictive and these companies know it. They're experts at luring us in. It's all algorithms, showing us what we like, and what we search for, keeping us hooked without us even realising it. Eventually, it's your loss and their gain. Think about it.

Guests from Seoul

One day, three guests from Seoul landed at our doorstep in Dubai — Song Lee and her two friends. We welcomed them with open arms and my kids were overjoyed to have new friends to chat and explore with.

For a month, they stayed as our guests, enjoying the lavish hospitality of Dubai, with accommodations in the iconic Burj Khalifa. Song Lee's visit was deliriously joyous for me. We were spending such an extended period together.

The first week was filled with laughter and adventure, but as time passed, a subtle tension began to surface. I'd encountered this before—the initial warmth fading into uncertainty. Yet, I remained patient, knowing storms often precede clear skies. Moreover, she was my closest friend and guest.

Looking back, I've noticed a pattern. In past relationships, I've observed that women who became easily angered initially presented themselves as very loving. Unfortunately, this seemed to be the case with Song Lee as well.

So far, our time together has been short. We had a wonderful few days in South Korea and the first week in Dubai was just as fulfilling. However, after that initial period, things shifted. There were dark clouds on the horizon. I chose patience. This approach kept things calm, avoiding any explosive arguments. The experience with my ex-wife had equipped me to handle the new situation. The dark clouds cleared off. But I was genuinely worried about what was happening between me and Song Lee.

Before their departure back to South Korea, we still managed to enjoy outings to places like Burj Al Arab and Madinat Jumeirah, even amidst the underlying unease

Song Lee left with an invitation for my children to visit Korea, which filled them with excitement.

During her stay, Song Lee gained a deeper understanding of my life, witnessing firsthand the authenticity of my words and experiences. She saw my business, met my friends and spent quality time with my family. This comprehensive picture, I believe, helped her feel confident that I was being genuine and not simply trying to impress her with exaggerations.

The agony and ecstasy of love

The occasional bumps in the road did not hinder my commitment to my relationship with Song Lee. Also, we planned to get married soon. I made regular trips to Seoul, spending a week with her every two months, despite the long flights and jet lag. The round-trip flight from Dubai to Seoul took a total of 18 hours. Our bond grew stronger with each encounter and thoughts of a future together lingered in our minds.

When it came time to plan trips with my children around the world, I eagerly invited her to join. “I’m planning to travel. Would you like to come along?” I asked. Her enthusiastic nod set the stage for our adventures in Hong Kong, Singapore, New York, Los Angeles, New Delhi, Kochi and Florida.

She once asked, her curiosity piqued: “You know so much on so many subjects, it’s unbelievable! Where do you find such accurate information and insightful perspectives?"

A smile played on my lips. "While I wouldn't call myself an avid reader in the traditional sense, the world itself is a rich source of knowledge. People and Nature are the best 'books' I've ever encountered. I gain information through conversations and discussions, seeing the world through others' eyes. It's like replacing books with people, but even better. You not only get the information, but also the stories and experiences of the person telling it, and potentially the experiences of those they've interacted with."

A thoughtful expression crossed her face. "And Nature?" she asked, leaning in slightly.

My gaze met hers. "Nature is another open book, waiting to be read. It offers fresh insights with every observation."

She held my gaze, a hint of admiration shining in her eyes.

While our relationship flourished through laughter and shared happiness, moments of discomfort occasionally crept in. I made it a point to address any disagreements before they escalated, valuing our connection above all else. I accepted her perspective with grace, knowing the deep bond we shared.

Thanks to regular exercise and the guidance of my personal trainer Subair, I transformed physically and mentally after my divorce, shedding seven kilograms and feeling rejuvenated. Song Lee admired the youthful vitality of my body, a trait held by many Korean women who prioritise the physical health and appearance of their partners.

Our relationship, while unconventional, blossomed into something beautiful. Ignoring the curiosity from others about our unlikely pairing, we chose to keep our love story private. Our relationship attracted some media attention. Journalists were curious about our story, with a Korean-Keralite romance being a hot topic. However, public exposure wasn't something we were interested in pursuing.

With each passing day, my mind mirrored the youthful vigour of my body. Moments spent with Song Lee became the highlight of my post-divorce life, filling it with joy and meaning.

For the first time, I donned the role of a true lover. Even in moments of absence, my thoughts were consumed by her, longing for her presence. During the whirlwind of love, as I flew back and forth between South Korea and Dubai, I experienced a blend of joy and sorrow.

Parting wounds

Every two months, I'd make the arduous journey to Seoul, an 18-hour round trip, just to see her. During one visit, I poured my heart out: "The sacrifice is immense. Taking breaks from work, all this travel—wouldn't it be better if you came to Dubai? We could build a comfortable life together."

The constant trips to Seoul over the years had worn me down.

Culturally rooted in Korea and the sole child of her parents, relocating wasn't an option for her.

Growing up as an only child, compromises and adjustments weren't as ingrained in her life as they were for me with siblings.

Plus, her rural upbringing wouldn't mesh with Dubai's urban environment. The cultural gap was a hurdle we underestimated. It wasn't just about language; it was a whole new way of life. Perhaps, with more time and effort, we could have navigated these differences.

I knew all this. But love, I believed, could rewrite the rules.

All is fair in love and war. I suggested a compromise—perhaps two months a year in Dubai?

Despite repeated attempts, she wouldn't budge. Frustration boiled over. "If Dubai isn't an option," I exclaimed, "find someone in Korea! I'm leaving."

The weight of her refusal and my anger was crushing. We parted ways with a heavy silence.

Back in Dubai, calls and messages went unanswered. This stubborn streak was familiar. When upset, she'd retreat into a shell, leaving a trail of silence that could last weeks or months. Love, when present, was smothering, and anger manifested in icy withdrawal—a double-edged sword.

Some friendships mirror this pattern. A single negative experience erases all the good times, transforming friends into enemies.

One wrong step, one harsh word, and the balance crumbles. Laughter fades, replaced by an icy silence. Past experiences, once a foundation of connection, become hollow echoes. Friends turn into distant figures, their warmth replaced by a chilling emptiness. These bonds, once seemingly strong, reveal their fragility in the face of discord.

I envisioned her as my wife, a loving mother to my children. The silence wasn't just sadness; it was a slow realisation of who she was as a partner.

The silence persisted. I tried to court logic—if she wouldn't meet me halfway, I had to let go. There was no other go. Sometimes, the bravest choice is acknowledging a losing fight. Chasing a dream that crumbles with each step is like pouring water into sand.

We all lose people we cherish, regardless of how deeply we hold onto them. But the truth of her importance only struck when she was gone. Her absence echoed in the deafening silence. Laughter that once filled the air had vanished, leaving a hollow ache in its wake. Familiar places held phantoms of her presence—a long-lasting scent of her perfume, a vacant chair where she used to sit. The world, once alive, felt muted, painted in shades of a lonely gray. Memories swirled like autumn leaves, reminiscent of a life unlived together. Her love, like a tenacious root, had burrowed deep within me. I missed her all the time and I'm sure she must have felt the same yearning.

Tiger departs

The news hit me like a physical blow. Upon returning from Korea, I learned my beloved cat, Tiger, wasn't well. The once-powerful creature, who used to greet me with playful swats and a rumbling purr, couldn't even walk. He was at the veterinary clinic.

Rushing through the sterile corridors, a wave of dread engulfed me. There he was, my magnificent companion, lying motionless, eyes closed as if in deep sleep. The spark of life seemed to have dimmed considerably. Tears welled up as I introduced myself to the doctor, my voice thick with emotion.

"We can't save him anymore," the doctor said gently. "He cannot respond to anything. His internal organs are failing him. He's old, and all he wants now is a peaceful departure, free from pain."

My jaw clenched, the world blurring around me. Tiger, my constant companion, the one I loved like a son, was going to die. A whimper escaped my lips as I reached out, my trembling hand hesitantly stroking his head, a gesture of comfort we'd shared countless times before.

As my fingers brushed his fur, a miracle happened. A faint, raspy meow, barely audible, twice repeated. It was a flicker of recognition, a final expression of love that arose from his failing body. The doctor's eyes widened in surprise. Even in this weakened state, Tiger acknowledged my presence, saying a silent goodbye. Those moments still hold a powerful charge, fresh and alive in my memory.

The weight of that moment was crushing. I retreated to another room, unable to bear the thought of witnessing his final moments. I instructed the doctor to proceed with the lethal injection, the words a choked whisper escaping my lips. Tears streamed down my face.

When the doctor called to inform me of Tiger's passing, a hollow ache settled in my chest. He offered to keep Tiger's body for burial, perhaps assuming I lacked the space. But the thought was unthinkable. "Land and a villa," I croaked, the words heavy with grief. "I'll take him for burial.»

Looking back, a pang of regret pierces my heart. Leaving his side during those final moments, a time when he needed the comfort of my touch, was a colossal mistake. Grief shrouded me in a suffocating fog, blinding me to the simple truth—sometimes, even in the face of immense sadness, presence is a gift, a final act of love.

Tiger's final "meow" still echoes in the caverns of my memory. It's a sound carved into my soul, a constant companion alongside the ever-present image of him on my laptop wallpaper. Since 2013, it's not a picture of my wife or children that graces my screen, but a magnificent portrait of my beloved Tiger. That picture will remain a permanent fixture.

He was more than just a pet; he was a favoured family member, a silent observer who witnessed the joys and tribulations of our lives. His presence loomed large during my children's formative years, a gentle friend who brought a sense of wonder into their world.

We miss Tiger more than words can express, Aryaan, Gautam and I.

Closing doors, opening paths

For years, my children and I resided in a 25,000-sq.-ft luxury home in Emirates Hills. While the villa boasted beauty, our experience inside wasn't as pleasant as expected. It seemed like we were gradually losing the joy and comfort that should define our family life. Sensing this shift, I decided to have a candid discussion with my children about our living situation. They shared the same sentiment. It became clear that we were all yearning for a more private and intimate setting to call home.

I make it a point to discuss family matters with my children, even though they're young. Sometimes, their perspectives surprise me! We approach problems differently, and their viewpoints can be refreshingly insightful.

More importantly, including them in conversations makes them feel valued. They appreciate having their input considered. This can have a lasting impact. By getting used to discussing things openly, they're more likely to carry this healthy habit into their own future families. It can empower them to make thoughtful decisions after carefully considering all sides of an issue.

A month after I decided to move from the villa to a new place, Rita, a real estate agent, unexpectedly called me.

"Dileep, a prominent person has shown interest in buying your villa. He wishes to see the whole house. You must allow. Never say no," Rita urged.

It was already 8.30 p.m. when Rita called. My children and I were engrossed in watching a cartoon movie in the upstairs theatre room. Beautiful moments with children are important to me. "Now is not the time to talk dry business," I told Rita before hanging up.

But Rita called again, insisting, "He is not just a trader as you think. When he comes there, you will understand who he is. Please don't say no."

With Rita's insistence, I reluctantly agreed, "My children and I are watching the movie now. It will be done at nine o'clock. Then tell him to come. And one more thing. He should be told specifically that he should take only 15 minutes."

At nine o'clock, Rita arrived with the Russian visitor, accompanied by his entourage. As he toured the house, he kept admiring each room, saying 'Karasho, Karasho..' which I later learned meant 'beautiful' in Russian.

With Rita's help, I struck up a conversation with him. "When I first saw you, I was convinced that you are a good man. We became friends in just 15 minutes," I said.

"I like your villa very much. There is no more to think about. Will you sell this villa to me?" he asked.

Taken aback, I hesitated before replying, "Tell me a price I can't resist, let's see."

Although I wasn't keen on selling the villa so quickly, I agreed to his price almost immediately. I must say that it was price I could not resist.

"Okay, I have sold you my villa for this price," I confirmed.

The Russian was taken aback by my swift decision, but he agreed. As we finalised the deal within minutes, he was amazed by the efficiency of our negotiation.

After sealing the deal, I suggested, "Let's drink tea and call it a day."

He chuckled and said, "Because you said 15 minutes, I kept that promise."

Laughing, I retorted, "Wasn't I the one who said 15 minutes to Rita? I can decide how long you stay."

The Russian found my remark amusing and later returned after chatting and sharing jokes. As he prepared to leave, he asked, "Nice villa. Good kids. Didn't see your wife."

Jokingly, I replied, "Both of us cannot be happy in one house. I am happy in this villa and she is in her villa."

Amused by my response, he asked if he could return to see the villa during the day, to which I readily agreed.

"We can hand over the house by paying the full amount within three months," I informed him, finalising the terms of the sale.

After the sale, he became one of my closest friends, still residing in the villa with his family. It was a surprising turn of events, considering his prominent stature as a businessman in Russia. I won't tell you the price of the villa, but I can reveal that it was one of the big real-estate deals in Dubai that year and for the next 10 years.

Whenever we meet, I playfully remind him, "I built that villa not for myself, but for you. I sold that villa to you because you deserve it," to which he responds with laughter.

Small space, big smiles

We decided to move into a new home in Meadows 4, living right by the Montgomerie Golf Club. It was a charming, modest-sized house spanning only 4,000 square feet in Meadows 4, offering a picturesque view of the golf course and conveniently close to the kids' school. Before settling in, we spruced up the interiors to match our tastes and preferences, transforming it into a lovely abode.

After the sale of our previous lavish villa, murmurs and false tales were circulating about our financial situation. Some speculated that business woes had forced the sale, but I chose to stick to my mantra of "let the naysayers say what they will". I simply didn't have the time or inclination to entertain baseless gossip that could drain my energy and happiness.

The move to our new home was a joyous occasion, especially with Subhash and Deepa Nanny by our side. In this smaller house, we found a sense of privacy and familial contentment that had eluded us in the grand villa. Our happiness in this new space was palpable, radiating positivity into every aspect of our lives.

We realised that we didn't need to seek validation from society or prove anything to the world. Our decisions were ours to make and our happiness was paramount. Prioritising the happiness of those within our close circle, we learned to tune out the noise of external opinions and focus on what truly mattered to us. Let the gossipers chatter away; their words hold no weight in our pursuit of genuine contentment

The Five Circles concept

Life can be a whirlwind of relationships, obligations and external pressures. But what if we could simplify things? This is the philosophy behind the Five Circles concept. It's a way to categorise the people and aspects of life that truly matter, allowing us to focus our energy and cultivate happiness.

The first circle, the foundation of everything, is the Circle of Love and Gravity. This encompasses parents, teachers and anyone who has played a significant role in shaping you. They deserve our deepest respect, love and support.

The second circle is the Circle of Inspiration. This includes friends, colleagues and even those we might consider rivals. Here, we exchange ideas, challenge each other to grow and find the motivation to keep pushing forward. Even those who might harbour jealousy can unknowingly inspire us to strive for greater things.

The third circle is the Circle of Responsibility. This includes our bosses, clients and anyone we have professional obligations towards. Here, dedication, hard work and a strong sense of responsibility are key to success.

The fourth circle, the closest to our hearts, is the Circle of Protection. This is our family, our spouse and our children. Here, love, care, and a sense of security are paramount. We nurture and protect those who depend on us.

Finally, the fifth circle is the Circle of Higher Purpose. This encompasses our faith in a higher power or a deep connection with Nature. It's the source of our core values, offering guidance and a sense of belonging in the grand scheme of things. Protecting Nature and living things becomes an extension of ourselves.

Just like the five senses we possess, these five circles provide a framework for navigating life. By focussing on these core relationships and responsibilities, we can simplify our lives and maximise our happiness. Those outside these circles shouldn't be a source of worry or concern. Chasing external validation leads to headaches and unnecessary stress.

The key is to find joy in even the smallest things that happen within these circles. The people within these circles are our true supporters. They celebrate our achievements, overlook our shortcomings and constantly encourage us to be our best selves. They are the ones who dream alongside us and rejoice in our victories.

This philosophy has personally helped me achieve my dreams. The encouragement and inspiration I've received from these five circles have been instrumental in my success. My purpose is to make these important people in my life happy and proud.

Focus on building a life you love, big or small. The world needs all kinds of people and your unique contributions matter, regardless of scale.

By prioritising your inner circles, you may create a more meaningful and authentic life. A smaller world for oneself may lead to greater fulfilment; a wider world often ends in disappointment. True happiness and success come from nurturing deep connections with those who truly care about you.

13

A European damsel

After my breakup with Song Lee, I found myself trying every avenue to reach out to her. But as the realisation sunk in that I may never catch her, I received an unexpected message on my phone. It was from Sofia, a beautiful European woman I had met years ago at the Dubai court while finalising my divorce. I thought she looked noble and kind. We never really connected beyond occasional messages. However, during my moments of heartbreak, her message seemed like a ray of hope. A flicker of surprise danced in my chest. A hesitant hope, a fragile butterfly, took flight in my stomach. Could this be a new beginning, a melody to replace the melancholic silence?

Without much thought, I invited Sofia to Zuma, one of the top restaurants in Dubai.

As expected, Sofia arrived at the restaurant promptly, and over lunch, I poured out my heart, sharing the details of my breakup with Song Lee. Sofia listened attentively, offering words of comfort.

"Oh, I'm so sorry to hear that. It must be tough for you," she said.

"Yeah, it's been rough. I thought she was the one, you know? But things don't always work out the way we hope."

"I understand," she said. "Relationships can be complicated. But you'll get through this."

We talked for hours, and when we parted ways that day, I felt a sense of relief, as if I had unburdened myself of some of the pain.

Soon after, Sofia and I began exchanging regular messages and within a week, we found ourselves dating. Sofia, though a beauty, didn't quite fill the void left by Song Lee. She lacked the intelligence and charm that had captivated me in Song Lee. Still, Sofia offered some comfort during this difficult time.

A renowned model from Europe, she had her charm, but I yearned for someone more grounded, someone without hidden agendas. As we continued dating and travelling around Dubai together, a nagging feeling persisted. Sofia didn't ignite the same spark of connection I shared with Song Lee.

On different wavelengths

Sofia and I spent time together, but throughout it all, a shadow stayed put. My connection with Song Lee was unlike anything I'd ever known. It brought a depth of happiness, peace and emotional understanding that simply wasn't present with Sofia.

This experience, however, served a purpose. It drove home a truth within me—no other woman I've met has even approached the way Song Lee captured my heart.

I couldn't shake off the feeling that something wasn't quite right. It became clear that Sofia harboured intentions of marriage, whereas I saw our relationship as temporary solace.

Certain things she said and did, along with some initial reservations I had, led to growing doubts.

One particular instance that raised a red flag was our first encounter at the courthouse. When I mentioned living in Emirates Hills, her immediate reaction by offering her number, rather than focussing on my name, made me question her motives. I wondered if her interest was more materialistic.

Holding out hope for a deeper connection, I hoped her behaviour might change over time. Unfortunately, that wasn't the case. As days turned into weeks, I increasingly observed clues that reinforced my initial concerns about her character.

From our first meeting, I sensed that her interest lay not in me but in my wealth. Yet, I gave her the benefit of the doubt. But as time went on, her true intentions became clearer. The disconnect was obvious.

Goodbye, lady!

The thought of Sofia as my wife, raising my children together, felt unimaginable, even in the most fantastical scenarios.

Eventually, I made the decision to end things with her. I explained my reasons to her calmly, emphasising that our relationship wasn't serving either of us well. Although she initially seemed disappointed, I hoped she would understand in time.

"My time and yours are very precious," I said with a smile. "Let's not waste any more time. I don't agree with you becoming my wife. This relationship is not going to do you or me much good. You know that too well. We have memories of good experiences of three months in our mind. We can part as friends with those good memories. You will realise later that what we have done now was a good decision. So you should happily go back to your life."

When relationships end, I believe in a clean break, free of animosity. My goal is to communicate my feelings honestly and respectfully, even if they're difficult. Parting ways doesn't have to mean becoming enemies. There may be hurt feelings, especially if the other person has caused you worry or pain. But holding onto anger or negativity only hinders your healing. Therefore, I strive for a decent and amicable conclusion. This approach allows everyone involved to move forward without the burden of resentment or hostility. Her face became red when she heard me. “What?” she shot back, pointing her finger at me. “How can you say that? You’re just trying to get rid of me!” “No, that’s not it at all. I’m being honest with you. We’re just not right for each other and it’s better to end things now before things get even more complicated.” “I won’t accept this! How dare you treat me like this? “I’m sorry if I’ve hurt you,” I said. “but I have to do what’s best for both of us.” Her reaction, however, caught me off guard. She played the nationality card, and accused me of deception and of manipulating the situation. She bristled, her voice sharp. “This is unbelievable! How could you do this to a European? How did you get the courage for it?” Her comment about her nationality stung. I met her gaze, my voice firm. “Hold on. We dated, yes, but it wasn’t because you were European. It was because of who you were as a person. Bringing nationality into this is unfair.” I stood my ground, refusing to be swayed by her tactics. “Look,” I said, my voice firm, “did we ever care about nationalities when we were dating? Did we check our passports each other? I wanted to end this amicably, but bringing up nationality now complicates things. Don’t try to intimidate me with your nationality card. We’re not in colonial times anymore. I’m an Indian, and India is a thriving nation on the world stage. We’re moving forward, not clinging to the past. Now, let me tell you, get out of here.” She became speechless. She left the room in a huff. I knew our relationship had come to an end. Months later, she reached out to apologise for her behaviour. Through this experience, I came to appreciate the depth of my feelings for Song Lee. No other woman could compare to her gentle grace. She was the one who had left a permanent mark on my heart and no amount of time with anyone else could change that.

Love calls me back to Korea

I felt that my connection with Sofia was intended to be an eye-opener. Maybe, its purpose was to teach me that no woman could replace Song Lee. It proved that no woman could love me as much as she did. Nor could I see a substitute for her in my mind.

Day by day, incident after incident, I missed her more. No new love could replicate the one we shared. I longed to see her. I decided to go to Seoul and see her. After breaking up with her, I've never been there.

As I boarded a plane to South Korea after a gap of one year, anticipation mingled with apprehension in equal measure. Thoughts of her flooded my mind.

The past year had not been easy for me. Every sunrise brought a fresh pang of absence, every crowded street a phantom echo of her laughter. Dating, travel, movies—nothing could truly distract me. I filled my days with activity, my nights with memories.

During the flight, I found myself lost in a sea of questions. Could I rekindle our friendship? What were the after-effects of the break-up? How would she respond? Would there be any trace of the warmth we once shared? The uncertainty gnawed at me, leaving me restless in my seat.

A familiar face broke through the haze of my thoughts. It was the Korean air hostess, familiar to me.

"It's been a while," she greeted, her voice carrying a hint of warmth.

"Indeed, it has," I replied, offering a faint smile in return.

I told her about going back to Song Lee. The air hostess knew about our relationship.

I was not in a mood to talk more to her. Tired, I tried to catch some sleep. The next morning, I woke up, freshened up, and prepared to disembark. The air hostess offered a genuine smile and a friendly wave.

"Good luck," she said.

I prayed that I should be lucky.

Upon arriving in Korea and checking into Grand Hyatt, I wasted no time in reaching out to Song Lee, hoping to bridge the chasm that had formed between us. I called her up. She didn't respond. I texted to her several times. The messages did not elicit any response. I wanted to cool her down.

"I travelled 7,000 km to see you, Song Lee," I texted to her, the words heavy with longing. Maybe, she thought that I was in Dubai and did not respond.

So, I sent her a photograph of me in the hotel room.

She texted back, "I knew you would come back one day in search of me."

I was relieved. "Yes, I can be stubborn sometimes. You are more stubborn than I'm. If a Malayali can be stubborn, why not a South Korean? It's a trait we all share, I guess," she continued to text.

She relented and came to the hotel next day and drove me around the city. It seemed that she was genuinely trying to repair the relationship. Suddenly, it felt like old times. Familiar landmarks triggered a cascade of memories—the cafe where we first met, the park where we picnicked under the cherry blossoms. Her laughter filled the car, a melody I hadn't heard in a year, yet it fit perfectly alongside the city's continual hum. For a stolen moment, time seemed to rewind. The ache in my heart softened, replaced by a flicker of hope, a fragile question mark hanging in the air. Could this spark rekindle the flame we once shared?

During our time together, she mentioned her mother's enquiries about me. Her mother had asked why I was not visiting South Korea any more. Her dad continued to dislike me.

I apprised Song Lee of all that happened in the past year, when she was not with me—except my brief affair with Sofia. Neither did she ask me if I got into a relationship with someone else.

A love story lost in geography

Song Lee and I decided to travel outside of South Korea again, hoping the experiences would make things better. We explored favourite destinations like New York, Hong Kong and Japan.

However, the geographical distance remained a looming challenge. The true test came in 2016 when we attempted to close that gap. My dream of Song Lee settling in Dubai clashed with her deep connection to South Korea. This fundamental difference led to our first parting. A year later, a spark of hope flickered. Touched by my sincerity, Song Lee returned to Dubai, and we reconnected as friends. Her kindness shone brightly during this time. The renewed bond notwithstanding, the core issue persisted. Her values, deeply rooted in her South Korean upbringing, made leaving her home a difficult decision. For me, Dubai, the land of opportunity and responsibility—with my business, children, and company ties—held an undeniable pull.

As the reality of our situation settled in—neither compromise (me moving to Korea or her settling in Dubai) seemed realistic—we made the difficult but mutual decision to end the relationship permanently.

We could feel our hearts beating.

As she spoke about the impact our relationship had on her, I couldn't help but feel a pang of regret deep within me.

"I never imagined someone could change me the way you did," she confessed.

I swallowed hard, the weight of her words settling heavily on my shoulders. "You've left a deep impression on my life as well," I replied, my voice barely above a whisper.

The decision was searing. We decided to part ways for good wishing each other well in the future. The pain of parting was unbearable.

A suffocating tightness gripped my chest. Tears welled up in my eyes. I found myself grappling with a sense of emptiness. The realisation that I would never again feel her touch, hear her laughter or share in her dreams was a bitter pill to swallow.

All of that happened between us since 2011 flashed through my mind as though a movie montage. Our first shy glances across a crowded room, the nervous excitement of our first kiss, the exhilarating laughter shared during our travels through major cities of the world—every precious moment flickered past, saying that a love story was reaching its final scene. The echo of her voice, the warmth of her hand in mine, the way her eyes crinkled when she laughed—these sensory ghosts haunted me. Each memory was a shard of a shattered dream. Yet, the weight of reality settled in—a life together was a beautiful fantasy, but an impossible reality. With a heavy heart, I accepted the truth: our paths were diverging.

The journey back to Dubai was a blur. My mind fixated on one question: could anyone truly replace Song Lee? Would an angel appear before me again?

Since our parting, I've met many wonderful women from diverse backgrounds. Each encounter, however, served as a stark reminder—none held a candle to Song Lee.

More time with kids

After parting with Song Lee, I got back into the swing of things at the office, focussing on business as usual. I made sure to spend quality time with my kids, taking them on holidays to various destinations. Our boys' trips became the highlight of our time together.

Watching my children grow up was a surreal experience. It seemed like they were sprouting before my eyes, both physically and emotionally. Our bond deepened as I shared life lessons with them, and in return, they offered me invaluable insights from their own experiences.

Like their dad, they had a knack for sports, particularly golf and tennis. On their free days, they dedicated themselves to honing their skills on the court and the green.

My children may not have topped the charts in every subject, but they always displayed a passion for learning in their own unique ways. They excelled in many areas. I prioritised creating in them a love for exploration and discovery, not just textbook memorisation. In my view, true education comes from real-world experiences, not just the ability to ace exams. I never believed in pressuring them to excel in studies.

I've always been skeptical of the traditional schooling system, where kids are turned into mark-producing machines. It destroys their souls. It kills their creativity. It restricts their naturalness. That's why I've made it a point to expose my boys to diverse experiences, especially through our travels and through meeting people from different cultures.

Since my divorce, we've journeyed to many corners of the globe. We've enjoyed every bit of it. Those were the best moments we spent together. I've gleaned wisdom from the people I've met and the cultures I've encountered during my travels. Life itself has been my greatest teacher. It has been my biggest university. In a world inundated with information from screens and pages, I've found that nothing beats the lessons learned from real-life interactions and experiences.

Across horizons, through friendship

Friendship has always been the cornerstone of my life. From my earliest days to my adventures in Mumbai, Dubai, different cities and countries, I've been fortunate to cherish meaningful connections with countless friends from all walks of life. As I've never tried to exploit my friends, the innocence in my relationship with them has been intact. Whether it's reminiscing about childhood antics, sharing school memories or simply catching up over a cup of coffee, these bonds have enriched my journey in countless ways.

I cannot forget my childhood friends Pramod and Prakash.

Pramod's absence left a void that I tried to fill in every way possible, even reaching out to his brother Prasad in hopes of finding him. Sadly, he remained elusive.

Then there are my village friends—Babu, Rajesh and Pradeep. While our paths may have diverged slightly over the years, our camaraderie remains intact. Pradeep's warmth could be baffling. He'd show moments of intimacy, followed by periods of aloofness.

I maintain close contact with my friends.

Whenever I'm in Edappal, friends reach out and I do the same. We catch up, share stories. I believe in intervening and helping friends in need, whenever possible.

My approach to helping others prioritises those closest to me: family, friends and neighbours. They're the ones who've known me throughout life's journey.

As the saying goes, we arrive in this world with nothing and leave the same way. Born with cries, we depart leaving loved ones in tears. It's the connections we create in between—with friends, family and loved ones—that truly matter. This short life compels me to extend a helping hand to those who matter most during our shared time here.

In 2018, I orchestrated a reunion of sorts, inviting my high school pals to Dubai. It was a joyous affair, filled with laughter and reminiscing about the good old days. Moments like these are priceless reminders of the beauty of friendship. My friends still remember the reunion.

We can never regain the past. It is over. We can never get our school and college days back. Time never travels back. It always moves forward.

The onus of travelling backward and revisiting the past is on us. Such reunions are crucial is bringing alive the memories of the past. What's more fulfilling than slipping into remembrances of the past?

The humid monsoon air of Edappal hangs heavy with the scent of freshly brewed chai and jasmine flowers.

Looking back, I realise Edappal isn't just a place; it's the very essence of who I am. I'm a product of my land and its people. Every person I know there has contributed to my growth as a human being.

I started the Edappal Tennis Academy with a two-fold purpose: providing a welcoming space for people from my hometown and around to enjoy tennis and offering underprivileged children the opportunity to develop their skills and potentially pursue their dreams on the court. The venture was inspired by my friend, Pankettan (Pankajakshan), a scientist in oceanography. It's my way of giving back to society, a small but significant step in fulfilling my social responsibility.

At the academy, we offer free training to many disadvantaged children, opening doors that may have otherwise remained closed. Witnessing their progress is truly rewarding; several of our students have even gone on to compete at district and state levels.

Through the Edappal Tennis Academy, we're not just teaching tennis; we're nurturing potential and empowering futures. It's a cause close to my heart.

While I've chosen to keep my charitable efforts private, I'm totally committed to helping those in need. However, handling this can be challenging. Sometimes, I feel approached for assistance in a way that feels transactional. I feel I'm seen as a money machine. It's not about blame. Perhaps, in their shoes, I might understand the impulse.

My request to them is to see me as a fellow human being, not as an 'Automated Teller Machine (ATM)'.

My approach is to prioritise what feels right to me. I want to offer genuine support, not simply function as a readily available resource. Ultimately, the decisions I make are based on my own values, not external pressures.

A R Shaji and Unni

I've maintained strong friendships with the comrades from my early days at the labour camp in Dubai. A.R. Shaji, whom I met there, remains a dear friend, though he's now settled happily in Kerala with his wife and two children. A. R.Shaji's a fantastic friend who's never taken advantage of our friendship. Whenever he calls, I always make sure to offer help, but he never asks for anything in return. It's refreshing to have someone so genuine in my life. He's yet to respond to my numerous invitations to visit me in Dubai, but I hold onto hope that he'll make the trip someday.

I lost my friend Unni to illness back in 2015. He was a skilled engineer and a dear friend. His absence is deeply felt.

While it's true that as we ascend in life, the number of true friendships may dwindle, I take comfort in the enduring bonds I've formed over the years. Names like Rajesh, Abu, Saifu, Bhasi, Jayan, Shaju, Akbar, Salam, Sudheer and Giri remain engraved in my heart as soulmates.

My connections from college days are equally steadfast. The roster of names like Aziz, Naser Kokodi, Naser Kapat, Viswan, Ajith, Ashok, Anand, Askar, Gopi, Ikku, Jayashankar, Jayagopal, JP, Jayakumar (Ammavan), Mehrunnisa, Vaheeda, Rema, Shaji, Radhakrishnan, Gafoor, Naser T., Ajith Kumar, Mini, Sabu Paul, Sreelatha, Suresh Babu, Muhammadali, Savitha, Unni and Radhakrishnan stands strong even after four decades.

The rise of mobile phones and social media has made staying connected easier, but it also highlights how easily connections from earlier times can be lost. Back then, without these technologies, we exchanged physical addresses, which unfortunately become outdated with life changes.

I've tried various means to reconnect with some dear friends, but some remain lost due to these circumstances.

Please know that losing touch doesn't diminish the value of our friendship. While this text may not mention everyone, it serves as a tribute to all the friends who have enriched my life's journey.

Some of my close friends are older than me. One such friendship began 20 years ago with Zakariaka, a kind soul from Kozhikode who is 15 years my senior. Conversations with Zakariaka, a wit, are filled with laughter and good humour, making time seem to fly by. I feel incredibly fortunate to have him in my life.

Through Zakariaka, I also met his nephew, Jamad Usman, son of Zakariaka's sister. Jamad Usman eventually became a close friend as well.

Maintaining friendships is a priority for me. I actively stay in touch with old friends and even try to reconnect with those lost over time. It's been truly rewarding, with many rekindled connections and even offering support to those struggling. Of course, there are exceptions. Sometimes, I distance myself from people with negative behaviour or those who seem to have ulterior motives in our friendship. It's important to be able to identify and avoid such situations.

Having strong friendships brings immense value to life. I've witnessed firsthand how wealth and fame can leave people feeling isolated, lacking true confidantes. It makes me deeply grateful for my own fortune. Throughout my life's journey, I've been blessed with great friends from all walks of life. My greatest hope is to nurture these bonds of love and friendship until the very end. It's a stark contrast to those who lack true connection. Without friends to share your heart with, what meaning does life's success truly hold?

A new plot in Emirates Hills

It's been four years since we said goodbye to that sprawling villa in Emirates Hills and sold it off. Sure, the big villa had its perks, but privacy became a bit of a challenge. Still, we can't help but reminisce about the good times we had there. The movie nights in our cozy theatre room, splashing around in the expansive swimming pool, hitting the gym together and enjoying the golf simulator—those memories shine brightly in our hearts.

Our youngest, Aryaan, felt the loss the most. He had so much space to run around and play in that villa.

The house we were in then was located right by the Golf Club in Emirates Hills. It was a beautiful place, but the current Meadows villa at 4,000 sq. ft, was starting to feel a bit cramped, especially as the kids grew up and brought their friends over. That's why I got my eye on buying land and building our own custom home. We snagged a plot in Emirates Hills with stunning views of the golf course and Dubai's skyline.

I bought the land from a Pakistani American businessman at the asking price, even though there was an old house on it that I planned to demolish. My vision was to craft a new home from scratch, tailored to our family's needs and preferences.

One day, I took the kids to see the plot we'd purchased. When they spotted the old house, they were a bit puzzled.

"Dad, did we buy this old house?" they asked.

I reassured them, "No, we're knocking this one down and building something brand new. Just focus on the location and surroundings. If you like it, we'll make it happen."

I wanted to involve them in the decision-making process and gauge their interests, and this will eventually help them when they grow up. After all, it's not just a business venture—it's where they'll call home.

My childhood friends Abu, Akbar and Salam at my Emirates Hills residence

Business magnates and dear friends Adel Zarooni, Ramesh Prabhakar and Naima Maya

A 2006 memory I'll always cherish—meeting the talented actor-director Sreenivasan while holding Gautam at our Meadow-9 residence in Dubai

Actor Sreenivasan visited our Dubai residence in 2006 when my son Gautam was just 2 years old

So happy to reconnect with Radhettan recently! His family's kindness in allowing me to stay at their home in Mumbai back in 1990 when I was struggling was invaluable

Reunited with Chandrettan! Remember him seeing me off at Mumbai airport for Dubai all the way back in 1991!

My kids making winter memories in South Korea

Korean pines reaching for the sky, just like my travel dreams did after seeing a similar scene in a book gifted by Cheriyachan. This view ignited the wanderlust within!

In South Korea during winter

A photograph taken during Eid celebrations of 2023

My children beside the statue of Abraham Lincoln at the Central Park West steps near the New-York Historical Society Museum and Library in New York city

The Dubai Creek Golf and Yacht Club

A father-and-sons trip!
With my children in London

A family photo, captured by cine photographer JP, during Diwali celebrations

My motivational lecture for final-year students of SSM Polytechnic College

Dreamland Dubai!
A breathtaking panorama of soaring skyscrapers and shimmering waters—as viewed from my office cabin. This land has given me everything in life

With MJ's parents and brother in the Philippines

When MJ and I met for the first time at the Address Montgomerie Hotel in Dubai.
Also seen are Alain and Joanna

Amma

Love in Singapore!
MJ and I in Singapore

Milestone achieved! Every new car gets parked by the Rashidiya Mosque, a token of gratitude for blessings received

Fond memories of quiet reflection at the Rashidiya Mosque. A beautiful place of worship in Dubai

Back where it all began! This Mumbai building, which housed the office I worked in, holds so many memories. A 2023 photograph

In a Mumbai local train—reliving old memories

The Edappal Tennis Academy I founded in my hometown, Edappal

My kids are having a blast with their furry companions, Rocky and Sweety, at our Meadows-9 residence on the day of shifting to a new house in Emirates Hills after my divorce

My cousin (Valiachan's son) Kuttan, the boy from the 'Kannimanga' story narrated in the book

Ashraf, my friend whom I helped relocate to Dubai in 1992

Teeing off with Cheyenne Woods, niece of golfing legend Tiger Woods

A long-awaited reunion! So happy to catch up with dear friend Pramod after 30 years, right here at my Kerala home

With cricket legend Kapil Dev in London

Catching up with friend and celebrity jewelry designer and watchmaker Jacob Arabo

Championship bond! With my best friend Walid Alattar
by the prestigious Ryder Cup Trophy

Sharing a moment with friend and Bulgarian professional tennis player Grigor Dimitrov

Enjoying a round of golf with friend and world number nine tennis player Hubert Hurkacz

Soaking up the atmosphere at Wimbledon with my family

What a legend! With Rory McIlroy, former world number one in the Official World Golf Ranking

Delighted to be with friend and actor R Madhavan

With friend and film director Balachandra Menon

In Heilbronn's office in Dubai Marina

MJ and I —our early days

This cricket bat, used by Sachin Tendulkar, was autographed and presented to me in 2011 by the legend himself

A day on the green with friend and cricket star Sanju Samson

On the green with Yuvi (Yuvraj Singh) and Ajay Bindroo! Learning from Yuvi, the epitome of perseverance, both on and off the field

More than a cricket star, Sreesanth is a great friend!

Journey time! Along with my family

MJ takes part in the World Amateur Golf Finals in Turkey

Clinched the chance to represent UAE at the 2019 Turkish Airlines World Amateur Golf Cup Tournament!

Lucky to learn from the best! With my amazing boss and mentor John Andrew Papadouris

MJ—before I met her

An old photo of MJ—before our paths crossed

With business magnate M A Yusuff Ali and my dear friend P M Naser in London's Kensington Garden

14

Mr Edappal meets Ms Philippines

After parting ways with my South Korean girlfriend Song Lee, I found myself lost. Every day felt like a struggle, as if I was nursing a wound that refused to heal.

In an attempt to move on, I tried befriending several women, hoping to convince myself that Song Lee was truly gone. Then one morning, out of the blue, my friend Anil called with an unexpected proposition.

"I've found someone special for you," he said. "Drop by my office and I'll introduce you."

Anil is a freelance project management consultant in Dubai. I've known him for over two decades, so I trusted him implicitly. Plus, he knows me inside out—my life, my stories, my quirks.

I had my reservations about falling for anyone after Song Lee, but something in my heart urged me to heed Anil's call. So, I made my way to his office.

As I entered, Anil ushered me into a room where Alain, his Senior Quantity Surveyor, and his team were hard at work. And there she was – a tall, stunning woman, radiating warmth and grace. Her smile, though rare, spoke volumes, and her demeanour exuded nobility and simplicity."

Anil introduced me to Alain but left out the introduction to the beautiful lady by his side—an Assistant Quantity Surveyor who worked with Alain. I too had started my career in Dubai as an AQS.

Later, I couldn't resist asking Anil about her.

"That's Maelyn Joy or MJ for short," he explained. "She's 22, hails from a small village in the Philippines."

Upon learning she was Filipino, I felt a pang of scepticism.

"She doesn't give a Filipino vibe," Anil remarked, with a knowing smile. "Actually, she's a mix of Filipino and Spanish."

Curiosity piqued, I inquired about her background.

"Her father's a businessman and civil engineer, her brother's studying civil engineering, and she recently moved to Dubai with her mother," Anil filled me in. "Oh, and she's a former beauty pageant winner and model back in the Philippines. She was Miss Philippines Earth Misamis Oriental Winner and National Finalist. Yet, she's as down-to-earth as they come."

Her story captivated me, but I couldn't shake off one glaring issue.

"There's a significant age gap between us—26 years, to be precise," I pointed out to Anil. "There's no way she'd entertain the idea of being with me."

Anil's response? A knowing grin.

"That's no hurdle. After all, haven't most of your girlfriends been younger women?" he quipped.

As a matter of fact, I was never looking for younger women. Just by chance, I ended up with them.

A quest for connection

Anil's behaviour left me feeling utterly betrayed. Not only did he fail to provide me with MJ's contact details, but he also seemed to be stringing me along, showcasing her like a prize without any intention of introducing us properly.

I couldn't shake the feeling that Anil was playing a cruel joke on me. He kept dodging the issue, coming up with excuse after excuse to avoid introducing us. It became clear that he was deliberately toying with my emotions and I decided enough was enough.

One day, I mustered the courage to confront Anil over the phone.

"What are your thoughts on me speaking to MJ directly?" I asked, catching him off guard.

He was put in a tight spot, unable to give a straightforward yes or no answer. I didn't even request her number; I simply sought his permission to reach out to her myself. Yet, he sidestepped the question, diverting the conversation elsewhere. It was evident that he got the message—I was done playing his game.

Knowing Alain, Anil's Senior Quantity Surveyor, to be a man of integrity, I decided to shift my focus to him instead. After several conversations over the phone and via text, I made it clear to Alain that my intentions toward MJ were serious.

"I envision her as not only my wife but also a beloved friend to my children. I'm looking for a mother for my kids. I've a straightforward nature. I dislike saying one thing and meaning another. I need to make a final decision about her soon," I explained.

Alain understood my sincerity and expressed his concerns.

"From what you say, she seems to be an ideal woman for you. But I'm not sure whether she likes a man of another nationality. She also has a martinet mother," he said.

But I reassured him, "Leave it to me."

Eventually, after much persuasion, Alain agreed to arrange a dinner with MJ. A few days later, he called to confirm that they would be joining me at the Address Montgomerie Hotel for dinner, along with Joanna, MJ's friend.

The one I adore

The anticipation was killing me as I waited for the moment Alain would arrive with MJ for dinner. From the minute their car pulled up, I was on edge, eagerly awaiting her appearance. Alain and Joanna emerged first, and then, like a vision descending from heaven, MJ stepped out behind them, leaving me utterly stunned.

It's hard to put into words the effect her presence had on me. She was like an angel, radiating beauty and grace with every step. Her pearly smile, her statuesque figure—I was completely mesmerised.

As I reached out to shake her hand, a jolt of electricity shot through me. It was as if that simple touch ignited a spark of love within me, setting my emotions ablaze.

I made a conscious effort to keep my composure. I wanted to make a positive impression. Nothing should put her off. I couldn't afford to let any hint of my inner turmoil show, not during our first meeting.

For MJ, this was a big step—her first encounter in Dubai with a man of different nationality. She'd managed to convince her strict mother that she was just having dinner with a friend from the office and she had to be back before 10.30 p.m.

Over dinner, I tried to break the ice by getting to know her better. We talked about business, family, but her reaction to my attempts at conversation left me feeling somewhat disappointed. It seemed like I was making little headway in leaving an impression on her.

Then, I mustered up the courage to ask her the question that had been burning in my mind: Why had she given up the glitz and glamour of the Philippines to come to Dubai?

Her answer took me by surprise.

"The glitz and glamour never brought me joy," she began. "The constant tension and stress were unbearable. All I yearn for is a simple life and a happy family. I have no grand ambitions or desires. Just the desire to lead a life of normality and contentment."

Her words struck a chord deep within me. In that moment, I knew—she was the one.

MJ wasn't your typical beauty queen. Even at the peak of her fame, humility shone through. Gazing at her, a thought bloomed in my mind: "She could replace Song Lee."

MJ shattered my belief that no one could fill the void Song Lee left. She challenged my perception of women entirely. I was determined to have her in my life, no matter what.

Taking a deep breath, I decided to be vulnerable. My confidence surged as I spoke, "MJ, listen. This comes straight from the heart. If you come with me, I'll protect you fiercely. I'll cherish you like a precious gem, love you until my last breath."

My voice trembled with emotion, each word punctuated by a hesitant stutter. After composing myself, I continued, "Let's be friends, good friends forever. I promise to make you happy, no matter what life throws our way."

The weight of my confession hung heavy in the air. Not just MJ, but Alain and Joanna who accompanied her, seemed speechless. A thick silence descended upon the dinner table. Alain and Joanna, convinced by my sincerity, likely envisioned MJ accepting my offer.

All eyes fixated on MJ, eagerly awaiting her response. Finally, she broke the silence, her voice soft but firm.

"No, I can't accept your offer," she began. "You might see a flawless exterior, but I'm far from perfect. When I was young, a mishap affected my hearing. Even now, I wear a hearing aid."

Carefully, she reached up and gently removed a small device from behind her ear, displaying it for all of us to see. The revelation hung in the air. A wave of emotions engulfed me—surprise, empathy and respect for this remarkable woman's honesty.

After being silent for a while, she continued.

"You're rich. Why choose me when you could have someone better?" she questioned.

But I was resolute. "Is it a crime to be wealthy? Is there an obligation for women to love only the poor? Shouldn't a rich man love and be loved?" I countered.

"I didn't mean that," she replied. "You might know a lot of women. Why don't you choose one from them to be your partner?"

"I actually have a story for you," I said, leaning forward a little. "Remember when I was traveling in Singapore? I saw this fascinating photo—11 snakes all tangled up together. It seemed like a big cuddle puddle! But then I read the caption and things got interesting. Apparently, there were 10 male snakes and only one female! The caption said the female would only choose one mate and...well, ignore the rest."

A slight smile played on my lips. "It reminded me of myself, searching for that special someone. Like that female snake, I've been looking for the one who truly clicks."

My gaze met MJ's, sincerity filling my eyes. "Then I met you. And something just feels different."

MJ's laughter filled the room, leaving Alain and Joanna at a loss for words. They listened intently, unsure of whose side to take or how to advise.

MJ politely declined my offer after dinner. Her conversation hinted at needing more time, perhaps to process my words. It was also nearing the curfew her mother had set.

After settling the bill, we prepared to leave. Reaching the parking lot, I offered, "Let me give MJ a ride home."

While Alain and Joanna didn't object, MJ seemed hesitant. "No, I'll go with Alain," she replied.

Concerned, Joanna took MJ aside for a private conversation that lasted about 15 minutes. When Joanna returned, she offered to accompany MJ, who then reluctantly agreed to ride with me. Thankfully, I was able to get her home well before her mother's curfew.

The art of waiting

My first encounter with MJ left a permanent impression on me. Not only did I gain three new friends–MJ, Alain and Joanna—but I also witnessed a type of womanhood I'd never encountered before.

Our friendship was just beginning and though my mind reassured me that things would evolve as I envisioned, it also reminded me to be patient. Sometimes, life has its own timeline and not everything aligns with our expectations. But that's the beauty of it—the unpredictability, the waiting, the eventual realisation. Rushing a process can sometimes create more problems than it solves. Yet, when things don't happen as quickly as we'd like, we often blame time itself.

The next day, I invited Joanna to lunch and she brought MJ along. We chatted for a while, and as I prepared to leave, I offered to drop MJ off at the office. Without hesitation, she accepted, and as we rode together, I said, "You can trust me! All that I told you yesterday is true. I wouldn't dream of fibbing about life."

I felt compelled to share some truths about myself.

"I don't smoke, rarely drink and don't gamble," I confessed.

MJ chuckled in response. "I'm wary of wealthy people. I come from a humble background and don't think I'd fit into your lavish lifestyle."

Her words lingered in my mind as I drove away. I knew she had reservations, but I sensed a glimmer of hope. She was laying out the reasons why we couldn't be together and I couldn't help but wait for the day she'd say yes.

Thanks to Joanna's efforts, MJ and I crossed paths many times after that. One morning, I offered to drive her to the office and after some persuasion, she relented.

During the ride, she revealed, "I need my mother's consent to date you. I don't want to pursue anything without her approval."

Understanding her concerns, I assured her, "No point talking to your strict mum. She'll never agree to the dating. I'll speak to your father here in Dubai. We'll make sure everything is right."

But she hesitated, explaining, "My father's tied up with his business in the Philippines. He won't be coming to Dubai anytime soon."

Her fear of wealthy individuals stayed. "It seems you are a family-oriented man. But I'm terribly afraid of moneyed people like you. I've heard stories," she said.

I replied, "You'll see, MJ. Not everyone fits the stereotypes. Please understand. One day, I'll prove it to you that all rich people are not bad and all poor ones are good. Good and bad permeate every section of society."

With that, I left her near her office, hopeful that one day she'd see beyond the misconceptions and take a chance on us.

A surprise phone call

I intentionally kept my distance from MJ and Joanna for a while, letting them mull over our previous conversations. I wanted MJ to ponder on what I had said, to truly understand my intentions.

After a few days, I decided to surprise MJ with a call. As soon as she saw my number, she picked up, probably curious about why I was calling after the hiatus.

But instead of speaking to her directly, I handed the phone to someone else nearby. When she heard his voice, she was astonished. It was her father. I was having lunch with him and her brother in her village in the Philippines. Her father was thrilled to chat with her.

"Your friend Dileep came all the way from Dubai to meet me," her father said, "We had a great chat about ourselves. He told me in detail about what he's doing. Turns out, Dileep and I are both civil engineers, so we had a lot to talk about in our field. Isn't your brother studying civil engineering? Well, he joined us too. So now, we've got a little civil engineering team going on here."

Her father laughed heartily.

MJ was taken aback by the unexpected call from her father, especially since he had such positive things to say about me. It shattered her preconceived notions and made her see me in a new light.

Even in her wildest dreams, she might not have thought that I'd go all he way to the Philippines to meet her father.

I owe Joanna a big thank you for sharing MJ's home address in the Philippines without her knowledge. Joanna and Alain knew my plan, but they played along and did not divulge it. And to bond with her father, who loved playing chess, I spent some time over a game at her house. He enjoyed it throughly. Delighted to have a guest, a fellow chess player, and someone to converse with after a long time, he felt a surge of happiness.

We ended our chess games after promising to continue them on my next visit to the Philippines. My mind whispered: the next time, I'd be here, it would be to ask for MJ's hand in marriage.

There was a sliver of hope. Perhaps this unexpected turn of events was a sign that things could be different, that her carefully constructed walls could crumble in the face of genuine connection.

When I returned to Dubai, I received a message from MJ, acknowledging my efforts and expressing her admiration for my persistence.

"You're one of a kind. I've never met anyone as determined as you, willing to go the extra mile to pursue what you want in life," she texted.

I took it as a compliment and a sign of progress.

The next day, I invited her to join me at the Emirates Golf Club. She arrived. We walked 11 km along the course and spent four-and-a-half hours together, watching a game between me and my dear friend Walid Alattar. I wanted her to take an interest in golf.

It was our first date. Perhaps, it's a coincidence that it happened on the golf course.

She wore a jeans and a T-shirt.

"If you wear a golfer's dress, you'll look more beautiful," I suggested.

I took her to Pro-Shop and got her a golf dress before taking her to the fairways. The new dress transformed her into a vision of elegance on the green. She had the looks of an international golfer.

As she was a model, any dress suited her. Any apparel enhanced her beauty.

She soon joined me in playing golf. I arranged a trainer for her. MJ and I spent a lot of time together, thanks to golf. She became an admirer of golf. I became hers.

The driving range and practice green soon became her happy place. Mine too.

As we discovered our shared love for food, trying various dishes from different restaurants, I realised how similar our tastes were. She enjoyed golf, sports and good food, just like me. We went to countless restaurants around, trying out different cuisines. It felt like we were cut from the same cloth, sharing not just interests, but a deep connection.

15

The beginning of us

After a few months, it became clear to me that there was a strong connection between us. MJ became my ultimate mission and purpose. All the friendships and romances I've had along the way have led me to her. It was through those experiences that I truly understood the greatness and love of MJ.

There's a truth to the saying that God has a plan. Though the path may be winding, with unexpected turns and experiences, it ultimately leads us toward our purpose. This has certainly been the case for me. Many things came before this moment, each shaping me and preparing me to find the love of my life.

Finally, the dream I held so dear has blossomed. This isn't just a single momentous occasion; it's the culmination of a life journey. It's a powerful reminder of perseverance and the belief that when you truly desire something, and work towards it, it can become reality.

But even the grandest dreams are richer when shared. Throughout my climb towards success, what I craved most was a partner in life, a soulmate who would understand and love me unconditionally. My heart overflows with gratitude that this ardent wish has come true.

Once her initial anxieties about becoming my girlfriend subsided, we had a candid conversation. "I'm older than you," I began, "and I understand the realities of you entering my life and the lives of my children. They are my top priority, but you come after them. We need to raise them together as if they were our own."

Her smile and unwavering agreement warmed my heart. More importantly, her behaviour and the love she showered on my children spoke volumes.

After we started seeing each other, I took MJ and the children on a visit to my hometown of Edappal. My mother was seeing me with a woman for the first time after my divorce. It was heartwarming to see MJ bond with my mother right from the start. I knew my mom would adore MJ, and their instant connection proved me right. My mother has an inherent ability to read people.

During her time in Edappal, MJ embraced the local culture wholeheartedly. She enjoyed the simple pleasures of life, like sipping tea, and having vada and pazhampori, at the local tea shop and exploring the wide range of Kerala's cuisine. The traditional feast (Naadan Sadya) and pappadam became her favourite dishes.

We decided to get married. Our wedding ceremony reflected this commitment, a simple gathering of our closest friends and family. With just the soft murmur of loved ones as a backdrop, we began this new chapter together, our love the sole adornment of the occasion.

We called on our dear ones. We called on Parutty Chechi and Devan and spent time with them.

MJ wanted to get a taste of the rest of India. We visited Kochi, Kumarakom, Udaipur, New Delhi, Mumbai and Agra. Witnessing her awe at India's rich history and cultural heritage was truly rewarding.

MJ quickly became not just my wife, but also my best friend, golf partner and confidante. Our relationship blossomed into a beautiful partnership. She's an invaluable partner in everything I do. From meticulously charting my meetings to ensuring a smooth-running household, her attention to detail leaves its mark on every aspect of our lives.

This journey together has been one of mutual learning. Just as I've grown from her dedication and organisation, I hope she's found value in my experiences and perspectives.

The knowledge I've acquired throughout my life, from MJ and from countless others, has become the driving force behind my achievements.

The desire to carve my own path has always been a defining aspect of my personality. I actively seek out knowledge and experiences from others. It's this constant learning and adaptation that allows me to stand out and conquer new heights. Following the well-trodden path may offer a sense of safety and predictability, but it prevents me from truly challenging myself and reaching my full potential.

While youthful dreams might sometimes be dismissed as mere fantasies, choosing to chase them can be life-changing. My own aspirations weren't just for myself; I envisioned a better life for my friends and companions as well. I trained my mind to dream big and persevere in pursuit of those dreams. Programming my body and work ethic to align with my mental aspirations played a crucial role in achieving a successful career and a higher quality of life.

The journey from having no rupees to becoming a millionaire is a proof of the power of focussed effort. My mind set the goal, and my body followed suit. Through sheer strength of will, I achieved what once seemed like an impossible dream.

I always wanted to be different, not just be an ordinary person. My mind and brain always worked in a way to be totally different from others.

A model couple

MJ and I are considered a model couple.

Our differences are stark. Nationality, age, wealth, lifestyle, language, even physical attributes like height—none of it seem to align. Yet, beneath the surface, a deeper connection blooms. Compatibility isn't about external factors; it is about the meeting of minds and the harmony of souls. Thankfully, we share a remarkable alignment in interests—games, food, travel. Hours, days, months flew by without a hint of monotony.

MJ, my confidante and open-minded friend, has become an integral part of my life. We share everything, from the intricacies of business to the joys and challenges of raising children. My decisions are informed by her perspective.

I see her family's initial reservations about us as a natural concern arising from cultural differences. But MJ, with her love and strong belief in us, slowly chipped away at those doubts. Within a year, they too were swept up in the warmth of our connection, becoming not just in-laws but friends.

MJ, with her adventurous spirit, has imbibed my love for golf and tennis, becoming a skilled player herself. Every two months, we go on week-long journeys to new destinations. Sometimes, these adventures take us further, prompting relocations to experience new cultures and refine our golfing skills.

With MJ by my side, life sparkles with supreme joy. Despite being in my early fifties, I feel a youthful energy in me, both physically and mentally. A commitment to healthy living has formed a central principle of our well-being. We have prioritised nutritious meals, regular exercise and a positive mindset. MJ's presence, a constant source of positivity, matches my own optimistic outlook.

The presence of children further enrich our lives. Whenever their schedules allow, we revel in spending quality time together.

I realise the importance of physical and mental health. Material wealth pales in comparison to feeling energetic and alive. To achieve this, we are both dedicated to a holistic approach to well-being.

Food, the cornerstone of health, receive our careful attention. We understand the impact of diet on our longevity and overall health. Nourishing our bodies with wholesome foods that nurture our internal organs is a non-negotiable. Mindful eating habits, avoiding anything that could cause digestive distress, ensure our bodies function optimally.

Just like a well-oiled machine, our hearts, lungs and brains have served us non-stop since birth. We nourish them with care, ensuring their smooth operation for years to come. Regular meal timings are another key element. We aren't slaves to the clock, but eat when our bodies truly need nourishment. Drinking half a liter of water every morning is a ritual, rehydrating after a night's sleep and kickstarting the body's internal systems.

An early dinner, between 6 p.m. and 7 p.m., aids sleep and digestion.

Sleep, too, plays a vital role in our well-being. Early to bed and early to rise has become our habit. Exercise hasn't been relegated to just golf and tennis; we've incorporated walking, yoga and gym sessions into our routines for a well-rounded approach to fitness.

Mental well-being is equally important. We actively cultivate positivity, banishing negative thoughts whenever they arise. Focusing on the good in life cultivates a sense of happiness. Another key element is refraining from blaming others. Negative thoughts manifest as hurtful words, poisoning relationships. Instead, we opt for encouragement and praise.

Life's greatest joys, I often ponder, are simpler than we imagined. Food and water, the most basic necessities, bring immense satisfaction. Perhaps, the ease of access, has made us take them for granted. The true value of water becomes evident when thirst parches our throats. Similarly, the absence of food highlights its importance, reminding us of the sheer pleasure of a satisfying meal. The joy of finally satiating hunger surpasses any other feeling. Nothing else matters more in life.

The sweetest moments, however, are created when MJ, the children, and I are together.

MJ's journey has been a fascinating one. She achieved national recognition as a beauty queen and model, but she has chosen a different path. Coming from a regular family, she never harboured grand ambitions for a life in the spotlight. This grounded nature is one of the qualities I admire most about her.

But, eventually, she has ended up living a great life though she had never dreamt of it.

Irreplaceable: the one and only

MJ and I find joy in the simplest of things, much like each other. We share a common understanding that true wealth lies not in material possessions, but in the quality time we spend with our loved ones. Love and time are the most valuable gifts we can offer each other and they bring us immeasurable happiness. Money may improve our living conditions, but it can never buy true contentment.

I can't imagine another woman who embodies honesty and simplicity as MJ does. The best part is that she has never loved money. There are moments when I'm genuinely awestruck by her grace and humility. It's almost as if she's one of a kind, like God crafted her with special care and decided she'd be the only one of her kind. I don't say this lightly—MJ truly feels like an angel sent into my life by a higher power.

MJ is not without her flaws. She's open about her hearing impairment, which can be challenging at times. But our communication has never suffered because of it. I love her for who she is, weaknesses and all.

Our age difference, rather than being a hindrance, has become a source of mutual learning and growth. I provide her with guidance and support when she needs it. And in return, she enriches my life with her unique perspectives and experiences.

Like any woman, MJ has her moments of tension and mood swings. It's essential for men to stand by their partners during these times, offering strength and support instead of criticism. Creating a peaceful and supportive atmosphere at home is crucial, especially during challenging moments.

Our children have wholeheartedly accepted MJ as their mother figure. They look up to her for guidance and support, and she handles their affairs with care. She's taken on the responsibilities of running our household and managing my affairs, demonstrating remarkable maturity and capability.

Since MJ entered our lives, our home has been filled with joy and harmony. She's restored the happiness and warmth that we lost after the divorce, bringing us together as a complete and happy family.

One day, curious about the spark in our relationship despite our apparent differences, I asked MJ why we clicked so well.

With a playful smile, she replied, "DK, you're intelligent, competent, smart, and handsome. Me? Well, I'm a bit of an idiot!" She chuckled, then added, "You know, like opposite forces attracting each other—positive and negative. That's the secret to our connection, I guess."

Her teasing response, though lighthearted, left me pondering. Perhaps there was some truth to her playful jab. Maybe our contrasting personalities, rather than creating friction, somehow balanced each other out.

A small smile crept across my face.

I can't help but feel grateful to have her by my side. It's as if God chose me to cherish His finest creation, and for that, I'll forever be thankful.

Footprints across continents

I've travelled to almost every corner of the globe, making countless trips since 1991—around 375 flights. But for me, travelling isn't just about ticking off countries on a map. It's about finding happiness in new places, experiences and people.

Every journey is an opportunity to refresh my mind and spirit, like a flowing river that's new every moment. Each trip brings new sights, new flavours and new lessons.

Travelling is like a pilgrimage, washing away all worries and problems. And wherever I go, I make it a point to help out those in need I meet during my travels.

Once, while in Beijing with MJ, we had trouble finding a taxi willing to take us a short distance. One driver reluctantly agreed. When we reached our destination, I handed him extra cash along with the fare.

MJ was puzzled. "Why give him so much when he initially refused?"

"He's struggling to make ends meet," I explained. "I noticed he had no legs—his artificial ones were in the cabin."

MJ was surprised. "How did you know?"

"I observed," I replied, "and felt compelled to help. This is a lesson for him. Never again would he turn away passengers on the grounds that the distance is too short. He must have realised by now that he might be recognised by someone he doesn't know."

This experience aligns perfectly with my philosophy on charity. I believe in giving directly to those in need, bypassing intermediaries. Timely assistance is crucial and bragging about good deeds diminishes their impact. These three principles—directness, timeliness and humility—are the highlights of my charitable giving.

The joy of giving transcends the material value of the gift. While what we offer might seem small to the recipient, the satisfaction we experience is immeasurable. It's important to remember, we are not gods; we can't solve everyone's problems. But within our means, the act of giving itself is a powerful act of compassion.

My travels have instilled in me a deep appreciation for culinary diversity. I greet the unique flavors of every country I visit, savouring each dish with an open mind. I take the extra step to seek out local specialties, understanding that these signature dishes are not just food, but a reflection of history, culture and tradition.

French fries and Onasadya

My travels have opened my eyes to a world of curious experiences. One question I frequently encounter from my foreign friends is, "Why do Indians eat with their hands?" It seems to clash with their cultural norms and dining etiquette. My initial response was always a simple explanation based on tradition: "This lifestyle has been passed down to us through generations."

However, this answer never truly satisfied me, leaving me curious about the deeper significance behind this custom. It was during a journey that I began to gather some clues about the secret of this habit.

Let me tell you about this dining experience at the luxurious Peninsula Hotel in Hong Kong. I was accompanied by my friend Rosalina, a fellow food enthusiast. As we sat down to enjoy our meal, something caught my eye: while Rosalina elegantly wielded her knife and fork for most dishes, she had a peculiar habit of reaching for her French fries with her bare hands.

Intrigued, I couldn't help but ask, "Rosalina, why do you only eat French fries with your hands?"

With a playful smile, she replied, "It's just a habit, I suppose. We, Asians, have always done it this way."

But her answer sparked a revelation within me, a revelation about our Indian tradition of eating with our hands. I decided to share my newfound insight with Rosalina.

"You see," I began, "when you eat with your hands, you engage all five senses. Touch, being the fifth sense, plays a crucial role in how we experience food. When we touch our food, we're not just feeling its texture; we're also sending signals to our brain about its temperature, size and quantity. It's a sensory experience unlike any other."

We can't even imagine eating a Malayali's favourite Onasadya (Onam feast served on banana leaves) with a spoon. The true essence of the meal is lost when using a spoon. Only by eating with our hands can we fully experience the rich and intricate flavours of Onasadya. To savour every taste and texture, the food must be picked up and enjoyed with our hands.

Rosalina's eyes widened with curiosity. "So, this is why Indians eat with their hands?" she asked.

"I guess so," I nodded. "It's about fully giving yourself to the flavours and textures of the food. And this is why you use your hands to have French fries. Your fifth sense comes into play even without your knowledge."

From that moment on, Rosalina looked at French fries in a whole new light.

Romancing the rain

One of the most fascinating things I've noticed during my travels is the uncanny connection I seem to have with rain. It's like wherever I go, the rain follows. It's become somewhat of a running joke among my friends, who've come to expect rain-soaked photos from my trips.

Take my trip to the U.S., for example. I started off in New York, where it poured down like there was no tomorrow. And when I moved on to Los Angeles and Florida, the rain followed me there too. It's like I brought a rain cloud along for the ride, hitting every city I visited.

But sometimes, there are surprises. Like that time in Hong Kong back in 2015. For five whole days, there wasn't a drop of rain in sight. My friend, who was in on the rain joke, couldn't resist poking fun as we headed to the airport. "Did you forget to bring the rain this time?" he teased.

I played along, but deep down, I had my doubts. Yet, as luck would have it, as soon as I stepped out of the car at the airport, the heavens opened up. My friend couldn't help but laugh at the sheer coincidence and I just shrugged it off with a smile.

These little quirks and curiosities of travel never fail to amuse me. And it's not just about rain; even the simple act of going to a hotel for a meal can turn into a head-scratcher. I'll walk into an empty restaurant, but by the time I'm done eating, it's packed to the brim. It's like I bring a wave of people along with me wherever I go.

I've developed a habit of jotting down my thoughts and experiences. Whether it's the sights I've seen, the people I've met or just random musings, putting pen to paper helps me make sense of it all.

But perhaps the most enriching part of my travels is connecting with the everyday folks—the hotel staff, taxi drivers, street vendors. I've always found their stories to be the true heartbeat of a country. It's through them that I get a real sense of what a place is all about and their recommendations never disappoint when it comes to experiencing the authentic flavours of a country.

Wanderlust and remarkable faces

Trusting my gut has always been my go-to, especially when it comes to dealing with people during my travels. One incident that stands out is when I was in New Delhi and had this amazing Uber driver whom we hired for a whole day when we visited Taj Mahal. Facing resistance from other drivers, he stuck by me and made sure I reached my destinations safely. To show my gratitude, I deposited a hefty sum into his account as a token of appreciation.

He folded his hands in a gesture of respect and said, "This is the first time anything like this has happened to me. Why did you give me so much money?"

Smiling, I replied, "You deserve every rupee of it. Honestly, it brings me joy to give to people like you. You were the only driver who didn't try to cheat me. When everyone else was arguing and trying to inflate the fare, you were different. That kind of honesty deserves to be rewarded."

In fact, I've encountered many such people during my travels and some of them have even found their way to Dubai, where I've offered them jobs in my company. Till they reached Dubai, many of them did not know who I was. Throughout my travels, I maintain a low profile, keeping my identity a secret from most people. This allows me to experience new places and cultures on a more personal level. On a trip to New Delhi, I met driver Parminder Singh, who, unbeknownst to him, would become a familiar face in the years to come. Impressed by his qualities, I brought him to Dubai and offered him a position as my driver.

I've always been impressed by the honesty and integrity of everyday people.

One particular incident in Vietnam left a lasting impression on me and MJ. Late one night, stranded without a taxi in sight, a kind watchman took it upon himself to arrange an Uber for us and even contributed his own money to cover the fare. His selflessness moved us and we knew we had to do something to show our appreciation.

We gathered some cash, along with a few other items, and went back to the restaurant where he worked and handed over the gift.

"Your love has moved us. Please accept this as a token of our affection. Keep my number. Any time you need anything, give me a ring," I told him.

Interactions like these remind me of the goodness that exists in the world and it's moments like these that restore my faith in humanity.

16

India: no place quite like it

It stings a bit to hear some Keralites bad-mouthing Kerala or India. It's as if the good stuff back home gets forgotten, replaced by the allure of what they see in Europe or America.

Those places, I agree, might have better infrastructure—smoother roads, grand bridges and gleaming skyscrapers. But do they have the deep social connections we cherish in India? Having visited those very countries they idealise, I seriously doubt it.

India offers something far more valuable than flashy buildings or spotless streets: the warmth of family bonds, the strength of friendships, an inimitable way of life rooted in compassion and a deep-rooted respect for one another. That's a treasure you won't find everywhere.

India's tradition of compassion is fabled.

In the unfortunate event of an accident, bystanders in India are more likely to step in and assist the injured, even if they lack medical expertise, compared to some Western countries. This willingness to help transcends bystander apathy. Indian families are renowned for their strong support systems. During times of hardship, family members come together to share the burden and alleviate suffering.

The tradition of caring for elderly parents within the family is also more prevalent in India compared to many Western nations.

India's strong social structure is a national treasure. Talk about traditions and history. We've got more historical monuments and cultural heritage sites than you can shake a stick at. India's glory transcends the dazzling beauty of its palaces and the heart-stopping majesty of the Himalayas. It's a land where the echoes of ancient wisdom reverberate in every grain of sand. Here, history isn't confined to dusty museums; it's a living force woven into everyday life. Millennia-old philosophical traditions like Hinduism, Buddhism and Jainism continue to guide the Indian way of life. Here, fellow feeling and care aren't enshrined in dusty tomes; they bloom animatedly in the daily acts of life.

Our hospitality is second to none. We welcome guests with open arms, even if they end up taking advantage of our kindness. Remember how the Portuguese, the Dutch and the British exploited our love and colonised us for over two centuries? But we eventually sent them out.

So before we start singing the praises of other countries, let's take a moment to appreciate the greatness of our own.

Because, at the end of the day, there's no place like India. It's a land of wonders, where history, tradition and warmth come together in a way that's truly unique. As some of my foreign friends have said, India has a vibe that you just can't find anywhere else.

To quote Pandit Jawaharlal Nehru, "Who lives if India dies? Who dies if India lives?"

The unforgettable granny of Rome

Whenever I hear people comparing India to other countries, it brings back a vivid memory from 2006 when I was travelling in Rome with my family. We were staying at the InterContinental Rome Ambasciatori Palace near the famous Spanish Steps.

Every day, as we left the hotel and returned in the evening, I noticed an elderly lady sitting alone in the nearby park. She seemed lost in thought, muttering to herself. After seeing her there for several days, I decided to approach her and strike up a conversation. I felt compelled to help if I could.

"Excuse me, do you live nearby?" I asked.

She responded in broken English, "No, not near. A little far."

Curious, I inquired further, "Then why do you always come here? I've noticed you here every day."

She tried to smile but her eyes betrayed her sadness. "My son and his family live there," she gestured toward a large building nearby.

"So, you come here to visit them?" I pressed.

Her smile faded and tears welled up in her eyes. "No," she choked out. "My grandson plays in this park. Whenever he has free time, he comes here to play. I never know when he'll come, but if I wait here, I might catch a glimpse of him."

Her words hit me hard. Here we were, in Rome, a city steeped in history and grandeur, yet witnessing the heartbreaking loneliness of this elderly woman waiting for her grandson. It made me question the true meaning of development and progress.

Rome boasts magnificent roads, bridges and buildings, adorned with marble statues that speak of its ancient glory. But what good are these accomplishments if they come at the cost of human connection and compassion?

Who else but us would recognise the true value of our country? Development isn't just about infrastructure; it's about nurturing the human spirit. India's greatness lies not in its monuments or highways, but in the compassion of its people. While Rome's legacy is carved in stone, India's spirit flows through generations. One builds monuments, the other builds relationships. True progress weaves both—a flourishing society with a soul.

Even though I travel extensively, my hometown remains my most frequent destination. There's no way I can imagine living without the connection to my country and its people. My family, friends, the serene landscapes and the love I feel for my homeland are all precious to me.

The world is an oyster

Each of us enters this vast world as a unique being. As for me, I'm not just a native of Edappal, Kerala or India, but a citizen of the world. Our existence transcends the boundaries of villages, towns and countries. This world is our playground.

Our perspective should extend beyond the confines of our immediate surroundings. Life is not meant to be lived within the narrow confines of our hometowns or nations. The world is vast and rich with diverse experiences waiting to be discovered. We should embrace the chance to see, learn and experience all that it has to offer.

We're not meant to merely exist, going through the motions like passengers on a bus tour. Travelling shouldn't be about just reaching a destination, ticking off boxes and heading back home.

For instance, we want to go on a trip to Munnar. Catching a bus to the Munnar station and back is just a way to get there, it's not real travel. True travel is about giving yourself completely to a new place. It's about exploring the breathtaking landscapes of Munnar, visiting its sights, interacting with the locals, tasting the local food and experiencing the unique culture. That's when a trip becomes an unforgettable adventure.

Our journey on this earth is akin to the spinning of the globe, constantly evolving and expanding. We should seek out new experiences, revisit favourite destinations and return home enriched with fresh perspectives.

For me, the Malayalam movie 'Love in Singapore' sparked a desire to explore the world. My first holiday trip was to Singapore, and since then, I've returned multiple times. Recently, I had the opportunity to attend a live concert by the renowned American singer Taylor Swift in Singapore, making my trip even more unforgettable. As the movie title mentioned, it really was 'Love in Singapore'!

Pencils and places

I've shared with you the role a simple pencil played in shaping my life. Remember how I mentioned that receiving a foreign pencil as a gift from Cheriyachan marked a significant moment for me? It was the first foreign-made gift I got.

That pencil sparked my wanderlust for exploring foreign lands. To honour that memory, wherever I go, I make it a point to collect pencils from that country as souvenirs of my travels from the hotels I stayed in and the golf courses I played in.

You'd be surprised where you can find these pencils. Sometimes they're readily available in plush hotels, while other times, I have to specially request them from places that don't normally provide them. I have a preference for pencils over pens, so I always ask for pencils, even if pens are on offer.

As of now, I've amassed a collection of more than 170 pencils from various countries, including ones from hotels and golf courses abroad. Interestingly, golf courses often hand out their native pencils for keeping score during a game.

I keep them not just as souvenirs, but as reminders of my past. It underscores my view: never forget the past.

Pencils, those unassuming writing tools, hold a surprising amount of variety. There's no single industry standard for pencil lead composition, meaning the feel of a pencil can vary dramatically depending on where it comes from. Let me take you on a journey through the world of renowned pencils across the globe.

Koh-i-Noor pencils of Czech Republic boast a rich history, using methods practically unchanged since the 1790s! The iconic Koh-i-Noor 1500, the world's first yellow pencil, debuted at the

Paris World's Fair in 1889 and then the Chicago World's Fair in 1893, influencing American pencil manufacturing.

Calepino pencils, crafted in the Loire region of France, are made by the sole remaining non-Bic pencil factory in France. They use FSC-certified Pulay wood and take their name from 15th-century scholar Ambrogio Calepino, known as 'Calepin', In French, 'calepin' means 'little notebook'.

Hindustan Pencils of India are the makers behind the popular Nataraj, Apsara and Sivo pencils. These pencils prioritise eco-friendliness, using soft woods like linden or poplar sourced from local farms and even residential areas. Hindustan manufactures nearly all its materials in-house, including the tiny screws on their sharpeners.

Japanese pencils are renowned for their exceptional smoothness and darkness. An HB pencil from Japan might feel more like a B or even a 2B from elsewhere. They typically boast high quality, featuring centred cores, California Incense Cedar wood, and meticulous finishing details (including an average of 14 coats of paint!). Japanese pencils often incorporate a bit of polymer in the graphite, making them less smudge-prone. Interestingly, many Japanese pencils have pre-determined designations like 'Master Writing' or 'Office Use'. This practice originated from a time with strict pricing regulations on school and office supplies.

The most famous pencil from Shahsons of Pakistan is the Goldfish Autocrat, which used to be delightfully scented like sandalwood!

The creative director of Viarco Pencils of Portugal designed their beautiful scented pencils inspired by the plants his grandmother grew in her backyard.

Milan pencils of Spain are known for their innovative designs, featuring unusual shapes and even combination pencils with graphite and highlighter functions.

Caran d'Ache pencils of Switzerland, offer excellent quality. They typically use California Incense Cedar (except for their exotic wood pencils) and are named after a 19th-century French cartoonist's pseudonym. Many US pencils use California Incense Cedar as well, but some opt for lower-cost wood alternatives. According to Guinness World Records, the largest pencil collection belongs to Aaron Bartholmey (USA) with a staggering 69,255 items. His passion began in first grade, collecting these affordable treasures at flea markets with his grandpa. His collection is meticulously organised by city and state, with a special place for pencils offering a glimpse into history.

I cherish my pencil collection dearly, keeping them safe in a special box at home. Sometimes, I entertain the idea of arranging and framing them on my wall as a unique piece of art. However, with new additions to the collection every month, courtesy of my ongoing travels, that dream seems elusive. After all, my journey will continue until the ultimate adventure of life comes to an end. And the pencils will keep coming till then.

To Kerala, to meet Babu

Reconnecting with old friends and relatives always brings a sense of renewal to my spirit.

Reminiscing about the past always brings me immense joy. Regular phone calls keep those memories alive, but there's nothing quite like sharing a traditional Kerala feast with friends and relatives. Every moment with them feels like a trip down memory lane, transporting me back to a time of carefree youth.

I stay in touch with Maniyettan and Kuttettan, two friends who have been part of my life for a long time. During my time working in Mumbai, I used to frequent Maniyettan's house regularly. They were like family to me during my stint in Mumbai.

Back in 1990, when I started my journey from Kuttipuram railway station to Mumbai in search of work, my dear friend Babu was there to see me off. I remember vividly how I rode on Babu's bike to reach Kuttipuram station that day.

Recently, when I tried reaching out to Babu, I couldn't get through to him directly. Instead, I received a message from his wife Bindu, informing me that Babu had suffered a stroke and was now in a coma.

The news shattered me. Babu had always been carefree about his health. Hearing about his condition shook me to the core. I assured Bindu that we, his friends, would do everything in our power to support him and arrange for his treatment.

"Babu is my closest friend. Don't you worry, let's do everything possible to get him back to how he was," I told her.

When I finally visited Babu's house in Kerala, it was heartbreaking to see him lying there motionless, barely able to breathe. The sight was unbearable. A tear escaped my eye, tracing a path down my cheek.

"I don't know if Babu knows you have come," Bindu said with a heavy heart.

"True, it would have been a great comfort to him if he had known that we friends had come to see him and were with him," I replied, a lump forming in my throat.

I made it a point to visit Babu whenever I was in Kerala, but sadly, his condition remained unchanged for a year. I often found relief in prayer, hoping that he wouldn't suffer.

After enduring a year in a coma, Babu bid farewell to this world. His passing left a void in my heart that was hard to bear, but I took comfort in knowing that he was now free from pain.

I'll never forget Babu till my last breath. No words can express what he meant to me. So close we were. I still can't believe that he is no more. Some friends leave such an impression on our lives that even in death, they live on as treasured memories.

Turkish Open World Amateur Championship final

In 2019, I was blessed with another stroke of luck, this time courtesy of the Dubai Creek Golf and Yacht Club. I had the opportunity to once again represent the UAE in the finals of the World Amateur Championship. It was an honour to wave the UAE flag proudly at the Turkish Airlines World Golf Final held in Turkey.

The day after my dear friend Babu passed away, I found myself on the golf course, playing the qualifying round for the Championship at the Dubai Creek Golf and Yacht Club in Dubai. It was a heavy day, with thoughts of Babu weighing on my mind. Was it right to be out here playing, just a day after his passing?

After much contemplation, I came to a resolute decision. If Babu were here, he would undoubtedly urge me to play. So, why not honour his memory and play for him?

I confided in MJ, expressing my sentiments. "If I win today and make it to the championship, it'll be a sign that Babu's spirit is guiding me. My victory will be a proof of his happiness."

With that resolve, I took to the course. To my amazement, I emerged victorious in all the qualifying contests, securing my spot in the World Championship. Not only did I win, but I clinched a hard-fought match, narrowly defeating my opponent to seal my qualification.

Representing the UAE for the second time in the World Amateur Golf Championship was a momentous achievement for me. I owe a great deal of gratitude to the Dubai Creek Golf and Yacht Club and to Shihabka, my old labour camp driver who first showed me a golf course. Winning all my preliminary matches at the Dubai Creek Golf and Yacht Club felt particularly sweet. It was on that very course, years ago, that the dream of becoming a golfer first sparked within me. This achievement felt like a beautiful full circle moment. Life connects things in unexpected ways. There's a pattern to be found if we pay close attention to the experiences that shape us.

Settling in Emirates Hills

In 2016, I made the decision to purchase a plot in Emirates Hills with the intention of building a house. However, construction hadn't commenced in the area yet. In the meantime, MJ, the kids, and I settled into a relatively modest house in Meadows-4, also in the vicinity of Emirates Hills.

The plan to build our dream home was put on hold, mainly because everyone felt that a large house wasn't necessary at the time. But our current residence in Meadows lacked adequate parking space, leaving three cars exposed to the sun without shelter.

Initially, the children were on board with the idea of a new house. But their priorities shifted when they expressed their desire to pursue higher education in London a few years down the line. They didn't feel comfortable with MJ and me living alone in a big house, and MJ herself wasn't keen on the idea either.

Considering everyone's sentiments, I decided to shelve the plan to build on the purchased land. Instead, we contemplated selling both the land and our current house. When we reached out to real estate agents, we received numerous offers, albeit below the price I had originally paid. Many suggested lowering the price to attract buyers looking for a profitable deal. However, after considering their offers, I opted to hold off on selling for the time being.

During a visit to the property with my eldest son, Gautam, after the Covid situation eased, he expressed his sentiment about the place. After thoroughly inspecting the existing house and its amenities, he shared his thoughts with me.

"Don't sell this place. It's unlikely we'll find a better spot in Dubai," he remarked.

I agreed. I realised that simply maintaining the old house wasn't my intention either. I proposed a plan to renovate the existing house according to our preferences and needs. We could start by building a new house on the land, with the option to move in later or sell it, depending on everyone's interests.

Thankfully, both my sons and MJ were on board with the plan. With no intention to sell the land, the idea of constructing a new house seemed like a promising venture.

The Covid-19 pandemic definitely played a role in my desire for a bigger house. As everyone, myself included, spent more time at home, the limitations of our current space became clear. The kids were growing up and needed their own areas to pursue hobbies and entertain friends. Similarly, I wanted guests to feel comfortable and have space to relax during visits.

As a property developer, I've never been one to hold onto vacant land for long periods. I always get an itch to design and build a new house on a plot. After all, what's the point of hard-earned money if it can't be used to enhance our happiness and enjoyment? This time, I wanted to build a house specifically tailored to my family's needs and desires, on land I had already purchased. While I knew there would likely be interested buyers once the house was complete, my priorities had shifted. The phase of selling every house I built for the family was over—this one was for us.

Like father, like son

My elder son Gautam is truly carving his own path, and I can't be prouder. He was offered the chance to study business management in London, but he made a bold decision to stay and study in Dubai while gaining hands-on experience as a part-time trainee at Heilbronn. His initiative fills me and MJ with immense pride.

When Gautam shared his decision with me upon receiving admission to London, I was pleasantly surprised.

"Dad, like you, I want to start working early in life. Attending a college in Dubai, shall I work part-time in your company?" he asked me.

His demand brought tears in my eyes.

His maturity and sense of responsibility have been evident at various junctures, especially in his caring relationship with his younger brother Aryaan. I proudly and wholeheartedly supported Gautam's choice.

"Absolutely, you can work on the site as you wish," I assured him.

While juggling college and work, Gautam diligently puts in hours under the sun, sacrificing the opportunity to enjoy the pleasant climate of London. It's not about income but learning first-hand from the site. However, I insisted that he take at least one day off per week, recognising the importance of balancing work and rest, especially at his age.

Gautam's willingness to work from a young age reminds me of my own childhood. While my friends played football, I accompanied my father to the farm, carrying the pipe of the motor on my shoulder, to improve the family income. Now, Gautam was working for the company sacrificing the time he could've spent with his friends.

My advice to him draws from the lessons I've learned over the years: "Strive for excellence in your work. Only by outperforming your senior managers can you rise above them. Survival is the ultimate lesson of Nature and living beings. Just observe the animal kingdom; the most successful are those who endure the longest. Similarly, in life, only those who adapt and persist thrive."

I acknowledge the sacrifices millions of Indian parents, like mine, make for their children's future, often at the expense of their own happiness. However, I advocate for a balanced approach, where parents enjoy the fruits of their labour without solely spending it all for their children. Our spouses, who support us tirelessly, deserve a share in life's joys and rewards. It's essential to prioritise self-care and well-being.

There's a misconception that financial security for our children means saving every penny. But that approach can underestimate their potential. Many children are talented, intelligent and capable of achieving great things. They might even surpass our own achievements! And they should. We shouldn't limit their drive and work ethic by leaving them with a massive inheritance. Let them build their own successes.

Of course, not every child will follow the same path. If your children are capable and driven, they'll find their own financial success. However, a large inheritance for someone who isn't prepared to manage it could lead to them squandering those resources.

The key is finding a balance. Leaving a comfortable legacy for your children can be a wonderful thing, but it shouldn't replace the valuable lessons learned through hard work and personal responsibility.

Hoarding wealth also hinders progress. Money sitting dormant in a bank or hidden away benefits no one. A healthy economy relies on the circulation of wealth and that circulation leads to innovation and growth.

Hello, new home

The journey from buying the plot to witnessing the completion of our new house in Emirates Hills was nothing short of a miracle. Within just 18 months, the Heilbronn company worked tirelessly to bring our vision to life.

It's almost impossible to recognise it as the same old house. The value of the property has soared, with offers pouring in at six times the original price. However, for me, this house is priceless—it's not just a property, but a home for my family.

To those interested in buying, I simply couldn't put a price on the sentimental value of our home. It's a place where memories are made, where every corner holds a story of its own.

A while back, I would have considered selling this house. But not anymore. No matter the offer, it wouldn't be enough. This place holds a value far greater than any amount of money.

"It just feels right," I'd tell potential buyers. "This is where I'm supposed to be, with my family by my side."

Moving from Meadows to our new abode was a significant transition. The amenities in our new house cater to every aspect of our lifestyle. From ample parking space for all my cars to a state-of-the-art theatre room, a play area, a snooker room and a refreshing swimming pool—we've created a haven for relaxation and entertainment.

One of my favourite features is the spacious bathroom with glass walls, reminiscent of my childhood days spent gazing at the sky and listening to the chirping of birds. It's a space where I often find myself lost in deep thoughts, much like I did as a child. Just like a jolt of reality used to snap me out of daydreams when Amma came to scold me as a kid, MJ's calls now have the same effect when I lose myself in thought in the bathroom.

As fate would have it, the numbers associated with our house hold a special significance in my life's journey.

Numbers seem to follow me around! In Emirates Hills, my old villa was number E183. Interestingly, the sum of its digits (1 + 8 + 3) is 12, which also happens to be my college registration number. This coincidence continued when I bought a villa numbered 12 in the Meadows-4 golf course community. Even now, the current villa I reside in Emirates Hills has the number HT15. Adding the digits of this number (1 + 5) results in 6, which, coincidentally, is my school registration number!

As we moved into the new house, Gautam's words struck a deep chord. "Dad," he said, his voice swimming in pride, "you've worked so hard for all this. Look at this beautiful house—it's all thanks to your savings. You deserve the very best in life. It's already overdue."

My eyes misted over as I pulled him into a hug. They weren't tears of sadness, but of quiet satisfaction. In that embrace with Gautam, the years of hard work felt truly worthwhile.

17

A 30-year search ends

It's absolutely mind-boggling to think about how friendships can weave through the most unexpected paths.

One morning, I was relaxing at home, scrolling through my phone, when out of the blue, I got a message from an unfamiliar number. I had the shock of my life. I couldn't believe it: the name of the sender of the message was Pramod.

Thirty years. It felt surreal. My old school friend, reaching out after vanishing without a trace for so long. My unending search, ignited by worry and a desire to reconnect, had yielded nothing. Rumours swirled—a failed business, mounting debts, then silence. Unable to pay up the debts, he left home. Yet, his pride did not allow him to contact me or his other friends. Perhaps he considered working hard, marshalling funds and clearing his debts. The image of Pramod struggling, unseen and alone, gnawed at me. Knowing his situation, we, his friends, contacted his mother and brother and told them to ask him to return to Kerala if he called. He owed some money to banks and a few people. I'd vowed to help if he ever reappeared, even promising his family to settle his debts. But he was unseen, leaving behind a trail of worried faces and unanswered questions.

We suspected that his mother and his brother knew where Pramod was. But they did not reveal his whereabouts, perhaps, fearing the creditors.

Imagine my astonishment when that message shattered the silence. My finger dialled the number without hesitation, and Pramod's voice, unchanged by time, filled my ears. It was like stepping into a time machine. The years must have painted lines on his face. All I could make out was the vibrancy of his youth replaced by the quiet hum of survival. He was still single at 53, scraping by with odd jobs in Chennai. Yet, beneath the weathered exterior, there he was—Pramod, with the same warmth, innocence and affection that had always marked our bond.

We spent hours catching up, the years vanishing, like floating bubbles, as we exchanged stories. Relief and a deep sense of joy ensued as I learned about his life. Finally, I insisted on helping him, setting up a monthly stipend to ease his financial burden. I asked him to send me his bank account details. Some might have written stories and made movies inspired by lives like his but the sad fact remained: Pramod still struggled to make ends meet.

As the call neared its end, a thought struck me—a bold proposition. Why not have a reunion in Kerala after all these years at our convenience? He agreed.

Even after hanging up, the weight of the moment settled in. Three decades of searching, punctuated by a constant, nagging worry. And here he was, back in my life. This was the moment I was waiting for in the past 30 years. The impact he had on my journey, the inspiration he provided as I transformed from Dileep of Edappal to Dileep Heilbronn—that bond remained. I wondered how I lived those 30 years without him.

Retracing my Mumbai days

Some journeys burrow themselves deep within your soul, not just for the sights, but for the least expected twists that rewrite your narrative.

My 2022 trip to Mumbai with MJ was one such experience. We were crisscrossing India, and Mumbai, the city inscribed in my very being, couldn't be missed.

Mumbai wasn't just a place; it was a living, breathing chapter of my life. Every street corner, every screech of the local trains, every inch of that tiny room I once called home—they were all fragments of my story. Stepping back into Mumbai felt like a homecoming, a chance to relive the familiar warmth after all those years that had flown by.

We went on a pilgrimage of sorts, revisiting landmarks that held immense significance for me. There was the office where I poured my sweat and dreams, the local trains that once carried me towards an uncertain future (a strange comfort, even with their familiar overcrowding!), and finally, the Ganesh Darshan building—a silent sentinel of a bygone era.

As we stood before the building, I became teary-eyed. I could see only ruins. It was like a physical blow—a part of my past, reduced to rubble. We spoke to some people lingering nearby, sharing stories and memories. We then moved on to the Flora building near the Bombay Stock Exchange, another silent witness to the hours I had invested there.

This trip to Mumbai was far more than a sightseeing tour; it was an exploration of my personal history. It was a chance for MJ to witness the battles I had fought, the aspirations I had chased and the sacrifices I had made to reach where I am today. And Mumbai, in its own way, touched her soul.

All that made Mumbai the dynamic, chaotic city was there—a wave of humid air thick with the scent of street food spices, exhaust fumes, brightly painted buildings adorned with Bollywood posters, crowds weaving through narrow lanes, the noise of vendors hawking their wares and the cacophony of honking horns. The experience left her breathless.

Debt of gratitude

When I think of Mumbai, Kuttettan's face is the first thing that pops into my head. He was more than just a friend and roommate—he was family.

After a bit of sleuthing, I finally tracked Kuttettan down and gave him a call.

"Hello, where are you? I'll come to where you are," he told me. He sounded the same old self, kind and gentle, I had met years ago.

Images of the past flashed through my mind—our old living quarter, the chapatis and the vegetable curry, with a hint of milk, he whipped up.

He soon showed up at The Oberoi, Mumbai, where MJ and I stayed.

Kuttettan had come a long way since our hostel days. He was running a painting company, while also serving as the secretary of a temple committee. Still a bachelor, he was living that simple, stoic life.

When Kuttettan sauntered into the hotel lobby, all neat and dapper, a flicker of uncertainty sparked in my mind. Forty-two years in Mumbai's infamous chaos—countless faces must have passed through the shared room we once called home. Could my name be just a distant echo in his memory, a wisp of smoke with no face attached?

But the moment our eyes met, the years seemed to vanish. A wide grin stretched across his face as he swept me into a bear hug

"Dileep...?"

His voice hitched, his gaze locking onto mine. A sheen of moisture formed in his eyes.

Over a meal at the hotel, we caught up on old times. And when I brought up his cooking, the memories hit him. He could not hide his tears.

I handed him an envelope with a hefty cheque inside.

As the time for departure neared, Kuttettan made a surprising request. “I have a wish,” he began hesitantly. “Can you make it come true?”

“Anything, Kuttettan. Absolutely anything,” I assured him.

He paused, then blurted out, “Can I see your room? I’ve never been in a five-star hotel, and I’m curious about all the fancy amenities.”

Speech momentarily left me. A wave of emotions swept through me as I grasped his hand and led him towards my room.

His eyes widened as he took in the luxurious space, his gaze eventually drawn to the window that showcased a breathtaking ocean view. Pointing towards the road stretching along the beach, Kuttettan’s voice held a hint of wonder. “Do you remember the days we sat on the street, dreaming of stepping inside this very hotel?”

A smile bloomed on my face. “Absolutely. It feels like yesterday.”

“Then,” he continued, a touch of awe in his voice, “you declared you’d stay in this hotel someday. And here we are! Isn’t God’s plan remarkable?”

A range of emotions flickered across his face—a mix of joy, wonder, and perhaps a tinge of wistfulness.

“For 42 years,” he said, a nostalgic sigh escaping his lips, “I’ve only seen this place from the outside. Now, I’m standing here, looking out from within. Thank you for making this possible.”

As he rose to leave, he added, “Though I haven’t known your wife for long, I can confidently say she’s one of the finest people I’ve met. You’re a lucky man.”

Kuttettan had confided in me earlier about his heart condition, a reason he preferred staying unmarried. "Who knows what the future holds?" he said softly. "Why drag someone else into potential suffering?"

I called a taxi for him and asked him to call back as soon as he reached his living quarter.

He did.

"Why the big cheque, Dileep?" he asked.

"You deserve more than this, brother," I replied. "And trust me, I can never repay you for everything you've done for me. But if you ever need anything, just give me a ring."

"Thank you, Dileep," he said. "I'll buy a gold chain with this. I had pawned mine last year to pay hospital bills."

After meeting Kuttettan, MJ and I returned to Dubai the next day. It was a heart-warming and satisfying experience for me and MJ.

Mumbai memories

I've never forgotten another face of my Mumbai days. When I first landed in the big city, feeling like a lost soul, this face gave me hope: Maniyettan. He was my only connection in that vast metropolis.

Maniyettan, along with his wife Sudha Chechi, now calls Pune home. Their daughter Nisha, whom I've always considered a sister, has made her nest in the U.S. with her husband. And it's all thanks to Maniyettan's hard work that they're living the good life now.

For ages, I've had this dream of bringing Maniyettan to Dubai. After countless attempts at persuasion, it finally happened in 2023. They accepted my invite and we welcomed them to Dubai with open arms.

It was an emotional moment when I showed Maniyettan the same suitcase he'd once lugged around for me back in Mumbai.

After a delightful few days in Dubai, Maniyettan and his family headed back home.

And then there's Radhettan (Radhakrishnan), a name written in my memory from my Mumbai days. He's the one who opened his doors and his heart, offering me a place to stay when I needed it most.

I miss Gopi. Mumbai in 1991. A rickety bus ride to the airport with Gopi by my side. I was heading for Dubai. We lost touch after that. I often think back to that journey.

These amazing souls have lit the way on my journey. God has sent them at the right time, at the right place. When I needed them, they were there. I've made it my mission to reconnect with as many of them as possible. But there's still one person missing: Anil, my old roommate in Mumbai who had his sights set on buying a welding machine. His whereabouts are lost to the labyrinth of time. I wonder if he ever got around to a welding machine or if he's still waiting for one. A deep sadness settled over me as I realised Babu and Prakash were gone. The thought of never seeing them again shattered me.

I'm still in touch with all my former room-mates at Ganesh Darshan, where I first lived in Mumbai.

An unexpected letter

One day, my cook handed me a letter. Our driver Sujit, a Bangladeshi who had been with us for over 15 years, gave the cook the letter and asked him to pass it on to me. The letter, addressed to me, threw me for a loop. In this digital age of emails and WhatsApp, receiving a handwritten letter looked downright odd. And as I scanned the handwriting, a sense of familiarity gripped me.

But when I flipped to the second page and saw the signature, my jaw practically hit the floor. It was from my ex-wife, written in her hand. As I went through the letter, I couldn't believe what I was reading. It was an apology, a heartfelt one at that. I took 10 minutes to read the letter. She owned up to her part in our divorce, expressing regret for not understanding me better back then. She showered me with compliments, thanking me for being the best dad our kids could ask for.

She wanted to move to London and asked for my permission to list me as a nominee on her assets declaration. It was a shock, yet strangely touching to know she still trusted me in that way.

She was sending a message years after the divorce.

After mulling over the letter, I decided not to reply directly. Instead, I shared it with our sons, explaining its contents and asking them to convey my response to their mom.

My reply was simple: "Thank you for your kind words, but it's best to prioritise our children as your nominees. They're your legacy, after all."

With that, I tucked the letter away in my personal collection, a memento of our shared past.

Though our divorce created distance, I've always emphasised to our children the importance of maintaining a loving connection with their mother. Financially, I'll always be there to help if needed, but they're her rock. I explain that while my legal and emotional connection with her might be limited, that doesn't diminish the bond they share. "Give her the love and support she needs," I tell them. After all, no court can sever the powerful tie between a mother and her children.

In 2018, she wrote to me about relocating to London. In December of the same year, the children told me, "Amma is returning to Dubai for good. It would be nice if an apartment is arranged for her to stay."

I remembered a promise I made during our divorce that I'd be around when she wanted help.

"Convey to your mum that I'll give her a villa of mine to stay. She may stay there as long as she wants," I told the kids. They became happy.

"Did she mention any financial needs?" I asked the kids.

"No," they chorussed. "She just needs a place to stay."

I offered her one of my villas and that's where she resides today.

My children have grown up witnessing the respect I hold for their mother, even after our divorce. This respect has, in turn, become the foundation of their relationship with her. They readily offer help and support whenever she needs them.

Children's most influential guides are their parents. It's from their parents that they absorb the most-needed values. This influence starts from the moment a child is born. Every interaction, every word spoken, every reaction displayed becomes a building block that shapes their character. From kindness and compassion to hardiness and responsibility, the values instilled in a child's formative years decide what they become.

Children are like impressionable sponges, soaking up the world around them. While lectures and reprimands have their place, true learning often happens through observation. When parents demonstrate kindness, honesty, and respect in their daily interactions, it becomes the foundation for their children's upbringing.

18

Heart on wheels

As a kid, I was obsessed with toy cars. Every time I spotted one in my friends' hands or on store shelves, I longed to have my own. But back then, fancy toys like that were a luxury my family couldn't afford.

Watching my children play with toy cars brought back a flood of memories. It's funny how something as simple as a toy can trigger such nostalgia. But back in my day, even those little cars were a big deal.

Growing up in Chennai, my craze for cars was an all-consuming passion. Crawling to school in our cycle rickshaw with my sisters, a slow crawl compared to the world around us, only intensified my longing. Our classmates would pull up in luxury cars, gleaming in the sunlight, and I'd find myself gazing incessantly. It was during these times that the desire to own such a car, a symbol of freedom and progress, first ignited within me, a dream that would propel me into adulthood.

From a young age, I made a habit of studying cars inside and out—colours, shapes, you name it. I even plastered my room with posters of my favourite models, losing myself in their sleek designs.

Our family's first car, an Ambassador, rolled into our lives in 1987, courtesy of my father.

Dubai's impressive car culture was a major draw for me. I'd often dream of cruising down its wide, open roads in a top-of-the-line vehicle— a stark contrast to the narrow streets and limited car options back home in Kerala.

Upon arriving in Dubai, I was initially captivated by the world of branded T-shirts. But as I acclimated to the city, my fascination shifted towards watches and, especially, cars. The realisation dawned on me: owning these coveted items required dedication and hard work.

Seeing others go about in style made me think, "Why can't I achieve that too?" The answer was clear—unceasing effort.

But it wasn't until I made it to Dubai in '94 that I finally got my hands on my own set of wheels. With a loan in hand, I snagged a Ford Tempo. I got BMW 3 Series in '99, followed by a Mercedes E Class in 2002.

Then, in 2005, my former boss Mr John surprised me by giving me his old Jaguar.

In 2007, my passion for high-performance cars took hold when I acquired my first Ferrari, a stunning F430 in classic red. The following year, a sunshine-yellow Lamborghini convertible joined the stable, and my love affair with speed and style was cemented. These two sports cars were just the beginning, as my collection gradually expanded to encompass automotive royalty: a Rolls Royce, the iconic Mercedes G Wagon, a sleek Porsche, a luxurious Bentley, a commanding Range Rover, and more. Today, my collection boasts 12 of the world's most prestigious automobiles.

But for me, it's not just about the flash and speed of these cars. My primary attraction is to their colours. Maybe, it is so because of my love for Nature. I like rare and unusual colours.

The captivating world of colour began for me with marbles—from my Chennai days. The swirls and specks within those tiny spheres ignited a lifelong interest. Now, I find myself drawn to the same dance of colour on a grander scale—the gleaming hues adorning cars that zoom past me.

My craze for cars has changed the course of my life. It triggered my passion for relocating to Dubai, working in a foreign company and later starting my own business. All these were for securing the cars I dreamt of. I realise that a single dream can change anyone's life.

From a childhood where a toy car was an unimaginable luxury, to owning coveted global brands today, the journey seems almost unbelievable. Perhaps it was destiny's hand at play. Maybe, instead of toy cars in my youth, there was a grand design to place me behind the wheel of these automotive icons. Only time, and the divine plan itself, will reveal the reasons behind this remarkable turn of events. God alone knows his plans for us!

My car and watch collection aren't about ostentation; they represent the culmination of dreams I once held close. Owning these things brings a sense of satisfaction that comes from achieving the goals I set for myself.

Owning several sports cars, I find myself drawn to a more leisurely pace behind the wheel. These magnificent beasts in my garage are like untamed stallions—raw power waiting to be unleashed. But unlike most, I find myself most at ease when I walk them at a gentle pace, appreciating their sleek form and luxurious comfort. My friends often joke that I'm "the slowest driver of sports cars on earth"!

My love for comfort doesn't stop at luxurious sedans. My collection will soon have some of the world's most coveted hypercar brands—Bugatti and Pagani.

In the world of high-performance automobiles, hypercars reign supreme. These incredibly rare machines boast horsepower exceeding 1,000 and price tags reaching into the millions.

Built with the utmost attention to detail, hypercars incorporate the most exotic materials available—carbon fibre, titanium, even precious metals like gold and rhodium. This commitment to exceptional materials serves a dual purpose: maximising strength for superior safety and handling during exhilarating performance runs, while simultaneously shaving off weight.

Aerodynamics is paramount in the design of a hypercar. Every curve and line is meticulously crafted to reduce drag, enabling these machines to slice through the air with minimal resistance. The result? Staggering performance. Top speeds exceeding 200 mph are common, with some hypercars reaching even 300 mph. Acceleration is equally impressive, with 0-to-60 mph times dipping below 3 seconds, and 0-to-100 mph achieved in under 7 seconds.

Exclusivity defines the hypercar experience. With fewer than 6,000 registered worldwide, ownership is limited to a select few. Production numbers are deliberately low and potential buyers are often carefully chosen, ensuring only the most elite clientele get behind the wheel. In fact, many hypercars are sold out before they even officially hit the market.

Hypercar production leans heavily towards the artisanal. Many are hand-built and offered in limited editions. Pagani, for example, restricts production to just 100 units per model, while Hennessey caps their Venom F5 at a mere 24 units. This dedication to rarity is another key element that elevates a car to hypercar status.

The pinnacle of personalisation, no two hypercars may be exactly alike. Buyers are often hand-selected before production even begins, allowing them to customise their dream machine to their exact specifications.

I did something different recently. Usually, people take supercars from abroad to India. I did the opposite. My prized possession, a dark brown Range Rover with a Kerala registration plate, recently made a sentimental trip from India to Dubai. This wasn't just any car; it holds a special place in the memories of me and my children. Bringing it here reflects a desire to keep the things we love close by.

A short video showcasing the Range Rover parked majestically in front of the Burj Khalifa went viral on social media. The clip opened with a close-up of the Kerala plate, then panned to reveal the breathtaking Dubai skyline. My accompanying post read: "A long journey from home. Our old Range Rover from Kerala is visiting us, and we're showing her around. Since 2011, she's been part of our family."

In another post, I shared the Range Rover's remarkable story. "She was born in England in 2011 and lived in Kerala, India, for 13 years," I wrote on Instagram. "Currently, she's having a great time in Dubai, UAE. Take care of your car, and it will take care of you."

The video garnered an overwhelming response online. One Instagram user commented, "Kids are taking UAE reg cars to Kerala. You're a legend for bringing a KL reg car to UAE." Another user captured the sentiment perfectly: "Omg, now this is true love. You have a really big heart."

And every time I buy a new car, I make a pilgrimage to Rashidiya Masjid to offer my gratitude for the blessings in my life. I park the car near the Masjid for a while.

It's a ritual that's become deeply meaningful to me, a moment of reflection and thanks for how far I've come.

I remain outside the Masjid and look at the sacred space inside. I'm sure the Supreme Power that all religions speak of listens to the musings of my soul. I'm convinced that I've come so far in life because of divine blessings.

"Why do you come here with a new car every time?" Gautam has asked me.

I've never given him the answer. Let him read this memoir and know the secret.

Ticking obsession

My fascination with watches kicked into high gear when I landed in Dubai. I still vividly recall the humble plastic watch I sported on my wrist when I first stepped foot in this city. Red and white dial, snagged from the streets of Bombay, for a mere pittance.

The second timepiece to grace my collection was an Esprit watch. It adorned my wrist for a spell before finding a new home with my father. After his passing, I brought it back to Dubai, where it holds the most sentimental value among all my watches.

Nowadays, my collection boasts an impressive array of luxury timepieces. I've got coveted brands like Audemars Piguet, Patek Philippe, IWC Schaffhausen, Rolex, Franck Muller, Richard Mille, MB&F, A. Lange & Söhne, Jaeger Lecoultre, Roger Dubuis, Vacheron Constantin, Breguet and Jacob & Co adorning my watch box. Each one tells its own story.

For me, collecting watches is akin to investing in treasure. Their value only appreciates over time and understanding the intricate details of each model adds to their charm. It's not just about the price tag; it's about the brand's legacy and the artistry behind each piece.

Passions and hobbies are essential for a fulfilling life, and for me, cars and watches top the list. Some may question the point of amassing such a collection, but for me, it's about more than just financial gain. It's about the sheer joy of owning something that brings happiness.

Recently, I received a truly special timepiece from Jacob & Co.—the Bugatti UAE Edition watch, customised just for me by none other than Jacob Arabo, the Uzbek-American jewelry and watch designer who founded the company. Among the prestigious clientele of his company, started in 1986, is none other than football legend Cristiano Ronaldo, for whom he created a similar bespoke timepiece.

Watches hold a special place in my heart, dating back to my childhood days in Chennai when my father gifted me my first watch. It was a plastic toy watch worth INR 1. Losing it was heartbreaking, but now, with watches from Jacob & Co. gracing my collection, life has come full circle.

I'm saddened when I see my friends without watches. That's why I've gifted timepieces from my collection to close friends like A. R. Shaji, Hari and my brother Abhilash.

Watches aren't just accessories; they're investments that can be passed down through generations.

I've always been fascinated by the world of watches—their designs, the history of the companies that craft them, the stories they tell on your wrist.

My love for aesthetics translates into how I wear my watches. I like to change straps to complement my outfit and even the car I'm driving. It's a way to express myself and find joy in the little details.

Some may find these hobbies niche, but for me, they bring immense pleasure. Everyone has their own passions and the true value lies in the happiness they bring, regardless of how others perceive them. After all, true happiness comes from within and material possessions can only take you so far.

Someone, playfully riffing on the watch collecting craze, asked, "Don't all watches tell the same time, no matter how expensive?"

I chuckled and agreed. "Absolutely! They all keep perfect time." But then I added, with a smile "The real difference lies in the history a watch holds and the craftsmanship behind it. And, perhaps more importantly," I said with a touch of jest, "it shows how good your time is."

While I've heard friends suggest I might be one of the first Malayalis to build a collection of both watches and cars, I can't confirm that for sure. However, my journey with watches began in 2002, followed by cars in 2007.

Regardless of whether I'm the first or not, I take immense pride in my collection, knowing I built it myself. It reflects my dedication and taste. Through it all, I feel a sense of gratitude—God's blessings have played a significant role in every aspect of my life, including this passion.

Keeping your prized timepieces in top shape requires constant vigilance. One challenge is ensuring proper storage. Watches, especially delicate ones, need protection from dust, moisture and extreme temperatures. Investing in watch boxes or watch rolls becomes crucial. Automatic watches require regular winding, either by wearing them frequently or using a watch winder. Battery-powered watches need timely battery replacements to avoid damage from a dead battery leaking. Perhaps the most significant challenge is servicing. Over time, mechanical watches require professional servicing by a qualified watchmaker to maintain accuracy and functionality.

Home treasures

My passion for sports has always ignited my admiration for sports stars and artists alike. I'm drawn to their positive energy and the joy they bring to countless fans worldwide.

Personally, I find the stories of athletes and artists more inspiring than those of the wealthy. Their dedication, struggles, and triumphs connect with me on a deeper level. Their journeys offer a sense of accomplishment that I find more relatable.

As my admiration for sports stars grew, so did my desire to preserve their legacies. It started as a small hobby, but soon grew into a vast collection of memorabilia, totalling around 100 items. Over time, I've shared many pieces with close friends and revered clients.

One prized possession in my collection is a cricket bat gifted to me by Indian legend Sachin Tendulkar himself, complete with his signature and a heartfelt message. "Best Wishes, Dileep!" he wrote I also have his used pad, adding to the sentimental value.

My collection also boasts 300 golf balls gathered from courses around the globe, including gifts from top golfers such as Tiger Woods, Rory McIlroy, Victor Hovland, Matt Fitzpatrick, Shane Lowry, Matthieu Pavon, Jorge Campillo and Thomas Pieters. and Thomas Peiters. Each ball holds a special memory of my own golfing adventures and encounters with the pros.

But it's not just golf memorabilia that fills my shelves. I've got shoes worn by football icons Messi and Ronaldo, as well as items signed by Usain Bolt, Pele, Muhammad Ali, Tiger Woods, Michael Phelps and F1 star Kimi Raikkonen.

From a helmet signed by Formula One champs Michael Schumacher and Max Verstappen, to a guitar autographed by the Rolling Stones, to photos and equipment signed by tennis legends Roger Federer and Rafael Nadal, my collection spans the sporting spectrum.

And let's not forget the jerseys signed by teammates from powerhouse football clubs like Manchester United, Chelsea and Arsenal. It's no wonder my friends jokingly refer to my home as a mini 'sports museum'.

The birth of a new golfer

MJ got her first taste of golf when she tagged along with me to the course. Little did we know, it would spark a new passion for her. Soon enough, she was hitting the greens herself and with practice, she became quite the golfer. Knowing her commitment to whatever she does, it was no surprise that she became so.

In 2019, she played a major role as my caddy during the Turkish Airlines World Amateur Golf Cup finals, where I represented the UAE. It was a warm experience, sharing the course with her by my side. When you have your dear one near you, will anything stop you from conquering what you set out for?

In 2023, MJ found herself in a tight competition during the qualifying round held in Dubai. There was fierce competition from both men and women, but she clinched a spot in the finals of the 2023 Turkish Airlines World Amateur Golf Championship. I've watched her journey from player to champion with admiration. And guess who was there to support her as her caddy? Her husband.

As a couple, we've been fortunate to share these golfing experiences together. From introducing MJ to the sport to representing UAE in the world championships, it's been a fulfilling journey. It just goes to show, you never know what life has in store for us.

Insta chronicles

In 2022, I found myself stuck in quarantine in the guest bedroom of my villa due to COVID-19. It was a challenging time, being confined to my own home and unable to go to the office or interact with family and friends directly. Quarantine was a new experience for me, and it left me feeling drained and restless.

During this time, I couldn't stand idly by, so I came up with an idea to start an Instagram account. I wanted to share inspirational and motivational content for the younger generation, drawing from my own life experiences and lessons learned. My goal was to be honest and transparent, sharing insights that could positively influence others without glorifying myself.

At first, I was hesitant about putting myself out there on social media. I'm a private person, especially living in Dubai where most people don't know me. I wasn't keen on making a big splash on a public platform. I decided to create posts without showing my face much, preserving my privacy while still sharing valuable content.

After three days of contemplation, I took the plunge and launched my Instagram account, '@dileepheilbronn', on June 17, 2022. I started with a photo from the terrace of my home in Kerala, setting the tone for what was to come. Over time, I learned the ins and outs of Instagram, adjusting my content to attract more followers and engagement.

Within a year, I reached 80,000 followers and in April 2022, I was thrilled to receive Instagram's verified badge. I got the blue tick after only 10 hours of applying. It was a validation of my efforts and the value of the content I was sharing. While I'm aware that some people buy verification badges, I'm proud to say that my growth has been organic and genuine.

Eighteen months later, my follower count has more than doubled to over 250,000. What sets my account apart is its authenticity. I've never resorted to buying views, likes or comments to inflate my numbers.

For new accounts struggling to find their voice or established ones facing a lull, buying a surge of engagement can be tempting. It offers a quick shot of validation. But the desire for instant gratification can mask the long-term drawbacks. It's a house of cards built on an inauthentic foundation. Bought engagement doesn't translate to real followers who are genuinely invested in the content. The facade may crumble.

My followers can trust that the engagement on my page is real and I'm committed to maintaining that integrity moving forward.

My 100th post

Every day, I'm diving deeper into the world of Instagram content creation. I've honed my skills in editing videos, making photos pop and crafting captivating captions, all thanks to the support and guidance of MJ and the boys. Together, we've learned the art of creating content that connects with the younger generation.

Instagram has truly been a game-changer for me, opening up new opportunities and connections that I never thought possible. I've had the privilege of meeting some fantastic people through the platform.

Those who know me in Dubai are often taken aback when they stumble upon my Instagram account. They scroll through my posts, amazed by the passion, hobbies and achievements they never knew existed outside of our usual interactions. From my collection of luxury cars to my rare watches, golf triumphs and snippets of family life, every post offers a glimpse into my world.

For my 100th post, I wanted to do something special—a reflection of my journey from 1991 to 2022. It was titled, 'The 100th Post—The Story of My Life'. It was a collage of milestone moments and life achievements. Everything got mention—my first job, the first car I bought in 1994, my first Ferrari, achievements as a golfer. The response was overwhelming.

This Instagram post turned things around for me. People who hadn't heard of me before started taking notice. It offered a window into my past. For many, these were the first pieces of my story. More than just personal snapshots, these photos were a testament to the hard work invested in getting here.

Instagram has become my personal time machine, allowing me to revisit memories and share them with the world. As I sift through old photos and videos, I'm transported back in time, reliving the highs and lows, the triumphs and tribulations that have defined my path. It's a journey filled with thorns and petals, obstacles and guiding lights, all of which have shaped me into the person I am today.

Instagram also reignited my passion for photography. Dusting off my skills, I began creating photos and videos. Crafting captions became a preferred hobby. Now, I share not just glimpses of my life, but also a piece of myself with every post.

To my followers, I'm not just a globetrotting Malayali; I'm also a farmer's son from Edappal, someone who has experienced some successes along the way while never forgetting his roots.

I got an invitation from RJ Fazlu of Radio Hit FM 96 for an interview in Malayalam. The interview, my first to a media house after starting my Instagram account, was a hit. I was thrilled to receive such tremendous feedback and comments from listeners.

From everyday folks to celebrities

My Instagram followers span from everyday folks to renowned celebrities. From American actor and TV host Terry Crews to

Indian actors like R. Madhavan, Balachandra Menon and Sanju Sivram, along with cricketers Yuvraj Singh, Sreesanth, Devdutt Padikkal, Herchelle Gibbs, Michael Vaughan and Sanju Samson. Actors like DD Neelakantan and Reenu Mathews, along with YouTuber Khalid Al Ameri, watch designer legend Jacob Arabo, badminton player Prannoy H.S. and actor-director Basil Joseph, make up just a fraction of my diverse follower base.

But it doesn't stop there. I've got world-class tennis stars like Grigor Dimitrov and Ben Shelton, along with other luminaries from the realms of cinema, sports, business, and vlogging, all following my journey on Instagram. And let's not forget my friend and follower, world number nine tennis player Hubert Hurkacz, with whom I've shared unforgettable moments on the golf course.

Other famous followers include Anirban Lahiri, Aalim Hakim, Manny Khoshbin, Ajmal Khan, Mo Vlogs, Neeraj Madhav, Shaz Mohammed, RJ Fazlu, Muhammad BinGhatti, Sameer Hamsa, Mohammed Irfan, Wealth and the Trillionaire Life.

Recently, I had the pleasure of sharing a meal and some quality time with none other than Grigor Dimitrov. Our chat at Burj Al Arab lasted a good two hours. It was a fascinating conversation, filled with shared passions for cars, watches and life's relationships. Time flew by unnoticed as we spoke about our common interests.

Through Instagram, I crossed paths with Balachandra Menon in 2022 and our lengthy conversation led to a deep friendship. Menon's film 'Aarante Mulla Kochumulla' left a deep impression on me during my college days, showing me that even those from humble beginnings can achieve success. When I told him how much this movie has influenced me, Menon was all smiles.

Little did I know, Instagram would spark my writing journey. This memoir is an extension of that spark. Its impact, however, extends beyond the personal. Instagram became a surprise source of family fun. Dinner tables transform into laughter factories as we dissect my posts, devouring comments together. Celebrity interactions, follower musings, the whole online buzz—it's become a family bonding ritual.

Forget the crass accusations of social media tearing families apart! Of course, we can use Instagram to bridge the gap, not widen it. Technology, used wisely, can be a powerful tool for connection.

It's humbling to think that even scientists from Antarctica follow me on Instagram.

For me, Instagram is not just a source of inspiration—it's a driving force behind my talents and endeavours.

With a follower count of 300,000 and over 70 million views for my posts and reels as I write this, Instagram has propelled me into the realm of celebrity status in record time. Among my most viral posts is a 19-second video featuring my beloved car, the Ferrari. In this heartwarming reel, I share a poignant father-son moment as I drive my first Ferrari, purchased in 2007, with my three-year-old son Gautam. Fast forward to August 2022 and Gautam, now 18, takes the wheel, driving his younger brother Aryaan to school in the same Ferrari—a reflection of the enduring bond between father and son, with Ferrari as the enduring symbol.

Followers said that this reel tugged at the heartstrings.

However, this journey wasn't without its twists. A collaboration with another Instagram account resulted in the disappearance of this valued video. Ignoring the initial setback, I persevered, re-editing and reposting the reel on my account. The response was overwhelming, with over 30 million viewers captivated by the tale. In hindsight, this ordeal only added to the story, as the reel garnered five times more viewership than the original collaboration.

I once again realised that no setback should put us off. They are all God's detours. Disappointment doesn't define us. He has bigger plans, paving a new path to success, even better than before. Trust His guidance.

19

Reunion of hearts

Finally, after three long decades of waiting, I met Pramod. I had been longing to see him, my dearest childhood friend, all these years. He texted to me from his exile only a few months ago. I heard his voice then after 30 years. I told him then that we should meet when I arrive in Kerala.

He agreed with some reluctance. He was not enamored of visiting Kerala after his business failed and debts accumulated.

I still wondered why he chose to remain incommunicado in those 30 years. One phone call and we, his friends, would have been by his side. No point talking about the past. I eagerly waited for our meeting.

In 2023, he boarded the Chennai Mail and made his way to my doorstep.

The anticipation was palpable as we stood face to face after all these years. Words seemed to fail us in that moment. At the same time, there was an undeniable sense of familiarity, as if no time had passed at all. It was like reuniting with a part of myself I thought I'd lost forever. It was a glorious moment. God is kind!

I did not express happiness, sadness or curiosity. My response was neutral. I ensured he felt welcome and comfortable. I did not blame him either for absconding. I treated him with good hospitality.

"Did you have breakfast?" I asked, breaking the silence.

"No," he replied quietly.

"Come, let's have breakfast. I've been waiting for you."

As we sat down to eat, the tension between us began to dissipate. I could sense a warmth that only old friends can share. We talked about my family, his life in Chennai, and slowly but surely, the years evaporated, leaving behind the essence of who we once were.

We instantly transformed back into our old schoolyard selves. We heard the sounds of a football game in the playing fields of the countryside. During the rain, we launched paper boats on the glistening puddles. The scratchy stems of the *Mashithandu* plant (Peperomia Pellucida) served as our erasers, carefully scrubbing away the markings on our slates plant. With a mischievous glint in our eyes, we ditched class. We wandered for hours through the bustling Edappal market. We watched movies at Govinda Theatres and Murali Theatres. Back then, movie tickets were a steal at a rupee each. We revelled in the thrill of breaking rules, hearts pounding under the stern gazes of teachers we both respected and feared. It was a return to the springtime of our youth.

In Pramod, I found the same kind-hearted friend I remembered from our younger days—honest, straightforward and incapable of malice. It was clear to me why he hadn't climbed the social ladder; his integrity and authenticity were too pure for such pursuits.

But in the grand scheme of life, such innocent people are God's chosen ones.

I remember the Biblical words: 'Blessed Are the Meek, for They Will Inherit the Earth.'

Those who are gentle will ultimately be blessed.

As the evening drew to a close and Pramod prepared to leave for Chennai, I couldn't help but feel a pang of sadness at the thought of saying goodbye once again. I gave him some money. I prefer to support my friends as their needs arise. While a large one-time sum might seem appealing, it often doesn't solve underlying problems. By providing targeted assistance, we can ensure the resources have a lasting impact. It allows me to tailor my assistance to their specific situations and make a real difference.

I promised to support him along. And as he left, I made a silent vow to myself to help him find a partner. Why should he walk all alone in life?

Driving down memory lane

I recently recalled my mentor in driving, Workshop Kuttettan (Kuttan), while posting my videos on cars on Instagram. Kuttettan was a dear friend of my father's and played a significant role in shaping my driving skills. Back in the day, he managed a car workshop in Edappal, where many folks learned the ropes of driving while taking the repaired cars out for a spin. He was generous to a fault.

A nostalgic trip down memory lane took me back to 1988 when Kuttettan patiently taught me how to manoeuvre our old Ambassador car. Today, I find myself effortlessly handling a fleet of luxury cars, all thanks to the invaluable lessons from my guru.

Last July, during my visit to Kerala with MJ, I made it a point to reconnect with Kuttettan. We spent quality time chatting and enjoying a meal together at his home. He was his same old self, his smile reflecting his huge heart.

Capturing the essence of the moment, I filmed a heartwarming video of my mentor. As 'Gurudakshina', a token of gratitude, I presented him with a gold coin and a cheque, which I could tell meant the world to him from the blessings in his eyes.

Upon returning to Dubai, I shared the video on Instagram, accompanied by a caption reflecting on Kuttettan's influence on my journey from novice to expert driver. "In 1988, he gave me the opportunity to experience the excitement of holding the steering wheel for the first time," I wrote. "Recently, I met him to express my gratitude and seek his blessings. He has taught hundreds of students in his life and I am one among them. Thirty-five years ago, we both were not aware that I was getting trained to drive the best cars in the world. Life can take you places you can't even imagine, but always remember where we come from."

To my surprise, the video garnered immense attention, reaching 1,000,000 views. What struck me the most was the outpouring of love and appreciation not just for me but also for driving instructors worldwide, sparked by Kuttettan's endearing presence in the video.

"It's a blissful moment," wrote a follower. "No words to say," posted another.

Yet another commented: "Such a great culture. Only possible by Indians."

True. In India, the guru is considered equivalent to the parent. Nay, to God.

The video featuring Kuttettan turned out to be one of my finest creations. It even caught the eye of Shamsuddin Mubarak, a senior sub-editor at *Malayala Manorama*, who reached out to me after stumbling upon my Instagram profile. Although he proposed a feature on me, I politely declined, preferring to stay out of the spotlight. However, fate had other plans when Shamsuddin, intrigued by my connection with Kuttettan, paid us a visit and ended up penning a feature that appeared in the Sunday edition of the newspaper on July 23, 2023.

"This feels more about me than Kuttettan," I remarked to Shamsuddin.

"Can't help it," he chuckled.

He had chronicled my life story, my journey from zero to hero, so that it would inspire youngsters.

The feature garnered widespread attention.

Unseen connections

Anto Joseph, the filmmaker, gave me a buzz sometime ago.

"Dileep, you got to check out this Malayalam film, 'Malikappuram'. It's good," he urged.

I was intrigued, so the very next day, MJ and I hit the theatre to catch 'Malikappuram'. Set against the backdrop of Sabarimala, the movie took me back to my childhood trip to the sacred site with my cousin Kuttan. Remember Kuttan? The one who imparted some crucial lessons in sharing through the 'Kannimanga' story. While I was 13, Kuttan's father, my Valiachan, took us to Sabarimala.

After watching the movie, I reached out to Kuttan. "Do you remember the pilgrimage to Sabarimala?" I asked.

"Of course, how can I forget?" he replied.

"Thought of you while watching 'Malikappuram.' Just felt like calling you. How've you been?"

"Nothing much. Just doing odd jobs. Currently, I'm at this small restaurant," he revealed.

His response hit me hard. He used to work with me at Heilbronn, but now he was toiling away at a restaurant. It didn't sit right with me. What happened? He shouldn't feel that there is none to help him.

"Stop slaving away at the restaurant. You've earned your rest. You shouldn't strain yourself at this age. Let's figure out how to cover your expenses," I insisted.

Relieved, he quit his job. But just when things seemed settled, Kuttan dropped another bombshell a few days later. He informed me about a growth in his intestine that needed surgical removal.

"Don't sweat it. Get the surgery done, and we'll sort out the bills," I reassured him.

After the surgery, the biopsy revealed there could be a possibility of cancer in the future. Chemotherapy was the next step.

I couldn't shake off the feeling of how interconnected everything was. Anto Joseph's call had led me back to Kuttan and now we were going through through these unexpected twists together. It made me ponder if there's some grand plan at play orchestrating these events.

Life's a puzzle, pieces scattered at random. A chance encounter, a forgotten comment, a wrong turn—these seemingly isolated moments can hold hidden links. We plant seeds of experiences, blind to the future they'll shape, or how they might connect with threads from faraway corners of our lives. The picture unfurls, a beautiful enigma, a proof of the unseen forces that weave the grand narrative of our existence.

My journey has been full of such interconnected incidents. Many people have held my hand when I needed it.

One such person is Unniyettan (Unni). Back in my Polytechnic College days, my friend Hari and I would often hit up a spot for some delicious masala dosas. Each dosa would set us back a mere two and a half rupees. But there were times when our pockets didn't quite match our appetites, and that's where Unniyettan, who ran a grocery store at Annakampad, came in clutch. We'd borrow 50 paise or 25 paise from him, promising to pay him back once we had the cash.

Years later, when I reunited with Unniyettan, it was a moment of genuine joy for both of us. I made sure to get his account number and sent him a sum of money.

"Dileep, why did you send me this?" he asked, clearly taken aback. "You don't owe me any money."

"Consider it a gift, Unniyettan," I replied.

Little does Unniyettan know that those masala dosas he generously fronted for were more than just meals—they were a lifeline for a hungry young student.

Wisdom of the wild

Observing Nature teaches us some important life lessons, the most crucial being that strength often prevails over weakness. The truth: survival of the fittest. Nature imparts to us the importance of sharing success and not fretting excessively about tomorrow.

Take a moment to observe animals. They live their lives in perfect harmony with Nature, devoid of stress and tension. Have you ever noticed how simple their existence is? Their primary concern is safety—constantly vigilant against potential threats. Only once they've ensured their security do they think about satisfying their hunger. After a meal, they seek out a cozy spot to rest. Finding a mate is their next priority.

Animals focus solely on these basic needs. They don't meddle in each other's affairs or waste time calculating potential gains. Regardless of how big a prey they catch, they remain indifferent. Their concern is only for themselves, living in the present moment without worrying about tomorrow. They take only what they need.

This simplistic approach to life allows animals to lead peaceful lives compared to human beings. The law of Nature dictates that the strongest survive while the weak are spared. Success stems from strength in both thought and action. Any sign of weakness invites failure, eagerly awaited by external adversaries.

Consider the intricacies of the food chain. When a lion hunts a herd of buffaloes, it targets the weakest prey. After the lion feasts, other predators like tigers and jackals scavenge what's left. Birds pick at the remains. Flies and worms come visiting and, finally, microorganisms break down the remaining organic matter, completing the cycle.

Unlike human beings, animals waste nothing. They don't hoard excess food for tomorrow but instead sustain themselves on what they catch for days or even weeks.

Forests erupt with life—a menagerie of creatures, from giants to the barely seen. Remarkably, in this consummate diversity, an unspoken truce holds.

That is why, I always look up to the animal kingdom and Mother Nature for answers to all my questions.

Human beings, supposedly the pinnacle of intelligence, grapple with something as basic as respect for each other. It begs the question: why can't we achieve similar harmony?

Beyond grammar

When I was just nine years old, my English teacher hit me with some harsh words. "Your English is terrible. You don't know any grammar or rules of the language. If you don't learn English, you won't get anywhere in life," she said, looking straight at me.

Those words got under my skin. For days, I dwelled on them, feeling crushed by the fear of failure.

But as time passed, I came to realise that my teacher's words didn't hold water. English isn't the be-all and end-all of success.

Just look at the many countries around the world where English isn't the primary language. Are their people all failures because they don't speak English?

As I grew older, I became even more convinced of the fallacy in my teacher's words. English is just one of countless languages spoken worldwide. Proficiency in it does not reflect your intelligence; it's just a language. Fluency in a language isn't about mastering every grammar rule; it's about being understood by others. I've travelled far and wide, communicating effectively in many countries using the same English my teacher scorned.

Nowadays, I'm proficient in Malayalam, English, Tamil and Hindi. I can even understand and hold basic conversations in Arabic, Korean and Tagalog, thanks to my life experiences, not textbooks.

Education is undoubtedly crucial, but today's generation spends the bulk of their lives in classrooms, absorbing information they'll likely never need. From the age of three to 40, this process may keep them occupied. The Internet has made knowledge readily accessible, rendering rote memorisation of capitals and equations obsolete. Cramming the names of capitals, sine theta and algebra formulas likely won't translate to real-world use for most students. With a single click, all this information is readily available online. They are wasting their precious time. Instead, we should turn to the greatest university of all: Nature, humanity and life itself. We should never stop learning from this varsity till we leave this world.

This university has no teachers, syllabi or exams—only invaluable knowledge and insights. This knowledge guides us through difficult moments and competitive circumstances.

Let's not forget that we're born champions, having triumphed over countless odds just to enter this world.

Conception holds a hint of competition. While it's true millions of male gametes compete to fertilise an egg, it's not quite an individual race. Male gamete motility and chance play a significant role. The journey from male gamete to baby is a remarkable feat of Nature, but not a competition we consciously 'win'. However, there's a beautiful metaphor here. Our very existence is a story of toughness. Our mother's body nurtured us through this early developmental stage, preparing us for the challenges of life ahead. This doesn't mean every subsequent situation is a competition to win or lose. Life offers a spectrum of experiences, from collaboration to overcoming obstacles. But that initial spark of perseverance reflects our inherent strength.

Every stage of life presents its challenges, and it's up to us to face them head-on, not by comparing ourselves to others, but by striving for self-improvement every day. We should compete with ourselves. And make every day special.

As Albert Einstein famously said during his visit to Japan, "A calm and modest life brings more happiness than the pursuit of success combined with constant restlessness.

The lessons of life

Everything I've shared in this book is straight from the pages of my own life. These are real experiences that I've lived through and each one has shaped me into who I am today. I've written about ways of living that made every day of mine better. I've shared success models from the cauldron of my own life. My goal is simple: to inspire the next generation with tales of success. If there's even a chance my story could resonate with the new generation, that makes sharing it worthwhile. I've never felt that others should know about my life. Nor is it a story I'd necessarily classify as 'great'.

I didn't start writing an autobiography just to boost my ego. My only intention is to offer hope and motivation to those who need it. Behind every achievement in my life lies a story of hard work, sweat and tears. It's these lessons and experiences that I want to pass on to others.

When I watched the movie, 'Slumdog Millionaire', I saw a reflection of myself in the protagonist. This movie takes viewers on a whirlwind journey with a Mumbai slum teenager. As he finds himself on the hot seat of a popular quiz show, his past is revealed. Each question acts as a trigger, unlocking a memory that reveals how his life on the streets unknowingly equipped him with the knowledge to answer the questions. Like him, I've drawn strength and inspiration from my own life's journey, as well as from Nature, friends, family, mentors and even adversaries. While his story may be fictional, mine is rooted in reality.

One life principle I've discovered is OMAR: Observe, Memorise, Apply, Repeat. 'Omar' fittingly means 'long-lived' in Arabic. Thanks to my dear friend Ahmed Saleh for helping me develop this acronym.

Truth is stranger than fiction. We gain insight into the depths of human experience only when we explore the lives of people. New facets come into the vision. Unknown angles enhance the understanding.

I want to connect directly with the younger generation through platforms like Instagram. If my stories can alleviate even a fraction of someone's life disappointments or cast light on their path, then that's the greatest contribution I can make.

My mission to interact with the new generation began at Tirur SSM Polytechnic College, where I once walked the halls as a student. Perhaps destiny ordained that the beginning for this should be made at my alma mater, where my dreams first took flight. Time seemed to rewind. Invited by my classmates Abdul Aziz and Nazar Kokkodi, I spoke to final-year students of all batches, on January 3, 2024, sharing my journey as a notable alumnus.

During the session, I encouraged the students to ask anything they wanted and I was blown away by their insightful questions. This generation isn't like mine; they possess a remarkable perspective on the world and their future careers. I was truly impressed by their plans and confidence.

I left them with a simple yet powerful message: don't compare yourselves to others and don't compete with them. Each of you is unique, with your own path to success. Discover your individuality, strive for excellence in your endeavours, and you'll become the benchmark for others to emulate.

The students responded with applause.

They favoured relatable success stories from real everyday achievers over generic motivational talks. This is quite understandable.

The principal informed that those who could not make it to the session have urged the management to convene another talk of mine.

Their feedback is heartwarming! It has buoyed my enthusiasm for connecting with younger generations.

A life in calendar

As a contractor and property developer, meticulous planning is my forte. Every project is mapped out meticulously, each phase detailed on a calendar with clear start and end dates. This method has spelled my success in the industry.

But in the hustle and bustle of construction, an important notion was shared with me by my former boss, Mr. Mohammad Vatuvara, when I was 24. He suggested applying this same meticulous approach to life itself—setting goals, charting a course and following it diligently. It was a notion that persisted, waiting for the right moment to take root.

That moment came in 2008, a year marked by unutterable loss. My father, the pillar of my existence, departed this world at the age of 75. His passing shook me to the core, awakening a realisation that time is a fleeting commodity.

In the wake of his departure, I heeded Mr. Vatuvara's wisdom and crafted a life calendar. With each stroke of the pen, marking off another week, the fragility of life becomes painfully apparent.

Embedded within the pages of my A3 sheet lies a truth: none of us arrived in this world with an eternal lease. Like all living beings, we have a definitive beginning and a destined end. Birth inevitably leads to death; it's the circle of life. If we were exempt from death, we wouldn't have been granted the gift of life in the first place.

Of all uncertainties in human existence, death reigns supreme. We don't know where, when or how our final moments will unfold, and this uncertainty casts a shadow of fear over mankind.

Yet, paradoxically, it's this very uncertainty that breathes vitality into our days. If we possessed absolute knowledge of our mortality—its time and manner—we'd likely wither away long before our time.

Each dawn, my calendar whispers a sobering truth: "You are inching closer to your inevitable end." From the moment of birth, we start a journey inexorably leading us towards the ultimate truth of death. Every step we take, every breath we draw, brings us nearer to that final voyage.

Each day, as I reflect on the names inscribed in my calendar—loved ones lost to the sands of time—I'm reminded of life's preciousness. Their absence points to the fragility of existence, urging me to seize every moment with gratitude. Each day granted to me, after some of my dear ones have left, is nothing but God's grace. It has brought this inner decision in me: do everything you want to do before your time is up.

As for the future, it remains shrouded in uncertainty. I cannot predict how many days I have left on this earth. But I vow to live each day with purpose and intention.

Perhaps I'll reach the age of 75, like my father did, and as my calendar has noted. Or I might meet my end before then. Conversely, I may surpass the age of 75 altogether. The truth is, I simply don't know what the future holds. Regardless of what lies beyond 75, I'll continue living one day at a time, updating my calendar for the next few days as they come.

Desert reveries

As I stood in the vastness of the Al Awir desert, memories flooded my mind like a swift tide. It was here, 33 years ago, that my journey began.

I was there to visit the labour camp in the middle of the desert where I once lived. My wife, my children and my childhood friend Pramod accompanied me on this recent trip to Al Awir. I had brought Pramod to Dubai for a few reasons, one being the hope that a few days immersed in the city's energy would pull him out of his recent slump. I've given him a job in my company.

The landscape in Al Awir had undergone a remarkable transformation. Where the dusty labour camp once stood, a bright fruit and vegetable market now bustled, flanked by modern buildings. Yet, remnants of the desert remained, stretching out endlessly. In 1991, the only landmark visible from this spot was the Dubai Trade Center. Today, a breathtaking panorama unfolds—the iconic Burj Khalifa pierces the sky, dwarfed by hundreds of other megastructures that have sprouted from the desert sands.

Dubai's metamorphosis from a modest settlement to a global metropolis within a few decades is nothing short of astonishing. This vision owes much to the foresight and leadership of His Highness Sheikh Mohammed bin Rashid Al Maktoum. His guidance has propelled Dubai onto the world stage. The success stories of countless businessmen, myself included, testify to the impact of his leadership.

In the silence of that desert, I reflected on my life's twists and turns. Each step, each moment, held memories of the past and hints of what was to come. I closed my eyes and compared my life then and now. I reminisced about the highs and lows. The silence around me deepened. My wife, children and Pramod were lost in their reflections.

As I traced the arc of my life, from clay sculptures in childhood to friendships with global icons, I couldn't help but feel a sense of awe. This moment of reflection was special. Pramod, my childhood confidant and silent witness to my journey, stood beside me as we shared a contemplative silence amidst the endless desert sands. Dubai has undergone unimaginable growth over 33 years. My own company has. Dreams I once deemed unachievable have become a reality. A far cry from the young boy in Edappal, I now stood as a member of a prestigious international golf club, surrounded by an enviable car and watch collections. The world had become my playground, with sporting achievements and a life of unbelievable luxury. My travels have brought me face-to-face with wonderful people from all walks of life and even some global celebrities have become friends. It's been a journey filled with remarkable encounters. It all began with a curious dream 50 years ago.

Four decades. Dreams translated into plans, then into sweat and action. Detours of doubt and setbacks unseen by others, driven by a stubborn hope that flickered even in the dark. All of these have been the outcome of my own efforts and decisions. I thank God for what I am today. I also thank all my fellow travellers.

Today, bathed in the warm glow of success, I was here in Al Awir, looking at the same desert sands.

Every choice, every move, a step on this path. This was my sweet victory. It was not an easy road, but I made it.

But amid the accolades and achievements, one thing remained clear: the importance of humility and gratitude. No matter how high I soared, I vowed to never lose sight of my roots, and to never forget the lessons learned in the crucible of life. True success is often built upon the foundation of past experiences. Losing sight of them can leave you ill-equipped for the future.

Since 2022, a deep commitment to empowering others has propelled me to share stories of perseverance and dedication. My aim is to provide a roadmap for success. This desire to motivate is what ultimately led me to write my memoirs.

If I can, so can you. Believe me. It's not an easy task but certainly not an impossible one. I want to convey to the younger generation the mantra of ethical business.

Through this book, I sought to share not just my successes, but also the struggles and sacrifices and the philosophy that guided me.

It wasn't an easy task, reliving 55 years of life within the confines of a book. A journey through the past is bittersweet. Compressing a lifetime of experiences into a handful of pages feels like trying to capture the ocean in a seashell. The emotions ran deep.

As you hold this book in your hands, know that it was crafted with love and care. It carries within its pages the essence of a life lived to the fullest.

While these pages hold a part of my story, there's always more to explore. I feel there's a lot more to be told. What has been written is a heartfelt effort penned in the midst of a whirlwind of business ventures, sporting events, global travels and moments with loved ones. As a first-time author, I poured my heart and soul into crafting this story. Countless drafts, revisions and edits went into shaping this book amidst my hectic schedule of travel, family, work and sports. Months of dedication went into every page and I truly hope you enjoy the journey. However, if I've stumbled along the way, please accept my gracious apologies.

20

Until we meet again

Vida! Piriyavitai! Alvida! Khuda Hafiz! Ma'ssalaame! Annyeong! Au Revoir! Paalam! Goodbye!

As I reflect on the chapters of my life, an ineffable sense of joy envelops me. To think that I've had such a meaningful journey in such a fleeting span of time is nothing short of wonderful. In this memoir, I've shared glimpses of this journey inexorably entwined with the lives of those dear to me, for they are a part of my being. Without them, I am but a solitary soul adrift in the currents of life.

These connections transcend the pages of this book, for they are the very essence of who I am. They are the words of encouragement on a quiet morning, the hand extended in the face of doubt, the shared memories that warm the coldest night. These connections are the lifeblood, coursing through the narrative. They are the guiding stars, forever marked on the map of my life.

Building a business in Dubai mirrored this spirit of connection. Heilbronn's growth, as a part of the flourishing Dubai market, felt like a shared accomplishment with my team. Innumerable projects, precious assignments, innovative implementation and happy clients. What more can a company hope for?

Yet surrounded by the skyscrapers and crowded streets, there remains a constant—I still use the same old office chair I used in Heilbronn's first office 22 years ago. For me, age has not withered its value.

Family, friends, mentors, rivals, even strangers—all have contributed their mark. I'm the sum of their love and support. I'm keenly aware of the touch of God permeating my whole life. I thank everyone who has made my life eventful and distinctive. I thank all who made me what I am.

I'm reminded of the silent companionship of Nature—the vast expanses of land, the whispering winds, the gentle rustle of leaves.

Looking back, I've led a fulfilling life. I've realised my dreams and desires. The faces and experiences of my past remain close to my heart. As long as I live, they will stay. They transcend mere characters and incidents in my autobiography, becoming an ever-present part of who I am. While writing my autobiography, a nagging worry persisted—have I included everyone who mattered in my life? To my readers, please feel free to add those special names to your mind's eye as you journey with me.

Imagine God asking, "Who would you like to be in your next life?" My answer is swift and clear: "Myself, Dileep Kumar, once again."

Discontent keeps us yearning for a fresh start, but true satisfaction whispers, "Live it all again".

I wouldn't trade my path—the eldest son of my parents in Edappal, the same siblings, playing with the same childhood friends, learning on the same school bench, the train to Mumbai, the flight to Dubai. These are the building blocks that shaped me, the foundation upon which I built a life of love, success and purpose. I yearn to work with the same colleagues, under the same mentors, soaring with business success with hard work. I'd be incomplete without reuniting with my wife to have the same children. And then I would want MJ and the children for company. The support of my friends, the thrill of golf, tennis and chess, the roar of expensive cars in the world's major cities—these are the elements that constitute me. I should be able to lead a life, totally happy and independent, and not competing with anyone else.

Given a hundred lifetimes, my choice is clear: to relive this very one. I want this very same 'janma' or life again and again. There's a deep satisfaction in knowing you've built a life so fulfilling you'd choose it again.

I can't imagine a Dileep Kumar without all that I described.

Life isn't just fragrant flowers; it's also the thorns we encounter. These punctures leave their mark on our souls, like weathered maps. They are the sudden squalls that force us to reef the sails.

There have been moments of indescribable loss and longing. The absence of beloved friends like Prakash and Babu weighs heavy on my heart. Prakash is not around to witness my successes. So are Unni, my first friend in Dubai, and Babu, my dear companion. But perhaps the greatest sorrow lies in an unfulfilled promise—a debt owed to Welder Anil, a friend whose simple wish haunts like a ghost. Though I've searched far and wide, his whereabouts remain elusive, leaving me with a sense of unfinished business.

I'm heartbroken that I lost touch with Gopi, my kind friend from Mumbai. We rode the public bus together, he carrying my bag all the way to the airport and seeing me off when I left for Dubai. Unfortunately, I lost his address.

But there is light—a light that shines bright in the form of all my relationships, memories and dreams. And it is this light that propels me forward.

The richness of relationships, family, a partner, and children—blessings far beyond my wildest dreams—have filled my life with joy. I pray their presence remains a constant source of love and happiness until the very end.

For my children, this book records the journey their father has undertaken before and after their birth, probably to guide them in their paths.

It's an everlasting whisper in their ears, the unseen threads that bind us together across time and space.

And for the new generation, it is my fervent hope that these words serve as a source of inspiration. It's a gift across generations. I'm committed to my mission to motivate. I'll continue doing this till my end. If this book ignites a spark in even one reader's heart, the effort is richly rewarded. That's all I ever hoped for, not personal acclaim.

As I close this book, a mix of emotions arises. There's a sense of completion, a satisfaction in having shared my story. Yet, there's also the recognition that life's journey is ongoing, filled with new possibilities. The plan to give away all proceeds from this book to people in need fills me with joy.

As I pen these final words, I am filled with a deep sense of gratitude—for the readers who have shared this journey with me, for the loved ones who have supported me along the way and for the divine touch that has guided me through every step of the way.

As I finish this book, the last sentence hangs in the air, a whisper before sleep. A content sigh escapes my lips, a sigh laced with the tang of endings and beginnings. The world outside my window throbs with the promise of a new day, a blank page waiting to be inscribed.

As we part ways, let us remember the moments shared, knowing that our paths may cross again in the grand scheme of life. Until then, may the blessings of the divine be with you, guiding you through every twist and turn of your journey. Be happy.

Glossary

Achan—Malayalam word for Father
Amma—Malayalam word for Mother
Achachan—Malayalam word for Paternal Grandfather
Valiachan—Malayalam word for Uncle, father's elder brother
Cheriyachan—Malayalam word for Uncle, father's younger brother
Chechi—Malayalam word for Elder Sister/Respectful term for an older woman
Chettan—Malayalam word for Elder Brother/Respectful term for an older man